THE STATE AND ECONOMIC LIFE

Editors: Mel Watkins, University of Toronto; Leo Panitch, York University

17 BRUCE CURTIS

True Government by Choice Men?
Inspection, Education, and State Formation in Canada West

The dramatic political transformations which followed the Rebellion of 1837–8 in the Canadas resulted in a centralized and bureaucratic state system. Such a system was dependent upon the acquisition of reliable information about conditions in localities and upon the 'education of the people' in the new conditions of government.

Fulfilling both these objectives was an army of inspectors who delivered regular and standard reports to state agencies about social, economic, and political conditions throughout the country. Foremost among these were educational inspectors. In this study Bruce Curtis traces the development and operation of the educational inspectorate in Canada West.

He begins with a general examination of the political changes occasioned by the Union of the Canadas, and then discusses the international models of inspectoral systems upon which Canadian politicians drew.

The political history of educational inspectors in the 1840s is a tempestuous one. Curtis documents their pioneering efforts at establishing educational discipline and details the operations of inspection at the local level. He also provides a collective biography of the province's first 37 educational inspectors and places them in a context of class, gender, ethnic, and cultural relations. A concluding chapter traces the emergence of a dominant model of 'good education' out of the perceptions, interests, values, and beliefs of a group of respectable men of property.

Curtis's analysis cuts across the disciplines of political sociology and political science, Canadian political history, history of education, and local Ontario history. He presents a systematic application of the insights of sociological theory (especially Marx, Weber, Durkheim, Gramsci, and Foucault) to archival documents and primary sources, and places Canadian political developments of the mid-nineteenth century in imperial and international context.

Bruce Curtis is associate professor of sociology and anthropology, Wilfrid Laurier University. He is the author of *Building the Educational State: Canada West, 1836–1871*.

True Government by Choice Men? Inspection, Education, and State Formation in Canada West

BRUCE CURTIS

UNIVERSITY OF TORONTO PRESS

Toronto Buffalo London

© University of Toronto Press 1992
Toronto Buffalo London
Printed in Canada

ISBN 0-8020-5967-8 (cloth)
ISBN 0-8020-6894-4 (paper)

∞

Printed on acid-free paper

Canadian Cataloguing in Publication Data
Curtis, Bruce, 1950–
    True government by choice men?

    (The State and economic life)
    Includes index.
    ISBN 0-8020-5967-8 (bound) ISBN 0-8020-6894-4 (pbk.)

    1. School management and organization – Ontario –
History – 19th century. 2. Education and state –
Ontario – History – 19th century. 3. School
supervisors – Ontario – Biography. 4. Ontario –
Gentry. I. Title. II. Series.

LB2891.05C8 1992   379.1'52'09713   C91-095140-3

Cover photo: Hamnett Kirkes Pinhey (Archives of Ontario, MU 940, Acc.9002)

This book has been published with the help of a grant from the Social Science
Federation of Canada, using funds provided by the Social Sciences and
Humanities Research Council of Canada.

Contents

Acknowledgments

This book has been published with the help of a grant from the Social Science Federation of Canada, using funds provided by the Social Sciences and Humanities Research Council of Canada.

The research on which the book is based was first discussed over a pint of Guinness at the Hop and Grape with Philip Corrigan in May 1984. Corrigan had recently come to the sociology department at OISE, having done (among other things) doctoral research on the English educational inspectors. A post-doctoral fellowship from the Social Sciences and Humanities Research Council had given me the respite from the casual academic job market needed to attempt archival research for what became *Building the Educational State*. Over the course of the following several months, we mapped out a joint research project.

A research grant from the Social Sciences and Humanities Research Council sustained our investigations, and a grant to lecture abroad from the SSHRC, combined with financial support from the research office at Wilfrid Laurier University, allowed me to investigate the roots of educational inspection using materials in the national libraries of Scotland and Ireland. Facilities were provided for me in Edinburgh by Ged Martin at the Centre of Canadian Studies, and by Andrew McPherson at the Centre for Educational Sociology. Wilfrid Laurier University supported the production of the book through a book preparation grant.

Relatively little research of the kind reported here has been done for Canada West. The reconstruction of the biographies of superintendents has involved a considerable amount of ferreting about in obscure local history collections, private papers, public libraries and, on occasion, graveyards. Much of this part of the research was executed by Robert Lanning with tireless enthusiasm, considerable ingenuity, and at the cost of some delay in his own innovative doctoral research.[1] Lanning produced a first draft of material on the inspectoral corps that figures centrally in the present chapter 5. Shmuel Shamai located and reproduced important texts.

Regular research meetings enabled Corrigan, Lanning, and I to integrate the large volumes of diverse material we uncovered, and sustained the kind of comradeship necessary for the project's execution.

Like all research activities, this project has drawn upon the knowledge and energies of a large number of people. I wish particularly to thank the staff of the Archives of Ontario and the National Archives of Canada, the national libraries of Scotland and Ireland, and the Research Office at Wilfrid Laurier University for research assistance. The following people and organizations have also contributed to the research effort: The Baptist Archives, McMaster University; The Baldwin Room, Metropolitan Toronto Reference Library; Gerald Boyce; Mary Buch; The Carleton University Library; Glen Curnoe; Bernadine Dodge; Peter Eglin; Curtis Fahey; The Frontenac County Educational Museum; Chad Gaffield; Robert Gidney; Ivor Goodson; Barry Gough; Allan Greer; Mary Hardeman; Alf Hecht; T. Boyd Higginson; The Hiram Walker Museum; Susan Houston; Ivona Irwin-Zarecka; Graham Knight; Local History Collections, Cobourg, London, Perth, and Woodstock public libraries; Wyn Millar; Pavla Miller; Mike Murphy; New York University Archives; *Ontario History*; The Ontario Institute for Studies in Education; Stephen Otto; Fiona Paterson; Alison Prentice; The Prince Edward County Educational Museum and Genealogical Society; Jud Purdy; The Queen's University Archives; The Robarts Library, University of Toronto; Pam Schaus; Bernard Shapiro; Robert Smart; The Simcoe County Archives; *Studies in Political Economy*; Gladys Troyer; The United Church Archives, Victoria University; Steven Walker; The Weldon Library, University of Western Ontario; Don Wilson; and The Woodstock Museum. I apologize to all those I've left out. Two anonymous reviewers for the Social Science Federation of Canada took the time to scrutinize the manuscript carefully, and it has been improved as a result of their efforts.

Chapter 1 has appeared in an earlier draft as 'Representation and State Formation in the Canadas, 1790–1850,' *Studies in Political Economy* 28 (Winter 1989), and chapter 8 is a much-revised version of a paper presented at the conference 'Social Change and State Formation in Canada, 1830–1890,' held at the University of Toronto in February 1989, and published as 'Class Culture and Administration' in A. Greer and I. Radforth, eds., *Colonial Leviathan* (Toronto: University of Toronto Press 1992).

Michèle Martin learned far more about inspectors than she ever wanted to know; rode around rural Ontario in the wretched heat of the summer of 1988 to look at derelict schools, old grist mills, educational museums, and headstones; sampled the oleaginous culinary delights along sections of Ontario's Highway 7, and did so with remarkably good grace. She did not type the manuscript, darn my socks, or cook my dinner more often than I cooked hers, but several chapters of the book have profited from her critical comments.

All errors in the text are my sole responsibility.

Bruce Curtis
Montreal, Quebec
June 1991

True Government by Choice Men?

Introduction

For much of his life, Dexter D'Everardo (1814–91) lived in the village of Fonthill in Pelham Township in the Niagara region of what is now the Canadian province of Ontario. His twelve-room house commanded a view of the mists of the Niagara River and of Lake Ontario. To the house he added a hundred-foot-long 'gymnasium' where he walked on wet days, preferring, in clement weather, a path from the house to the end of the concession. He was a familiar sight on these outdoor walks, invariably with his head bent at a peculiar angle, eyes trained on the ground, right arm swinging vigorously, and left arm held tightly to his side. To facilitate this pursuit, he constructed a long plank walk, but, to his dismay, it was regularly invaded by people of the neighbourhood.

D'Everardo was a Quaker and a strict vegetarian who subsisted upon cereals, potatoes, and cheese. He carried his own food while travelling and never ate with his neighbours outside his own house. He collected and labelled bags of corn and oatmeal on his travels and, for his meals, might command from his cook Thorold oatmeal or Welland cornmeal. He was able to taste the difference. At table, D'Everardo consistently placed his watch in front of him so he could monitor the time he spent chewing each mouthful of food. He slept in a circular room lit by a skylight and without ventilation, had large amounts of money out on loan in his neighbourhood, and threw an annual New Year's ball for people in the region.[1]

For five years in the 1840s, D'Everardo was in a position not only to cultivate his own eccentricities but also to encourage moral and intellectual 'improvement' in the Niagara region. Appointed inspector of education in 1846, he supported the development of a centralized elementary educational authority. Draft school acts were sent to him by the chief superintendent of education for his comments. D'Everardo promoted the adoption of tax-supported 'free' schooling and, at his own expense, supplied every school under his supervision with an educational periodical. His report on the condition of common schooling in his district in 1847 was taken as a model by the central authority.

D'Everardo's counterpart in the Belleville region was William Hutton (1801–61), the youngest son of a leading Irish cleric, cousin to a Canadian prime minister, and designer of the census of 1861. Hutton agitated actively for the control of educational matters by 'choice men' like himself. He supported administrative uniformity and central control over curriculum and teacher training on the model of the Irish National Board of Education. Hutton promoted agricultural improvement in his prize essays and pamphlets and applied the methods he advocated to his own farm, which, unfortunately, never paid off his debts. Like many men of his class in the 1830s and 1840s, Hutton was land-rich and cash-poor, but he affected a tutelary relationship to those around him, especially to those of more modest means. He hauled cart-loads of manure onto his land, manure that the Belleville innkeepers were in the habit of dumping into the Moira River, and urged his neighbours to defecate in privies. With the aid of his cousin Francis Hincks and on the strength of his agricultural publications, Hutton gained the lucrative position of secretary (deputy-minister) of the colonial Bureau of Agriculture, Registration and Statistics, and before his premature death, organized the Canadian census of 1861.[2]

Samuel Brown Ardagh (1803–69) supervised popular education in the vicinity of Barrie, Canada West. Born in Co. Tipperary and the eldest son of the rector of Moyglare, Co. Meath, Ardagh entered Trinity College, Dublin, in 1820, supporting himself as a tutor and graduating AB in 1827. He became his father's curate in that year, and in the next married Martha Anderson, the daughter of a half-pay dragoons officer. He took his AM in 1832. An active proselytist, Ardagh narrowly escaped popular violence on a number of occasions. When a recently exhumed child's head was found outside his door with a note pinned to it, promising Ardagh a similar fate if he did not cease his activities against Catholicism, he emigrated to Canada West, arriving in Shanty Bay in October 1842 with his wife, mother-in-law, seven children, a governess, and several servants. He was appointed rector of Barrie, which had one of the endowed rectories created by Colborne in 1836, and worked to improve what he considered to be the generally degraded educational condition of his parishioners.[3]

These three men were members of a new breed of state servants that made its appearance in the Canadas of the 1840s and 1850s: namely, inspectors. Before the Act of Union of 1840, there were few public officials called inspectors in the Canadian colonies, and fewer still who actually inspected anything. In the two decades after the Act of Union, many dimensions of Canadian economic, social, and political life came under the gaze and investigative activities of such officials. Frequently ambitious and public-spirited men, inspectors travelled the Canadian countryside, explored city and town alleys, entered village shops and crossroads taverns, sampled the contents of barrels and ships' holds, checked the design of buildings and the safety of boilers, and evaluated the sanitary condition of houses. They examined food and clothing in jails, scrutinized the treatment of inmates in private asylums, disposed of dead bodies, posed questions to schoolchildren, verified the accuracy of weights and measures, and oversaw the conduct of public employees. They also wrote reports; for pay, for pleasure, and to satisfy the gnawing appetite of new central state agencies to know the local fate of their policies.

The growth of international commodity markets created pressures for the standardization of commodities and for the improvement of communications. Some of the colony's inspectorates were a direct response to these pressures. Many inspectors were appointed, with government sanction, by boards of trade in cities and towns involved in the colony's export trade. These officials inspected and graded such export staples as wood products, ashes, butter, meat, and flour. Other officials, often appointed locally, enforced standard weights and measures and regulated transport and communications throughout the colony. Inspection formed an important part of the infrastructure of the developing capitalist economy. A by-product of these activities was the generation of detailed import and export statistics, which informed developing colonial state agencies about political economic conditions.

The Canadian colonies were also in the throes of a major political transition in the 1840s, which led to a vastly expanded state system. State agencies undertook to create, organize, and regulate new social policies and new public institutions. Paternalistic government by members of appointed élites was giving way to a system of representative government with heightened colonial political autonomy. Elected bodies with new powers replaced many appointed bodies in the colony, and alongside them there appeared new state bureaucracies. This was a period of political centralization and state formation. Newly created central state depart-ments undertook systematic social policies, often using local government bodies as management agencies. The success of centralization came to depend, in part, upon the appointment of inspectors to examine and to report on the fate of central policy initiatives at the local level.

The development of inspection in mid-nineteenth-century Canada is thus both a component part and an index of a process of state formation. By state formation, I mean the centralization and concentration of relations of economic and political power and authority in society. State formation typically involves the appearance or the reorganization of monopolies over the means of violence, taxation, administration, and over symbolic systems. In mid-nineteenth-century Canada, state formation involved the extension of capitalist relations of production and liberal political democracy, with their coincident bureaucratic forms of administration and policing. The development of such relations entailed what Corrigan and Sayer have called 'cultural revolution': a fundamental transformation of the ways in which individuals and groups understand, value, and experience their relations with themselves and others.[4]

This book concerns the formation of the Canadian state in the crucial decade of the 1840s. To illuminate the process of state formation, I focus upon the development of the largest and most important inspectorate in the colony: the district superintendents of education in Canada West, appointed under the school acts of 1843 and 1846. The book examines the political context, both colonial and international, out of which inspection as a practice of government arose. It undertakes a collective biography of the thirty-seven men who served as educational inspectors, examines their activities, and retraces the process whereby practices pioneered by these men came to be institutionalized as 'efficient' educational administration.

The 1840s and 1850s were the decades of the Canadian nineteenth-century 'revolution in government.' The Rebellions of 1837–8 in the Canadas and the growing importance of the Whig-Radical alliance in England demonstrated the bankruptcy of colonial rule by an appointed élite. Political reforms carried out in the United Canadas led to the replacement, in certain areas, of appointed with elected government officials, the development of new kinds of central–local government relations, and the elaboration of bureaucratic governmental procedures.

Concurrently, systematic efforts were undertaken by the imperial government and the colonial Parliament to educate 'the people' in the ideological, moral, and behavioural requisites of the new forms of governance. Representation and bureaucratic administration demanded new forms of individual and group consciousness and comportment, including the willingness to cede legitimate political activity to representatives, to follow procedures, and to respect the legitimate rights of others. The substance of legitimacy was a matter of contest, but adequate or proper political conciousness and comportment came typically to be marked off as 'good moral character.' While such moral character remained the ascribed attribute of men of property and professional status, political theorists came to believe that it both could and must be implanted in 'the people' generally through training in state institutions – that is, if 'the interests of commerce,' the 'security of property,' and 'political and religious liberty' were to triumph.

A focus upon public educational inspection also finds its logic in the doubly political character of public educational institutions. The democratization of political participation demanded the instruction of the population in its 'rights and duties,' the creation in the population of a respect for the practical limits to democractic government imposed by allowing men of property to speak for society as a whole. Such was the ideological thrust of schooling.

At the same time, educational administration was seen to implicate the population in a practical process of training in 'self-government.' Educational administration would involve people (adult men especially, but not exclusively) in acting regularly and predictably, in following procedures, in behaving consistently. Bureaucratic administration was seen by political liberals as a practical education, a 'normal school' for 'the people.' Not only did middle-class activists argue that the generalization of bureaucratic behavioural patterns was an essential support to a 'free' government, but many of them also took pleasure in adopting such habits in their own lives. With the exception of an insightful (and neglected) article by Alison Prentice, this key aspect of nineteenth-century liberal thought and bourgeois culture receives only passing attention in recent Canadian work.[5]

Educational inspection played a central role in the formation of new state structures capable of connecting central authorities and local agencies, and educational practice, both as ideology and as administration, was fundamental to the existence of representative government. Educational inspectors, typically respectable, Anglo-Saxon men of property, were strategically placed to effect changes in structures and practices of governance. They were placed to promote and, at times, to enforce their cultural conceptions, their moral standards, their sense of justice, and their aesthetic sense as models for the rest of society. Tendencies towards educational standardization embodied their standards.

Educational historiography in Ontario has recently begun to turn away from the hagiolatry that, for more than a century, has centred upon the person of Egerton Ryerson (1803–83), educational reformer and long-time chief superintendent of education for Canada West (1846–76).[6] Yet, the pioneering educational inspectors of the 1840s remain virtually unknown. The official historian of Ontario education, J.G. Hodgins, accorded them scant attention. Hodgins frequently excised those of their views not narrowly related to state schooling, along with their critical opinions, from his collection of educational documents. Few of these men appear in the pages of the *Dictionary of Canadian Biography* or in other biographical compilations, and, when they do appear, it is not by virtue of their educational activity. Even in their own autobiographical accounts, their work as educational activists receives little attention.

But I think this invisibility is a consequence of their success. The contribution these inspectors made to a central educational authority was such that many historians have been able to present educational development as a product of central authority alone. Early inspectors did not possess the characteristics of bureaucratic expertise that later came to be the measure of state servants. When they looked back upon their lives after bureaucratic expertise had become normal, these inspectors tended to denigrate their own early educational activities. But I will argue that it was out of the culture; language; ways of seeing, valuing, and doing of these men, in a context of social struggle, that a particular conception of expertise and proper procedure was developed and institutionalized. Much of what these men and others of their class valued, believed, and understood became legitimated as *the* worthy, valuable, credible, and real – and not only in the domain of public education.

The thirty-seven men who served as district superintendents of education in Canada West between 1844 and 1850 were peculiarly well placed to shape educational practice. They were active at a period in Canadian political history when the state system itself was in a phase of accelerated formation. These thirty-seven men were placed to make and enforce political determinations about what needed to be done and known to organize the efficient 'education of the people.' They were leading activists in the extension of a new tutelar relationship between state and citizen, a relationship of intellectual, moral, and paternal guardianship. These men shared a broadly common social-class background and cultural experience that linked political order to the diffusion of sound moral character in society. They found their models of morality in the values of their own class. They worked consciously to transform these values into common or mass personal habits, which they called 'national character,' by encouraging the spread of didactic practices. In the course of these activities, they were involved in the elaboration of administrative methods and procedures as they interpreted and attempted to give effect to official educational policy. Their activity, in a particular context of policy initiatives and conflicts between nascent central and local educational authorities, laid much of the basis for what became neutralized as educational 'efficiency.'

One of the objectives of this book is to identify and examine the initiatives of regionally active state servants in the formative period of public education in Canada West. Their perceptions, interests, experiences, and identities figure largely in what follows. The class position of inspectors is discussed at length in chapter 5, as is the utility of various criteria for classification. I tend to use the terms 'middle class,' 'middle class in formation,' and 'bourgeoisie' interchangeably. This is not out of thoughtlessness; most of the people I'm concerned with were middle class in the sense of being midway between large landed property and wage labour; were members of a class in formation, in that the structure and culture of their dominance was in process; and were bourgeois in values, if not always in relation to the means of production. I am dealing with people whose political loyalties to and theoretical understanding of the 'interests of education' were often of more significance than their ownership of property. While I argue that these 'interests' were squarely based upon a (sometimes progressive) bourgeois view of the world, they were also relatively autonomous. The development of state administration created new resources and social groupings, state servants among them. The reactions of such groupings to social conflicts were shaped by their own place in the developing public domain. To put it differently, class and other social conflicts were fought out, in part, on the terrain of public education, but in an idiom that became increasingly 'educational' as the system of public education was itself solidified. The more general process of creating state interests, detached, to a certain extent, from their class origins, is a constitutive element of state formation.

The study of biography and collective biography is central to the methods of analysis elaborated by Philip Abrams in his *Historical Sociology*, which I attempt to follow here.[7] Abrams reminds us that social and historical development are inevitably processes in which people, formed through social institutions, re-create and modify the very institutions that formed them in the first place. He calls this a process of 'structuring,' a dialectic whose terms are human agency and social structure. The historical reconstruction of this process demands that one attend both to people's conscious activity in pursuit of social interests and to the unintended consequences of this activity for themselves and others. But to understand what people attempt to make of the circumstances in which they find themselves, Abrams insists, we must know how the people in question were themselves made. Biography and collective biography are thus essential elements of historical sociology. Within the conditions imposed by scattered and often fragmentary historical sources, I attempt to identify the educational inspectors in what follows.

While a focus upon educational inspectors makes the present work a history 'from above,' its concern with the process of structuring distances it from 'social control' approaches to social history. This book is about 'passive revolution,' revolution made from above, but made in the face of radical agrarian and republican agitation. I see social development as a process of conflict and contradiction. To argue that educational inspectors worked for certain social objectives and that these activities had real social consequences is not to argue that everyone else in society was thereby neutralized, nor is it to argue that inspectors had a free hand. Unlike 'social control,' the concepts of conflict and struggle imply limits to the wills of social classes and groups.[8]

Unlike those who see state education simply as a form of social control, I follow Philip Abrams's suggestion that the state may best be studied as a *process* of rule. Abrams distinguishes between the state system as a palpable set of institutions, organizations, buildings, and bureaux, and the state project: the lending of legitimacy to the ultimately illegitimate domination of a class (and, one should add, of a sex and a race as well). Rule, Abrams insists, is an activity, a continuously problematic effort to justify, through ideological and material means, the unjustifiable.[9]

'The state,' Weber echoes, 'is a relation of men dominating men [and women and children, I hasten to add], a relation supported by means of legitimate (i.e., considered to be legitimate) violence. If the state is to exist, the dominated must obey the authority claimed by the powers that be.' Like Weber, I pose the question, 'When and why do men [and women and children] obey? Upon what inner justifications and upon what external means does this domination rest?'[10]

I write about a period in which the assimilation of political practice to the 'neutral' domain of universal public education was in process. To male capitalists and intellectuals, the class, national group, and gender in society that should make determinations about educational questions was a matter of political power. The kind of world they valued and sought to entrench was one in which 'choice men,' the 'right kind of persons,' people without 'early prejudices,' would guide and lead the rest. To a small minority of them, 'choiceness' was a matter of inherited class position, from which the vast majority of people were excluded by nature. These people tended to work against the educational project. For others, 'choiceness' was something that the right kind of education could produce in men (not in women in the same way), and men so trained might safely be offered a role in political governance. Having served a political apprenticeship under the careful gaze of a tutelar state, men of the lower classes might act as political guardians in their turn, guardians of the inequitable distribution of property, of women's subordination, and of the dominance of the 'white' races. In these views, the superintendents of education as a group expressed the broader transformation under way in the Canadian colonies from political governance by small, appointed élites to political governance by elected representatives of respectable men of property.

In the case of Canada West, a select group of men of property and their allies worked to legitimate their dominance in part, through the construction of educational administration and practice. Developing state structures allowed for the connection and organization on a province-wide basis of activities formerly conducted, if at all, by members of isolated local élites. The construction of class hegemony, Gramsci reminds us, involves functions that are 'precisely organizational and connective,' which tie together members of the dominant class in institutions and practices that allow for leverage over social activity.[11]

Inspection was just such an organizational and connective force. Inspection, which ideally involved the sending of reliable agents to local sites and agencies for the gathering of standardized information and for ideological activity, became commonplace in most European and American countries in the first half of the nineteenth century. Rule by a centralized national state demanded the creation of local governmental bodies and of mechanisms for verifying the operation of central policy in the locality. Inspectoral practice was a major element in the transformation of nineteenth-century government. The generalization of inspection signals the increasing importance of what Foucault has called 'panoptic' modes of power, power based upon the making visible of the activities of individuals, institutions, or agencies to regulatory authorities. Panopticism heightens the importance of bodies of knowledge in governance, while it also seeks to regulate individuals and groups by arranging the spatial and temporal dimensions of their activities.[12]

Educational inspection led the way in the Canadian colonies. Beginning in 1844, inspectors travelled throughout Canada West, visiting schools, examining teachers, agitating for 'improvement' and collecting information that was reported to the central education office. Inspection allowed the central authority to monitor the local operations of policy, to identify innovation and resistance, to form defensible conceptions of 'what needed to be done.' Inspectors were placed to take initiatives about educational practices and relations. Given that inspectors were themselves initially little regulated by the central authority, their perceptions, attitudes, values, and interests affected the conduct of education and the elaboration of policy. The knowledge about educational conditions generated by inspectors was an important resource in the bitter political struggles over public education that characterized the 1840s.

While the organization of educational inspection and the larger political project in which it was embedded developed in a particular manner in Canada West in the 1840s, it would be misleading to regard this story in a simple sense as 'Canadian.' In other states, political centralization equally demanded the reconstruction of central-local relations. 'Canada' as a national state and as the basis for the elaboration of a political identification had an, at best, unstable existence during this period. Most of the superintendents of education, for instance, perceived themselves to be 'British' or 'English' men, although some of them also argued quite explicitly that state education might create a sense of 'Canadian' national identity: 'a common centre,' as Colonel Thomas Higginson, the Ottawa District inspector, called it.

The Canadas were English colonies in the period studied here, and what happened in the colonies was intimately connected with events and processes in the imperial state, refracted through the prism of proximity to the American republic. Educational inspection developed in England and Scotland in the 1840s as well, based on models of inspectoral practice elaborated by the English colonial administration in Ireland in the 1830s. Attempts were made to impose these models on the Canadas. But this Irish practice, in its turn, and contemporary

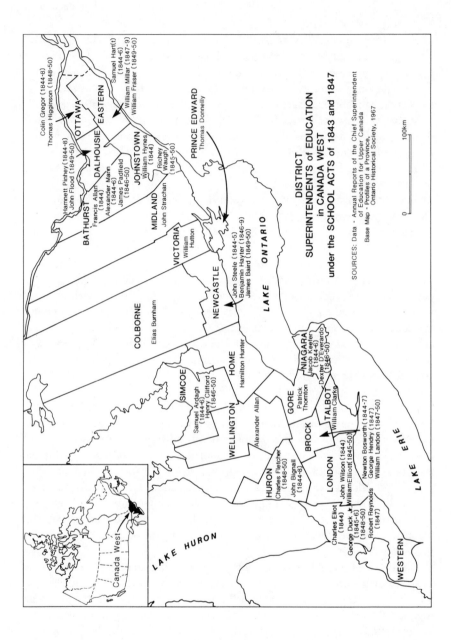

DISTRICT
SUPERINTENDENTS of EDUCATION
in CANADA WEST
under the SCHOOL ACTS of 1843 and 1847

SOURCES: Data - Annual Reports of the Chief Superintendent
of Education for Upper Canada
Base Map - Profiles of a Province,
Ontario Historical Society, 1967

0   100km

LAKE HURON

Canada West

WESTERN

Charles Eliot
(1844)
George Duck Jr.
(1845-50)
Robert Reynolds
(1847)

LONDON
John Wilson (1844)
William Elliott (1845-50)
Newton Bosworth (1844-7)
George Hendry (1847)
William Landon (1847-50)

HURON
Charles Fletcher
(1848-50)
John Bignall
(1844-8)

BROCK
William Clarke

TALBOT
Dexter D'Everardo
(1846-50)

NIAGARA
Jacob Keefer
(1844-6)

GORE
Patrick
Thornton

WELLINGTON
Alexander Allan

SIMCOE
Samuel Ardagh
(1844-6)
Henry Clifford
(1846-50)

HOME
Hamilton Hunter

LAKE ERIE

LAKE ONTARIO

NEWCASTLE
John Steele (1844-5)
Benjamin Hayter (1846-9)
James Baird (1849-50)

COLBORNE
Elias Burnham

VICTORIA
William
Hutton

MIDLAND
John Strachan

PRINCE EDWARD
Thomas Donnelly

JOHNSTOWN
William Hynes
(1844)
Richey Waugh
(1845-50)

BATHURST
Francis Allan
(1844)
Alexander Mann
(1844-6)
James Padfield
(1846-50)

DALHOUSIE
Hamett Pinhey (1844-8)
John Flood (1849-50)

OTTAWA
Colin Gregor (1844-8)
Thomas Higginson (1848-50)

EASTERN
Samuel Hart(t)
(1844-6)
William Millar (1847-9)
William Fraser (1849-50)

District Superintendents of Education for Canada West

Alexander Allan (1775–1855), Wellington District, 1844–50
Francis Allan (1793–1844), Bathurst District, 1844
Samuel B. Ardagh (1803–69), Simcoe District, 1844–6
James Baird (1823?–89), Newcastle District, 1849–50
John Bignall (c.1798–?), Huron District, 1844–8
Newton Bosworth (1778–1848), Brock District, 1844–6
Elias Burnham (1812–71+), Colborne District, 1844–50
William Clarke, Sr (1801–78), Talbot District, 1844–50
Henry A. Clifford (1810–1901), Simcoe District, 1846–50
Dexter D'Everardo (1814–91), Niagara District, 1846–50
Thomas Donnelly (1816–70), Prince Edward District, 1844–50
George Duck, Jr (1821–59), Western District, 1845–6, 1848–50
Charles Eliot (?–1858), Western District, 1844–5
William Elliot(t) (1817–1905), London District, 1845–50
Charles Fletcher (c.1808–85), Huron District, 1848–50
John Flood (1811–71+), Dalhousie District, 1848–50
William Fraser (1800–92), Eastern District, 1849–50
Colin Gregor (1808–64), Ottawa District, 1844–7
Samuel Hart(t) (1796–1871), Eastern District, 1844–6
Benjamin Hayter (1791–1862), Newcastle District, 1845–9
George Hendry (c.1810–47), Brock District, 1846–7
Thomas Higginson (1794–1884), Ottawa District, 1848–50
Hamilton Hunter (1810–81+), Home District, 1844–50
William Hutton (1801–61), Victoria District, 1844–50
William Hynes (1794–1862), Johnstown District, 1844–5
Jacob Keefer (1800–74), Niagara District, 1844–6
William H. Landon (1805–76), Brock District, 1847–50
Alexander Mann (1800–84), Bathurst District, 1844–7
William Millar (?–?), Eastern District, 1847–9
James Padfield (1802–79), Bathurst District, 1847–50
Hamnett Pinhey (1784–1857), Dalhousie District, 1844–9
Robert Reynolds, Jr(?) (1819–?), Western District, 1847
John Steele (1796–1876), Newcastle District, 1844–5
John Strachan (1800–75+), Midland District, 1844–50
Patrick Thornton (1797–c.1866), Gore District, 1844–50
Richey Waugh (1820–82), Johnstown District, 1845–50
John Wilson (1807–69), London District, 1844–5

practice in the United States were heavily influenced by developments in Prussia and Holland, while Prussian and Dutch practice had been shaped by the revolutionary propagandistic efforts of the French empire. One could continue to trace the filiations of inspection further, arriving ultimately no doubt at the suggestion that the earth cooled, and then there were inspectors. I do not wish to argue that educational inspection was *the* first instance of inspectoral practice, or that to discover such a first instance would be to understand all instances of inspection. But any account of inspectoral practice in the Canadas in the 1840s remains partial without the recognition that there was an international process under way to which Canadian practice was connected in myriad ways.

'Capitalism's cultural revolution,' Philip Corrigan called it in work preliminary to his publication, with Derek Sayer, *The Great Arch: English State Formation as Cultural Revolution*. And has it not frequently been the case, for those who have followed closely Màrx, Engels, and writers of the second and third internationals in the attempt to articulate a practical theorization of the state, that the yearning for a working-class internationalism has tended to overshadow the historical reality of bourgeois internationalism? 'Working men of all countries, unite!' cried Marx and Engels in 1847: in matters of state, by the 1840s, members of the rising national bourgeoisies were already in close collaboration. Those interested in the complex project of 'improvement' – reshaping cultural institutions in the image of bourgeois values of regularity, orderliness, predictability, reliability, sobriety, intellectualism, respect for property, religion, and the ever-elusive 'cheerful and willing obedience' to authority – were connected through a wide range of media: specialized periodicals, government reports and commissions, travel literature, tours, exhibitions, immigration, and others. Canadian state formation must be understood as a global process.

The thirty-seven men who served as inspectors in the twenty colonial districts (each district usually contained two counties) are listed on page 13, and the map on page 12 shows the parts of the colony in which they were active.

Charles Poulett Thomson (1798–1841), Baron of Sydenham and Toronto, sought to bring the Canadian state system into line with liberal reforms in England. One of his projects for the Canadas was the organization of a system of public instruction based on the one imposed upon Ireland in the 1830s. (Archives of Ontario, S.2180)

Francis (later Sir Francis) Hincks was author of the Canada West School Act of 1843 and supported Egerton Ryerson's School Act of 1850 against the left wing of his Reform party. His father was master of the élite Belfast Academical Institution and a strong supporter of the Irish National school system. (Archives of Ontario, Acc.6011, S.14854)

Rev. Egerton Ryerson (1803–83), assistant and chief superintendent of education for Canada West and Ontario (1844–76), argued that the power of government in public education lay in its control over finance and inspection. (Archives of Ontario, S.627)

Thomas Jaffray Robertson (1805–66), one of the first Irish school inspectors, played an important role in the development of educational inspection in Canada West. As he was principal of the Toronto Normal School (1847–66) and, from 1855, one of two grammar-school inspectors, his views of inspectoral practice were widely published and influential. (Archives of Ontario, Gov't. Doc. Ed.)

Malcolm Cameron (1808–76), MPP for Lanark in the Bathurst District, led the unsuccessful challenge of the left of the Reform party against Ryerson's centralized educational system in 1849. His break with the Reformers late in that year cleared the way for the School Act of 1850. (Baldwin Room, Metropolitan Toronto Reference Library, T.31101)

John Wilson M.P., William Elliot's caricature of his predecessor as school inspector. (McIntosh Gallery, University of Western Ontario)

Bottom right: William Elliot (1817–1905) succeeded John Wilson as school inspector in the London District and as district judge. Elliot was active in local cultural and scientific institutions like the London Mechanics' Institute and the Agricultural Society. He was renowned for his quick wit and for his caricatures of local figures, although these exposed him to suits for libel. (Baldwin Room, Metropolitan Toronto Reference Library, T.31932)

John Wilson (1807–69), the London District superintendent of education in 1844, was a central figure in the politics and government of London, Canada West. Famous for having killed his opponent in the last-known duel fought in Canada (1830), Wilson practised law before being elected to Parliament in the late 1840s. He ended his career as district judge. (Baldwin Room, Metropolitan Toronto Reference Library, T.16864)

Like many of his fellow inspectors, William Elliot was an advocate of Temperance. His *Spectacle in a Tavern in Mosa 1845* portrayed some of the township's drinkers. (McIntosh Gallery, University of Western Ontario)

Entertainment by William Elliot. Hotels and inns were rare in the back townships of Canada West in the 1840s, and school inspectors were dependent upon local residents for accommodation. Elliot regarded 'promiscuous lodging' as one of the worst conditions of his work as inspector, and his watercolour sketch provides a rare view of the living conditions of the population whose schools he inspected. The note reads: 'a log house in the Township of Williams in which I lodged at night in 1845 on several occasions when acting as school supet*n*'. (McIntosh Gallery, University of Western Ontario)

SCHOOL NOTICE.

ALL TEACHERS OF COMMON SCHOOLS

IN THE

EASTERN DISTRICT,

Are hereby notified that the GovernmentGrant to Common Schools for the current year, shall be paid at

MRS. CHESLEY'S HOTEL, CORNWALL,

AS FOLLOWS,

The Teachers of Glengarry shall, be paid on Tuesday the 21st of this month,
Those of Stormont, on the following day,
And the Teachers of Dundas, on Thursday, the 23rd of the same month.

An order will be given, at the same time, to each Teacher on the Collector of his Township, for the amount due his School Section of the District School Rate, if the order of his Trustees will authorize the whole of the amount due the School section to be paid to the bearer.

But, let it be remembered, for fear of fraud or imposition, that no claim shall be admitted without a certificate from one of the Clergy, Councillors, or Magistrates of the township, certifying that the said Teacher is or has been teaching this year in the School Section mentioned in his order. However this will not be required of any Teacher, personally known to the Superintendent.

WM. FRASER,

Superintendent of C. Schools E. District.

Cornwall, August 2, 1849.

Rev. William Fraser (1800–92), the Eastern District school inspector, summoned teachers to Mrs Chesley's hotel to receive their shares of the annual government school grant. Their control over the government grant and their right to examine teachers allowed the inspectors to shape the conduct of schooling. Here Fraser announces that a certificate from a member of the local élite is necessary for any teacher whom he did not know personally. (Archives of Ontario, RG2, C-6-C, Box 7)

William Hutton (1801–61), the Victoria District superintendent and a gentleman farmer, thought only 'choice men' who, like himself, were 'without early education prejudices,' could form sound judgments in educational matters. Hutton's publications on agricultural improvement and his close friendship with his cousin Francis Hincks led to his later appointment as secretary to the Bureau of Agriculture and Statistics, from which position he designed the Canadian census of 1861. (Hastings County Historical Society Collection)

Rev. Samuel Brown Ardagh (1803–69), the Simcoe District school inspector, came to Canada West as rector of Barrie after violent popular opposition to his proselytizing activities forced him out of Ireland. He subsidized his work as inspector out of his own pocket and was dismayed at what he considered the degraded educational condition of his parishioners. (Wilfrid Laurier University)

Thomas Higginson (1794–1884), the Ottawa District superintendent, was a farmer, amateur astronomer, poet, MPP, and railway promoter. The silhouette was made by his nephew, Thomas Tweed Higginson, about 1849. (T. Boyd Higginson)

Rev. Alexander Mann (1800–84), the Bathurst District superintendent, did not inspect the schools under his charge, sided with Egerton Ryerson against the district council in a dispute over school taxation, and was forced to resign. (Verna Ross McGiffin)

A broadside directed against Dexter D'Everardo (1814–91), the Niagara District school inspector. A disgruntled arch-Tory teacher, unable to make Egerton Ryerson act against the inspector's alleged 'Yankee' bias, threatened to expose D'Everardo in *The Magic Lantern*. D'Everardo was a Quaker whose adopted daughters were rumoured to have been kidnapped. (Archives of Ontario, RG2, C-6-C, Box 7)

THE TOWN OF PERTH, CO. LANARK, U.C. 1853.
From an oil painting by Field.

The town of Perth in the Bathurst District was settled by assisted Scottish weavers. 'Scotch democracy' was strong in this district, from which challenges to central control over public education were launched. (Baldwin Room, Metropolitan Toronto Reference Library, T.15348)

Rev. James Padfield (1802–79) was a grammar-school master and master of the preparatory school at Upper Canada College before joining the Church of England ministry. He was rector of Beckwith at the time of his appointment as Bathurst District superintendent. (Baldwin Room, Metropolitan Toronto Reference Library, T.16737)

James Padfield lived in Franktown in Beckwith Township while serving as school inspector, and his home church was what is now St James Anglican, originally constructed in 1822. The upper half of the tower is a later addition. (Author's photo)

Rev. William Landon (1805–76) superintended the schools of the Brock District. An elected Baptist elder, Landon scrambled to make a living by running private schools, editing a newspaper, enumerating the town of Woodstock for the 1852 census, and hawking railway shares. He was active in attempts to 'guide the popular voice' and made common cause with Egerton Ryerson in educational reform. (Woodstock Museum)

One of the earliest known views of Woodstock, Canada West, a flourishing regional
centre and the district town for the Brock District. (Woodstock Museum)

Hamnett Kirkes Pinhey (1784–1857) served as Dalhousie District superintendent and as district warden before being named to the Legislative Council in 1847. A retired English grocer and liveryman who had been educated at Christ's Hospital and decorated for running the Napoleonic blockade, Pinhey was at the centre of a local 'compact' composed of retired army and navy officers. He used his position to block tax-supported education in his district and to work against Ryerson's educational plans. (Archives of Ontario, MU940, Acc.9002)

An early view of 'Horaceville,' the village established by Pinhey on the banks of
the Ottawa River and currently a historic site run by the Pinhey's Point Foundation.
Pinhey's imitation-stone manor house and his mills are visible in the centre of the
sketch. Pinhey also built the church to the left at his own expense, and it was one of
James Padfield's first clerical charges. (Archives of Ontario, MU940, Acc.9002)

Richey Waugh's stone house and store at Oxford Mills in what was the Johnstown District. His grist and shingle mills, on the south branch of the Rideau River, were nearby. Many of the superintendents of education lived in commodious stone or brick houses, while the supporters of the schools they inspected were in log cabins. (Author's photo)

1 'The Great "Normal School" for Training the People'

The principles of governance were reconstructed and the state system was radically reformed in the Canadas of the 1840s and 1850s. The Rebellions of 1837–8 demonstrated forcefully the failure of the Constitutional Act of 1791, under which a prestigious colonial aristocracy was meant to contain the popular clamour for 'democracy' that had led to the loss of the American colonies. Imperial politicians attempted to limit colonial demands for governmental autonomy while extending to the colony some of the governmental reforms under way in England and while experimenting with other reforms. To a certain extent, the Canadas became proving grounds for political and administrative changes sought by English political parties.[1]

New agencies and instruments of government and new ideological justifications for political domination were created, struggled over, and entrenched in the 1840s and 1850s, in a context of rapid population growth and capitalist accumulation. The discrediting of the dominance of individual proprietors, priests, and professionals holding appointive offices for life involved struggles to legitimate both the elective principle and rational bureaucratic administration.

There were continuities and discontinuities with earlier forms of rule in this transition, and it was neither perfect nor complete. But it was real and important. New agencies of government were created, and old agencies reformed. A board of works; a bureau of agriculture; a board of registration and statistics; a system of prisons and jails, lunatic asylums, public-health bodies, new financial institutions, registry offices, local governmental bodies, and educational offices were organized. Much of the state system that characterized the Canadas at Confederation in 1867 was elaborated in this period.

A key element in this transition was an expanded role for elective political representation and the reorganization of central-local state relations. Wider powers were claimed by the representatives of naturalized adult white men of property. Largely elective state bodies came to organize key elements of governance in the locality, and regular, stable, and increasingly precise connections were established between central and local authorities.

State formation in the 1840s involved political centralization, a process that paradoxically depended for its success upon a new kind of political decentralization and created potentially competing or antagonistic interests in centre and locality. Effective political centralization demanded the creation of local government bodies able to execute central policy. But, once in place, such local bodies might pursue their own interests.

This process proceeded very unevenly in the two Canadas. In Canada West, the District Councils Act of 1841 led to the creation of local governmental bodies, and the failed Municipal Bill of 1843 attempted to extend their powers. Councils gained greater control over the appointment of their own officers with reforms in 1846, and the Municipal Corporations Act of 1849 created the system of county municipalities that remains in existence in the province of Ontario. In Canada East, effective local governmental organization was successfully blocked by entrenched élites in most areas until the mid-1850s, and feudal land tenure survived until 1855.

Still, the increasing scope afforded representative government took place at the expense of two earlier forms of governance: communal self-management and control by notables. On the one hand, the room for manoeuvre earlier gained by selected proprietors, who ruled according to personal and often idiosyncratic conceptions, was restricted by the development of bureaucratic structures and procedures. On the other hand, the powers of local communities, in Canada West especially, for self-management and for informal plebiscitarian democracy with a universal franchise, and the coincident communitarian culture, were also marginalized by new political institutions.

Representative government allowed selected men of property to speak for society as a whole. It did not create democracy in the sense of immediate rule by the people. Rather, the system of representation changed and broadened the basis and the mechanisms of political selection. Members of Parliament were still elected on a franchise limited by gender, property, age, and residence, and were themselves subject to a substantial property qualification. Similar limitations applied at the district level. The union of the Canadas did not include the principle of 'representation by population.' Under representative government, more men of property were allowed to engage in political activity than had earlier been the case.[2]

The system of representative government was accompanied by the growth of bureaucratic state administration. Alongside the elective principle, there appeared selection according to 'expertise,' entrenched in theory by the Civil Service Act of 1857. In many areas of social administration, boards of examiners were established to screen candidates for administrative positions. The practice of examination was most completely developed in the domain of elementary education in Canada West, where, from at least 1850, all prospective teachers were subjected to it. 'Expertise,' which involves the appropriation of domains of competence by individuals and social groups, constituted a further barrier between the governed and those who govern.[3]

Social dominance based upon religious allegiance was also under attack in Canada West in the 1840s and 1850s. Successive governments acted to limit the holding of secular offices by clergymen subsidized from the Clergy Reserves fund. After a protracted political struggle, the Reserves themselves were secularized in the mid-1850s. In Canada West, the provincial university became formally non-sectarian in 1849, and in both parts of the colony public educational institutions were based on a 'common Christianity.' The decade of the 1840s involved attempts by a number of activists opposed to the existence of a state church to translate general Christian tenets into an effective civic morality. Religious practice tended towards greater formality.[4]

There were important continuities between bureaucratic and non-bureaucratic governmental forms in the colony, in personnel and in the class basis of political power. The transition was itself promoted by many visible proprietors, professionals, and intellectuals active in political leadership roles both in appointive governmental office and in communal institutions. These were men whose social-class positions ranged from respectable artisanal workers to large capitalists and landholders. In terms of cultural outlook, however, these men were solidly bourgeois: that is, without exception they supported private property in the means of production; the wage relation; and the individual accumulation of capital, rational religion, and self-help. There were differences among them within this domain of consensus, but there was such a domain of consensus. The prestige enjoyed by many of these men was influential in promoting the governmental transition, and for many of them it was a means of personal enrichment.

For the mass of the population in the Canadas, the project of representative 'self-government' entailed the development of new forms of government of the self, i.e., of moral regulation and self-discipline. Bourgeois democracy would degenerate into chaos if the formal universality of citizenship were pursued as substance. Effective representative government and bureaucratic administration demand the renunciation of the actual, and acceptance of the theoretical, right to govern by the mass of the population. This renunciation was organized in the Canadas through public education, through processes of popular 'self-neutralization' that involved the attribution of competence and authority to 'experts' in the moral as in the administrative domain.[5] These attributions were as much usurpation, facilitated by ideological practices, as they were 'voluntary' acceptance. They were successful claims to rule by certain classes and groups. Representation for most people in the Canadas was political exclusion and limitation, but exclusion and limitation to which they were encouraged to agree by new state agencies. The organization of a civil administration in the decade of the 1840s involved the making of a social 'consensus' through disciplinary practices aimed at the population as a whole. Public education, I have argued elsewhere, was the leading instance of public discipline, but there were also attempts to reorganize and extend the powers of militia and police forces.[6]

State formation in this period was shaped by the earlier failure of the imperial state to establish in the colony a workable version of the modalities of rule prevalent in the imperium, known as 'Old Corruption.' Armed rebellion was followed by a nineteenth-century Canadian 'revolution in government.'

The development of a centralized state system, in which local government executed central policies, demanded the establishment of connections between central and local agencies. A novel kind of connection became a regular part of the Canadian state system in the 1840s: inspection.

Representation, Education, Inspection

The structure of colonial government under the Constitutional Act of 1791 worked against three elements, which, by the 1830s, if not before, were taken by English Radicals and Whigs and some Canadian Reformers to be central to the solidification and maintenance of class hegemony. I call these, respectively, the 'educational idea,' 'representative government,' and the 'inspective function.' The first two refer to the growing consensus among members of the governing classes that social order must be based upon the practical habituation of the population to the operation of parliamentary and narrowly representative forms of rule. In a broad sense, this consensus arose out of the 'crisis of moral economy' consequent upon the generalization of commodity production and exchange.[7] 'Free labour' could no longer be governed through direct supervision and personal contact between rulers and ruled. New relations of production created a new physical and political distance between classes.

In this condition, bourgeois political activists sought to base political rule on the subjectification of the population through a double educational process. On the one hand, direct socialization in habits and beliefs congenial to bourgeois hegemony would take place in schools for the bulk of the population. On the other hand, the management of limited agencies of local government (including schools) would train 'the people' (adult male proprietors directly) to conduct aspects of their own governance in limited representative forms.

This liberal theory of government allowed men of property, chosen through processes of election, to represent, define, and pursue the interests of society as a whole. Men of property were to govern propertyless men through new public institutions, and men generally would govern women and children through their dominance in the household.

The 'inspective function' refers to the development of connections between central authorities and local sites that centred upon knowledge/power relations. The capacity of central government to execute policy and to carry out policing came to be seen to depend upon the supervision of local provision by loyal agents charged with gathering and transmitting intelligence and with exercising leadership. Such intelligence gathering and leadership would enable the central authority to monitor local provision, to identify sources of conflict, to discover and generalize administrative innovation, and to intervene to overcome barriers to the realization of policy or the success of policing. At the same time, the practical activity of inspection would educate inspectors and would lead to the creation of a certain kind of expertise. Inspection became general in England in the 1830s, and a very large number of inspectorates were organized in the Canadas in the following decades.

Most of the population in Canada West in this period was employed directly or indirectly in the production of the colony's two main staples: wheat (on the rise) and timber (in decline). Many people had access to land, although landholding was supplemented for many small farmers by wage labour of various kinds. Wage rates remained relatively stable throughout the 1840s, but land prices tended to rise, cutting larger numbers of people off from access to land. Public works, extended as part of the imperial package to encourage the Act of Union, employed a large wage labour force. The expansion of village industry contributed to the growth of the class dependent upon wages, as did the wave of migration created by the Irish famines. The population of Canada West increased from about 450,000 in 1841 to about 950,000 by 1852.[8]

Governing the Canadas, 1791–1840

The nature of governmental forms in the Canadas was at the centre of colonial political struggle, at least until the granting of parliamentary autonomy in the late 1840s. Before the Union of 1840, the Constitutional Act of 1791 sharply limited the powers of local representative governmental bodies. It also weakened the central authority.

The authors of the Constitutional Act understood the eighteenth-century American Rebellion as the product of local democratic government in the absence of the salutary influence of a hereditary aristocracy. The institution of the New

England town meeting was seen to be particularly culpable as a forum for the fomentation of democratic 'excess.' As Lord Grenville, secretary of state for colonies, argued in his outline of a proposed constitution for the Canadas,

to the want of an intermediate Power, to operate as a check, both on the misconduct of Governors, & on the democratical Spirit, which prevailed in the Assemblies, the defection of the American Provinces, may perhaps be more justly ascribed, than to any other general cause which can be assigned. And there seems to be no one point of more consequence, in this country, than the labouring to establish, in the remaining provinces, a respectable Aristocracy, as a support, & safe guard to the Monarchy, removed, that is, at so great a distance, & on that account, so much less powerful, in its weight and influence upon the people at large.[9]

Lord Dorchester, governor of Quebec, suggested that the Crown retain parcels of five thousand acres in every township 'to create and strengthen an Aristocracy, of which the best use may be made on this Continent, where all Governments are feeble and the general conditions of things run to a wild Democracy.'[10] Dorchester claimed that even 'people of property' in the United States had come to realize 'the evils rendered by' the absence of an aristocracy 'and would bring forward an adequate remedy, did they know how to carry it into execution.'[11] However, both the governor of Quebec and the secretary of state for colonies were constrained to accept the political principle established by the American rebels: 'no taxation without representation.' Until the reforms of the 1840s, elected assemblies were needed to initiate money bills.

Still, the framers of the Constitutional Act hoped for the creation of a Canadian aristocracy through the distribution of colonial lands. Grenville sought a Canadian parallel to the English Lords, a hereditary aristocracy 'unlimited in point of number,' which would occupy the colonial Upper House and whose local activity would form the basis of governance. However, Dorchester opposed this, and eventually members of the colonial Upper House, the Legislative Council, were appointed for life during good behaviour. Dorchester regarded the attempt to use land and inheritance as reliance on unstable mechanisms for the creation of an aristocracy. Given the 'fluctuating state of Property' in the colony, which would 'expose all hereditary honors to fall into disregard,' it would be safer to select members of the Legislative Council 'from among the men of property, where talents, integrity, and a firm attachment to the Unity of the Empire may be found.' In the western part of the colony, this selection method came to involve the granting of lands to military officers on half pay.[12]

The constitution bestowed upon the Canadas by the act of 1791 was considered by the Colonial Office to be exceptionally liberal. The representative of the King, the lieutenant-governor, was to be advised by an appointed executive council, holding office during pleasure.[13] Parliament was to consist of an appointive legislative council, whose members held office for life during good behaviour, and an elective House of Assembly, whose members were adult male property holders. Both the Legislative Council and the governor-in-council exerted powers of veto over enactments of the elective branch, although money bills originated in the latter. After 1831, the elected assemblies also controlled the Civil List, that is, the payment of representatives of the Crown.

Town and township meetings of naturalized male proprietors were created in the Canadas, and the franchise was set at forty shillings freehold. However, the officers these meetings could appoint were functionaries without powers either of policy formation or of taxation: pound keepers, assessors, collectors, path masters, fence viewers, and so forth. Local powers of taxation and administration were mainly in the hands of appointed justices, either singly or assembled in Quarter Sessions. Justices were aided and informed by grand juries composed of male property holders. Officers appointed by town meetings executed functions specified either by justices or by acts of Parliament. The magistracy was not itself stipendiary, nor were other local governmental officials salaried. In practice, once appointed, the local judiciary was largely independent in its day-to-day operations.[14]

Limitations of Central Authority

The capacity of the central authority was sharply limited in the period before 1840 by the absence of regular connections between centre and locality.[15] Physical obstacles, especially the lack of roads and other means of communication, were exacerbated by administrative obstacles. Although census and assessment information of some sort was collected more or less systematically from the 1810s, there were relatively few central social-policy initiatives undertaken, or indeed that could have been undertaken, before the 1840s. Despite the desires of the framers of the Constitutional Act, class relations in the Canadas did not approximate those in the imperial state. With the limited exception of the seigneurs in Lower Canada, no colonial aristocracy came into existence, and *relatively* easy access to land freed the 'lower orders' from direct dependence on their social superiors, in Upper Canada and in some of the new townships of Lower Canada. In practice, in Upper Canada especially, the result was the absence both of a dominant class of proprietors capable of translating central policy into effective local practices and of the representative governmental powers that existed in the United States.

Local élites certainly existed in Upper Canada, and access to governmental office was severely restricted.[16] In many parts of the colony, leading proprietors acted in ways that sustained an authority structure based upon private property in the means of production, patriarchy, and official religion. But the structure of governance characteristic of England, in which local authority was sustained through the social and economic dominance of small élites (a notion already under serious attack from the early 1800s), was not replicated in the Canadas.[17] Many large land grants were held by absentees. To the absence of representative local government and to the policy of creating Crown and Clergy Reserves was attributed the relative economic and social backwardness of the Canadas in comparison with the United States.

In practice, the absence of both a local aristocracy and representative government meant that the execution of most central policies and projects was supervised locally through the appointment by Parliament of special or extraordinary officers, usually called commissioners or overseers.

There were important exceptions in Upper Canada. Appointed district boards of education were created in 1816 and were subordinated to an appointed general board of education in 1823. The importance of a central educational intervention was recognized by the colonial governing classes quite early, and attempts were made to regulate local schools. However, the General Board itself was disbanded in 1833, after persistent attacks upon it by Reformers, and district boards of education followed no consistent educational policy.[18]

The provincial penitentiary, created by an act of Parliament in 1832, was supervised by a board of five inspectors, who were to meet every two months in the institution and who were to submit an annual report. The inspectors could formulate rules and regulations for the institution, but there was only one penitentiary and the inspectors were unpaid and performed their functions haphazardly at best.[19]

Inspectors appointed by the lieutenant-governor under an act of 1803 were to issue licences and collect fees from the distillers of alcholic beverages and the keepers of billiard tables. These district inspectors had no funds for contingencies, for hiring deputies or for paying informers, and had few inquisitory powers. Interested applicants came to them, and, as a parliamentary commission of 1839 reported, 'thus the whole business of the District, no matter how populous or extensive, is thrown on one man alone, and unassisted in his labours.' The result was that large districts were 'utterly free from inspection.'[20]

Finally (and given an analysis of knowledge/power relations, importantly), assessors, clerks of the peace, and district treasurers were chosen by annual town meetings, and these officials collected and transmitted reports of classes of households and categories of persons to the central authority. This aspect of central governmental capacity attracted regular parliamentary attention, and, in

1823, a joint committee produced legislation that systematized the information-gathering and reporting procedures. Parliament specified the categories of information collected, but, until the creation of a board of registration and statistics in 1847, no central state agency was charged with interpreting this information.[21]

In Lower Canada, the cholera epidemic of 1832 led to the creation of a number of sanitary inspectors concerned with the quarantine of vessels, but the impotence of the central authority to gather information or to execute systematic policy was general. As Jean-Marie Fecteau has remarked of Lower Canada in the 1820s, 'le pouvoir exécutif n'a aucun représentant véritablement efficace au niveau local. Les juges de paix, traditionnellement investis de cette fonction, sont répartis sur un immense territoire, et sans moyens réels pour assurer la régulation locale et le respect de l'ordre.'[22]

In Upper Canada, with some rare exceptions, each of the relatively few projects undertaken for local improvement demanded a special act of Parliament to set it in motion, and each involved the naming of special overseers or commissioners to manage it.

In the domain of communications,[23] justices of the peace were initially appointed commissioners of roads, with fairly broad powers for planning and taxation. This system failed to produce much improvement in internal communications and, by the 1830s, when Parliament was appropriating fairly large sums annually for road construction, commissioners were appointed at the district level to supervise road building and to account for monies. Overseers of highways elected by town meetings kept lists of those liable to statute labour and arranged for its compounding. The construction of bridges, such as those over the Trent, Don, Humber, Grand, and Thames rivers, was centrally financed and supervised by commissioners appointed specially in each case by the lieutenant-governor. Separate acts of Parliament named commissioners to supervise the improvement of internal navigation and the construction of particular canals, the dredging of particular harbours, and the building of individual lights. Macadamized roads were established by special enactment as well, and, in 1840, trustees of these roads were united into commissioners of district turnpike trusts.

Appointed commissioners supervised the construction of Kingston General Hospital, subsidized by Parliament in response to the cholera epidemic of 1832. But, since no local authority existed to maintain or fund the actual operations of a hospital, the building sat empty until 1841, when it was temporarily occupied by Queen's College. Appointed commissioners were to supervise any asylum constructed under an enabling act passed in 1839, and special commissioners were to regulate the pretended Bank of Upper Canada.[24]

These special commissioners and overseers were casual. Their activity was little routinized, and they were not travelling functionaries. Their activity was bound to a particular locality and project. They did not accumulate information about all projects in a particular class, nor about matters other than the particular bridge, road, harbour, or light for which they were commissioned.[25] Thus, the capacity of central government to form a general view of local improvements, or to implement colony-wide policy was limited.

The absence of systematic organs of local government seriously limited the capacity of the central government to institute and carry out any social policy and policing on a continuous and regular basis. A similar lack in England was compensated for, to a degree, by the existence of and extensive powers granted to large proprietors. But, even in the English case, the 1830s saw important alterations in the relations of local governance known as 'Old Corruption.'[26] In the *comparatively* democratic conditions of the Canadas, the influence of property in the locality was less marked, not the least because of a high degree of absentee holding.

Education and Central Capacity

Before and immediately after the Rebellions of 1837–8, the absence of central capacity in the locality was seen as problematic, both to the Colonial Office and to members of colonial political parties. Such was particularly evident in the area of educational policy, which, in both parts of the colony, came to be seen as a key means for the maintenance of authority relations based on 'security of property.' In Upper Canada, Reform efforts in this regard were capped by the Duncombe report of 1836 which urged a systematic program of popular education. Duncombe's school legislation assumed the creation of local organs of representative educational government. The legislative councillor Robert Baldwin Sullivan attributed the Rebellion of 1837 to the absence of state-directed education, but the Legislative Council vetoed Burwell's School Act of 1839 on the grounds of excessive taxation.[27] The Gosford Commission of 1836, sent to investigate the turbulent conditions in Lower Canada, was officially enjoined by Lord Glenelg to attend closely to educational conditions.[28] All of these plans and projects assumed the existence of substantial organs of local government. In Lower Canada, the direct appointment of schoolmasters by Parliament was sharply criticized.

That is not to insist that representative local government was a *uniformly* popular demand. We do not know what the majority of the Canadian population thought or felt about this question. The absence of representative government, on the one hand, encouraged the development of various forms of communal self-management, forms that were destroyed through the establishment of representative institutions.[29] On the other hand, the Upper Canadian Legislative Council was strenuously opposed to local representative institutions. In 1839, the Committee of Council that examined Lord Durham's *Report on the Affairs of British North America* argued that the Rebellions were caused not by any defects in the structure of colonial government, but rather by 'the proximity of the American frontier – the wild and chimerical notions of civil government broached and discussed there' – and American immigration.[30]

Yet other sections of the colonial governing classes clearly sought to create structures in the locality that would allow for social and economic 'improvement' and for disciplinary practices. Both the Durham report and Radical opinion in the imperial Parliament urged the creation of institutions of local representative government in the Canadas, and, as early as 1839, this was a Whig policy. Popular demonstrations in the Canadas supported the Durham report. Both Reformers and moderate Tories in the colonies, and Whigs and Radicals in the imperial state, regarded oligarchic rule from the centre as ineffective and inefficient.

Until Ajzenstat's *The Political Thought of Lord Durham* called such a position into question, debate over the Durham report in Canadian historiography had focused upon its role in the coming of 'responsible government' (ministerial autonomy) in the late 1840s. Martin and Ward, for instance, criticized earlier views that attributed a central role to the report, both by subjecting Durham's own conception of 'responsibility' to scrutiny and by locating Durham, Buller, Wakefield, and others on the periphery of English political debate. Yet the Radicals advocated *just* the form of *local representative government* that was adopted in the Canadas after the Act of Union of 1840. While Ajzenstat attends little to questions of social class and tends to conflate Durham's 'the people' with 'everyone,' she demonstrates forcefully that representative government involved a radical centralization of political power, even as it broadened the basis of representation.[31] This new political infrastructure was to accompany and facilitate capitalist development.

Representation as Discipline

Durham and the members of his commission insisted that the absence of local governmental organization and state education was at the root of colonial unrest. The absence of powers of local government impeded 'improvement.' Schools, mills, churches, and roads were lacking because local proprietors did not have the governmental means to organize them. More important, the absence of such governmental structures meant that there was no 'room for talent' to find expression within the state system. Arthur Buller, charged with investigating the educational condition of Lower Canada, reported that 'talent' in the locality could find 'no outlet under the present system' and hence was 'endangering society by its irregular outbreaks.'[32] Charles Buller took a similar line in *Responsible Government for Colonies*. Colonial political disputes, he claimed, were made particularly heated since one of the few paths to individual betterment was central governmental office, while appointed officials were corrupt and incompetent.[33] These views were expressed in a particularly influential form to the English Cabinet by Edward Ellice.[34] All of these writers were agitating for political structures that would incorporate, and, at the same time, discipline, men from the class of small capitalists, farmers, and the petty bourgeoisie.

John Stuart Mill publicized the Radical position in a series of articles on the Durham mission that appeared in the *Westminster Review*. There were four measures, 'all of first-rate importance, all such as ought to have been given, even though not asked for,' which Durham had been about to institute when his mission was cut short, Mill claimed. These were 'free municipal institutions,' a general scheme of public education, a registry act for titles to landed property, and the commutation of feudal tenures in Montreal. Mill described elected local government as 'not only the grand instrument of honest local management, but *the great "normal school" to fit a people for representative government.*'[35] Radicals and Whigs, Reformers and moderates, all accepted these points: representative local-governmental institutions were productive of a twofold 'improvement': first, in standards of material life; second, because, as *educational* institutions, they would prepare and train 'the people' in loyalty to and in the operation of the dominant modes of their own self-government and subordination. As a system of rule, representative government was seen to operate reflexively, a kind of self-minding machine of power. The state of liberal political theory was inevitably a tutelar state in which participation in the institutions of governance (including schooling) would habituate 'the people' to consent to and support such institutions.

Lord John Russell emphasized these points in communications with his Canadian governor general, Poulett Thomson (later Sydenham and Toronto – the desire for a colonial aristocracy lingered) and included a detailed local-government plan in his draft of a bill for the union of the Canadas. Russell did not propose colonial political autonomy, but he did insist on the necessity of representative government. In official instructions in September 1839, Russell assumed Poulett Thomson would agree that English local governmental institutions were the only 'mode in which local affairs can be ... properly administered, and ... they form ... the most appropriate and effectual means of *training the great body of the people* to the higher branches of legislation.'[36] A month later, while urging Poulett Thomson to oppose any push for 'responsible government,' Russell again stressed that the imperial government was 'intent on giving to the talent and character of leading persons in the colonies, advantages similar to those which talent and character employed in the public service, obtain in the United Kingdom.'[37] People with 'talent and character' were, of course, men in the capitalist and professional classes. For the 'lower orders' in England at this same moment, Russell and other members of Cabinet were proposing the Irish educational system, and Poulett Thomson followed suit in the Canadas.[38]

Poulett Thomson was himself intensely critical of the government of Upper Canada. 'Much as I dislike Yankee institutions,' he wrote, 'I would not have fought against them, which thousands of these poor fellows, whom the Compact call rebels, did, if it were only to keep up such a Government as they got.'[39] But, to Poulett Thomson's chagrin and dismay, the Union Act of 1840 did not include a local-government clause. Imperial Tories, led by Peel and Stanley, forced the Whig ministry to abandon the clauses in question.[40] 'No man in his senses,' complained Sydenham, 'would think for a moment of the Union without its being accompanied by some sort of Local Government, in which the people may control their own officers, and the executive at the same time obtain some influence in the country districts.'[41]

Poulett Thomson highlighted the twin dangers of attempting to govern the Canadas without the disciplinary and mediating influence of local government. Parliament was forced to adopt 'powers equally dangerous to the subject and to the Crown,' and, he continued,

The people receive no training in those habits of self-government which are indispensable to enable them rightly to exercise the power of choosing representatives in Parliament. No field is open for the gratification of ambition in a narrow circle, and no opportunity given for testing the talents or integrity of those who are candidates for popular favour. The people acquire no habits of self-dependence for the attainment of their own local objects. Whatever uneasiness they may feel ... affords grounds for complaint against the executive.

Representative government, Poulett Thomson stressed, would remove 'Government' from this dangerous contact with 'the people.' He continued,

while the Government is thus brought directly in contact with the people, it has neither any officer in its own confidence in the different parts of these extended provinces from whom it can seek information, nor is there any recognized body enjoying the public confidence with whom it can communicate, either to determine what are the real wants and wishes of the locality, or through whom it may afford explanations.

Hence the readiness with which a demand for organic changes in the constitution has been received by the people.[42]

Institutions of representative government were not seen by their partisans as 'democratic' institutions. They were not intended 'to bring government to the people' in any simple sense of freeing and empowering. Rather, representative governmental institutions were to stand between 'the people' and the 'Government' or ruling class, disciplining the former, habituating them to the limitation of their political power, to the containment of their 'ambition' in 'a narrow circle,' situating the source of their potential complaints in their own activity. At the same time, through representative institutions, the 'Government' was informed about local activity, a mobility channel was created for the ambitious, and the infrastructure for commodity production and exchange was formed.

The anomalous character of the colonial political economy was strongly impressed upon Poulett Thomson, Lord Sydenham, for he had been active in overcoming such political economic conditions in England itself. He was a man eminently experienced in the substitution of 'rational' bureaucratic procedure for the patterns of governance known in England as 'Old Corruption.' Working already in the timber trade in St Petersburg at the age of sixteen, Thomson joined the Political Economy Club in London in the 1820s and studied with McCulloch.[43] His close associates were Mill, Hume, and Warburton. His election to the seat for Dover in 1826 was aided by Jeremy Bentham, who personally conducted the canvass. Thomson took the posts of treasurer of the navy and vice-president of the Board of Trade in 1830. In the following year, he revived the office of inspector general of imports and exports and attempted to transform the Board of Trade into the main statistical branch of the English state. He introduced the practice of double-entry accounting for the keeping of public accounts in 1831 and altered the manner in which trade bills were presented to the House. Thomson was heavily involved in both the Bank Charter and Factories Regulation acts of 1833. The factory inspectors (Leonard Horner among them) were supervised by the Board of Trade, of which Thomson became president in 1834. Thomson also instituted a school of design at Somerset House in 1837 and, in the summer of that year, spent two months touring Ireland in anticipation of the Irish Poor Law.[44]

Thomson's brother, Poulett Scrope, remarked Thomson's intimate relations with Durham. They were on 'confidential terms' in 1831 and were involved in commercial treaty negotiations with France. Thomson was primed for his Canadian tour by discussions with Durham and Buller.[45]

What Thomson attempted to do, both as dictator of Lower Canada before and as government leader after the Union, was to bring the conditions of Canadian governance broadly into line with administrative and ideological initiatives undertaken in England itself. While his long-term success was quite uneven, the reforms he put in place were, in large measure, those sought by most English

Whigs, by the Radicals associated with Durham, and by moderate Canadian Reformers. These reforms were extended and consolidated in the decade of the 1840s, even in the midst of debates over ministerial responsibility.

That is not to suggest that Canadian state formation in the period immediately upon the Union is to be read simply as the unfolding of Thomson's or of imperial political interests. Tory opposition in England prevented a local-government clause in the Act of Union; for at least a decade after 1840, local-government reform in Canada East was blocked by colonial resistance. Reform opposition in the Canadian Parliament impeded Thomson's educational plans; opposition by large landholders and *habitants* led to a ferocious '*guerre des éteignoirs*' in Canada East.[46] Nor did central policy initiatives become effective local practices simply by legislative enactment. But there was a Canadian governmental 'revolution' in the decades after 1840 that involved the disposition of novel administrative and ideological agencies and practices. The administrative, ideological, and political infrastructures accompanying capitalist development were elaborated in this period. How this took place in one area of government will concern us throughout this study.

Despite the general support of the Colonial Office, Sydenham was left to engineer the passage of a local-government act through the first session of the united Parliament, a feat he claimed was possible only because, as dictator of Lower Canada before the Union, he had first been able to dictate it for that part of the colony.[47] In the midst of acrimonious debate, the first sessions of the united Parliament laid much of the groundwork for a complete transformation in the organization of colonial governance and economic development. In addition to the District Councils Act, a new board of works, a new system of county courts, a new system for regulating granted lands, and a school act for Canada East and West were created. Divisions among parties and classes remained: Reformers struggled unsuccessfully for the election rather than the appointment of district wardens, clerks, and treasurers, for instance, but succeeded for a time in sharply curtailing the centralized educational organization proposed by Sydenham. None the less, from 1841 the main prerequisites to the systematic extension of central governmental capacity existed in the Canadas. Local bodies existed with taxation powers and relative autonomy for the pursuit of specific improvements. Central government could *potentially* use local bodies both as sources of intelligence and as means for the execution of colony-wide policy.

Again, these *possibilities* had to be translated into effective practices. This was done in part through inspection, which became the main connection between newly created central and local authorities in the Canadas of the 1840s and 1850s. Before the Act of Union of 1840, there were effectively no governmental inspectors. Legislation in the two decades after 1840 created at least twenty-one different inspectoral corps. Inspection became a central regulatory and administrative practice in many domains of social and economic activity.

Inspection enforced that standardization of commodities demanded by the growth of exchange in the rapidly developing domestic and international markets. Inspectors of weights and measures were accorded police powers of search and seizure. Parliament specified standard weights and measures for various commodities. Inspectors appointed by boards of examiners graded export commodities such as butter, timber, masts, staves, deals and boards, pot and pearl ashes, beef and pork, fish and oil, and flour and meal.

Inspection aimed to regulate the health and safety of the colonial population. Inspectors of ship machinery and railways were accorded the power to prevent ship sailings and to close sections of railways if they judged them to be unsafe. Inspectors of prisons, jails, and asylums visited all public and private institutions of this class and possessed broad powers to order changes in institutional conditions and practices. Public-health inspectors were empowered to enter private dwellings, to examine the inhabitants, and to order their removal and the destruction of their belongings for sanitary purposes. Inspectors of anatomy collected the bodies of those who died without relatives in public places and delivered them to doctors for dissection, returning periodically to ensure that the remains were disposed of appropriately.

Inspectors of tavern licences and of houses of public entertainment regulated popular meeting places and could limit their number and the activities taking place in them.

Centrally appointed inspectors audited the accounts of agricultural societies. They supervised agencies in the Crown Lands department and investigated the construction of colonization roads. They examined the claims of those demanding compensation for the activities of the Board of Works and for losses suffered during the Rebellions.

The activities of these inspectors resulted in the accumulation of enormous amounts of intelligence at the centre of government about social, political, and economic conditions throughout the colony, and their reports remain a key source for the investigation of nineteenth-century Canadian political economy. No central state agency could govern a population about which it was ignorant; inspection provided indispensable elements of intelligence to state agencies. Inspection was a key political innovation of the period after 1840. The Board of Registration and Statistics, a state agency concerned to collect, analyse, and distribute statistical information about Canadian society, was created in 1847 and drew its raw material from the enumerations and agricultural inspections of 1848 and 1852.

Inspectors were not intended to be neutral reporters, at least not in the domain of social policy. Many of them possessed police powers, which they were expected to exert. Inspectors in many domains were meant to articulate and to agitate for needed 'improvements'; to report to the centre what needed to be done; but also to mobilize support for such improvements in the locality.

The Inspector of Registry Offices

Inspection developed most completely in the 1840s in public education in Canada West. But there were similar developments in other domains. The inspection of registry offices is a case in point. The absence of a reliable system of registration for titles to property was seen by English Radicals and Canadian Reformers as a major obstacle to the accumulation of capital in land and as a major support to feudal tenure and the seigneurial system in Canada East. The establishment of registry offices was one of the four major reforms listed by J.S. Mill as essential for Canadian government. Registry acts for Lower Canada were passed in the early 1840s, and inspectors of registry offices were appointed and required to report annually to Parliament.

The brief report of E.A. Clark, the inspector of registry offices for Canada East, delivered in June 1847, is a model of the intelligence generated by inspection. Clark presented a brief history of registration in the colony. Before its introduction, titles were in such 'a deplorable state of confusion and uncertainty' that land could not serve as a source of security for loans. Various attempts to correct this situation were discussed, all of which had failed. Landed proprietors in Canada East remained able to mortgage their estates without subsequent purchasers having any reliable means of discovering whether such mortgages had been arranged.

Clark discussed the effects of the Registry Act, identified obstacles to its extension and success, and suggested remedies. He pointed to the existence of general mortgages, to the insufficient designation of estates, to the difficulties of determining liabilities, and to the freedom of the seigneurs from compulsory registration as factors that prevented registrars from keeping indexes of titles. Together, these things meant that 'many persons with ample capital have been delivered from investing it in the beautiful agricultural districts of this portion of the Province, from the fear of involving themselves in the supposed intricacies of a tenure unfitted to the spirit and intelligence of the age.'

Clark warned that many registry offices were liable to destruction by fire, pointed to the difficulty of determining titles if the records were destroyed, and called for the equipping of offices with fireproof vaults. He recommended amendments to the act to require all registrars to produce quarterly abstracts of registrations to be sent to the inspector, who would then produce a general index of titles. He presented a model of such an index and urged the publication annually of a volume containing all registrations in the province. 'The concentration in this mode of all the operations of the system, would place it in so clear and tangible a shape as to facilitate its supervision by the Legislature; which would thus be constantly in possession of a mass of information and requisite minute details, in connexion with the Registration of the Real Estate of the country, unattainable by any other means.' Finally, Clark urged the keeping of different registers for different kinds of title, and the central location of registry offices.[48]

Inspectoral reports like Clark's presented central state agencies with more or less clear statements of the history, current condition, and means of improvement of many dimensions of social and economic policy. Inspectoral practice made centralized government possible.

Educational Inspection in Canada West

The largest and, in many ways, most innovative Canadian inspectorate in the 1840s was the educational inspectorate in Canada West. If education was at the heart of the reform of Canadian government, inspection was at the heart of educational reform itself. It was in the domain of public education that many of the political conflicts and social struggles surrounding representative government and the development of a centralized state system were fought out in the 1840s. Public education was a domain in which bureaucratic innovation took place in advance of its occurring in many other branches of the state system. Audits were routinely made of school units from 1850, five years before the passing of the Canadian Audit Act. Well before the principle of examination was enshrined by the Civil Service Act of 1857, elementary-school teachers routinely appeared before licensing bodies and wrote qualifying examinations. Detailed annual reports of school activities in the colony were generated from the mid-1840s.

This study examines the organization of inspection in education in Canada West in the 1840s. It examines inspection as a political phenomenon, and educational inspection as *a particular instance* of this phenomenon. It sees inspection in education as an instrument and practice wielded and shaped by a particular group of men in keeping with their own biographies, cultural experiences, and interests. But I argue that educational inspection was about state formation: the creation, stabilization, and normalization of relations of power, authority, domination, and exploitation.

If educational inspection led the way in the Canadas, inspection was by no means a Canadian invention. Nineteenth-century Canadian activists 'learned from abroad.' Many of them travelled widely and examined social and political developments in other countries. An active press and publishing industry extolled international experience in educational organization. Canadian activists frequently attempted to apply or to adapt European and American models to the social conditions they encountered.

To understand the course of inspectoral development in nineteenth-century Canada, it is necessary, first, to investigate the international experience upon which Canadian activists drew. Chapter 2 presents an overview of the most important early nineteenth-century experiments in educational inspection.

2 The 'True Kind of Government for Schools': Educational Inspection in an International Context

In 1825, an anonymous author contrasted the educational condition of eighteenth-with that of early nineteenth-century Scotland. Through much of the eighteenth century, a 1696 act that required the appointment of parish schoolmasters had produced peace and public order, wealth and social development. Soundly educated, the skilful and intelligent Scots everywhere advanced with no evidence of vice. Able men were attracted to schoolteaching because it was a step to the ministry.

But, in the early nineteenth century, this advancement was undermined by urban capitalist development. 'During the last half of the last century, the towns in Scotland were not merely small, but were as orderly and well regulated as the country. The young not only well instructed, but living, as the fashion then was, under the eye of parents or of masters; – apprentices living generally in the house, and forming a part of the family of every shopkeeper, tradesman, and even manufacturer.' Yet, by 1825, 'the whole of this private control over the town population' had entirely disappeared and 'apprentices ... had no connexion with masters, except by their attendance at shop or work hours.' In place of peace and tranquillity, there arose 'a boldness of speculation in politics and in religion ... The press started into new life and activity ... The fashionable scepticism of the days of Hume ... came to be presented in later times by Paine.' The influence of the town was spreading over the countryside, and the dangers of this spread had been seen in the French Revolution. If Scotland were to be saved from a like fate, systematic educational reform was imperative.[1]

Large sections of the rising middle class in Europe shared this analysis. Capitalist development provoked a 'crisis of moral economy.' Close supervision of the governed by their social superiors in the household was incompatible with new relations of production. Many rising capitalists and professionals came to believe that, if respect for property, political authority, and Christian religion were to be preserved, new and impersonal forms of public order would have to replace household government. Throughout the first half of the nineteenth century, in Europe and America, bourgeois activists worked to reconstruct the institutional, administrative, and cultural bases of rule. They sought new routines, procedures, and practices of government that would consolidate a hegemonic position for them.

One of the leading forms of the new public regulation was 'public instruction,' centred on, but not restricted to, schools. Centrally organized school systems were regulated, in part, through the practice of inspection. Inspection became an important element of political governance, and many inspectors were influential political activists. The former secretary to the English Privy Council Committee on Education, Sir James P. Kay-Shuttleworth, argued in 1853 that effective educational inspection had been a main cause of 'that political repose which has characterised the English poor, while the whole of Europe has been threatened with a Socialist rebellion.'[2]

Eighteenth-century political theorists had promoted the reform of government and had advocated the supervision and inspection of the governed by members of the ruling classes or their agents. But most eighteenth-century writers sought to activate existing authority, to use to the fullest powers already held by priests and constables. This was the aim even of more forward-looking writers such as Cesare Beccaria, Adam Smith, and Patrick Colqhoun. It was early nineteenth-century writers, on the whole, who agitated for the mechanisms of government with which this study is particularly concerned.[3]

Canadian educational practice was especially influenced by the experience of Ireland, Scotland, Prussia, Holland, England, and the United States. I will deal with each in turn.

Irish Precedents

The role of Ireland as a centre of social experimentation for the English ruling class is well known. Irish inspectoral practice and educational organization were precocious and widely debated in England and Scotland. Large parts of Irish experiments were adopted in Canada West in the 1840s. The deputy-superintendent of education was sent to study in the Dublin model school, and one of the first Irish school inspectors was headmaster of the Toronto Normal School from 1847 to 1866. The Irish school books were adopted in the colony and were the basis of the official curriculum for twenty years. Many Irish-trained teachers also worked in the Canadian colony.[4]

The exigencies of colonial rule by isolated Protestant English planters surrounded by a hostile Irish Catholic population contributed to the development of novel forms of governance. Methods of central regulation of the colonial population and of connecting isolated members of the ruling class informed later attempts in England to regulate the developing internal colony, the industrial working class.[5] From the seventeenth century, colonial rule contributed to the elaboration of forms of social mapping and policing. William Petty's experience as surveyor general of Ireland in the 1650s underlay his formulation of the new 'science' of statistics: political arithmetic. Mapping Ireland encouraged the elaboration of new forms of political mapping in England itself, and the influence of Irish social experimentation stretches clearly to the nineteenth century and beyond. Peel's attempts to organize an effective police for Ireland in the first two decades of the nineteenth century, for instance, shaped his later plans for English police.[6]

By the last decades of the eighteenth century, schemes for the formation of a national educational system for Ireland had become commonplace. Most of these were based in some way on a plan articulated by Thomas Orde in the 1780s. Orde (1751–1814; from 1797, Lord Bolton) was secretary to Hely-Hutchinson, the lord lieutenant in the middle 1780s, a tumultuous period in which political disruptions surrounding the American War allowed Irish liberals to push for an Irish Parliament. Orde had earlier been auditor of the Duchy of Lancaster, secretary to the Treasury, and from 1786 sat on the Board of Trade. As secretary to the lord lieutenant, he was particularly interested in engineering a commercial union between England and Ireland.

The existing organization of Irish schools, penal institutions, and police was sharply criticized in this period of rising nationalist sentiment.[7] In notebooks from 1785, Orde entertained the 'idea of attacking the Roman Catholics by [educational] means and indeed of making their Leaders in some degree dependent upon Government.' However, it was out of his interest in the development of effective systems of police that Orde's concern both with education and with inspection grew.[8]

Orde argued that punishments in Ireland were severe, but did not 'prevent the Perpetration of the most atrocious Acts.'[9] Drawing upon the model of the French constabulary, he argued that effective police demanded the creation of information channels and agents. His proposed Police Bill included the suggestion that magistrates be educated in the law, and have attached to them 'an Enquirer; who should be a very active sensible Man whose Business it is to go on the spot and make such Enquiries as the Justice shall think proper to direct': a police inspector, in other words.[10]

There was a direct connection between police and educational reform. Effective police demanded that the poor know they would provoke violent repression through illegal activity. Parliament had 'been obliged to correct the unfortunate consequences of a want of education with a rude and severe hand,' but through instruction could substitute 'a remedy of more gentle, but not of less efficacious influence.' The lower classes were 'the foundation for the superstructure of the state' and, by educating them, Parliament could 'render that foundation not only more beautiful, but more secure and permanent.'

To execute this political education, Orde urged the creation of a new system of inspected diocesan schools. 'No object whatever can be more important,' he wrote, 'either with a view to the establishment or to the maintenance of every proper regulation, and the faithful discharge of duty, than a certainty and frequency of impartial visitation and inspection.'[11] In part, such inspection might be done by established authorities in the neighbourhood of schools, but Orde was not content simply to activate existing authority. He also proposed the creation of a 'College of Visitors and Inspectors' connected with his proposed university and suggested that Irish educational reform should begin with the appointment of such officials. Inspectors would formulate rules and regulations for the schools and would conduct 'a general Survey of the actual State of instruction &c in all part[s] of the Country.'[12] They would be 'frequently employed in making the circuit of the kingdom' and visiting all schools under government protection. They would conduct 'the strictest enquiries into all the circumstances of material consequence respecting the discipline, good order and economy observed in these societies, and be satisfied of the sufficiency and conduct of those persons to whom the care of the establishments in various respects shall have been entrusted.'[13] The inspectors were to examine the accounts of schools and to enquire 'generally into the state of' such institutions, including the numbers and performance of the scholars.

The character of inspectors was of central importance. Orde suggested that they be recruited outside the country, if necessary. The position was to be one of liberal support and large prestige, so that people would compete for it. The college designed to house these officials was conceived as 'a happy and honourable asylum' for those too old to teach, yet 'still competent to engage in the business.'[14] While inspectors were to be well-paid and honoured, care was to be taken 'against temptation, to evade the duties, because of the sweets of the situation.' Orde proposed to ensure diligence by creating some form of mobility channel within the inspectoral corps itself. In this way, the college would avoid the sinecurism characteristic of the Charter schools.

Orde's educational legislation was initially debated in Parliament in April 1787, but, before the next session, Orde left the country, and the educational scheme was abandoned. It was repeatedly debated in the turbulent decades that followed, although growing Irish nationalism and religious toleration made the state church an increasingly inadequate framework for education.[15]

Richard Lovell Edgeworth's Education Bill of 1799 called for the establishment of a national board of education with broad powers to support schools, license teachers, and publish books. The Irish Parliament had resolved before the reading of the bill that 'one or more Visitors should be empowered to in-pect these and all other Parish Schools once in every year.' However, the bill was dropped after second reading, ostensibly on financial grounds, although the clause calling for state aid to Catholic schools was probably seen as menacing after the Rebellion of 1798.[16]

Plans for Irish social reconstruction multiplied after the defeat of the Rebellion, but despite the recommendations of many observers for the establishment of non-sectarian state schooling, Dublin Castle began funding Protestant proselytist societies in 1799.[17] The London Hibernian Society and the Association for Discountenancing Vice received state funds and connected instruction with the conversion of Catholics. In 1815, the largest share of the lord lieutenant's Irish school fund began to go to the Society for Promoting the Education of the Poor in Ireland, or (from the location of its offices) the Kildare Place Society.

The Kildare Place Society

'One of those three alternatives,' wrote H. Mason in the Kildare Place Society's manifesto, 'is necessary to the conducting the machine of government in every State: either, preserving the ignorance of all the peasantry to subjugate them by force; flattering their prejudices to enslave them by art; or, enlightening their understandings to maintain them contented in their necessary state of due and liberal subordination.' Mason argued the third was the only possible means to govern Ireland, especially given the unregulated growth of popular literacy.[18]

The Kildare Place Society was founded on 2 December 1811 with a voluntary management committee of twenty-one, primarily middle-class, Protestants. It proposed non-denominational education on a monitorial model for the poor, with the daily reading of the Scriptures without note or comment. The society began by building a model school and publishing a version of Lancaster's plans for school management and a spelling book. It operated a depository for the distribution of school supplies and managed a Cheap Book Society, for, as Henry Mason argued, to prevent popular literacy leading to the consumption of seditious literature, sound books had to be produced and distributed to the peasantry.

As early as 1813, one commentator urged 'the propriety of the Society appointing inspectors, to visit the different Schools, annually, and from their observations, to make reports, of the general state of education in Ireland.' To pay these inspectors would be beyond the means of the society, but it was hoped 'some public spirited gentlemen, of independent fortune, might be found, who would qualify themselves for the task, and combine it with curiosity for seeing the country, and that whilst they were making the tour of their own country, gratifying and instructing themselves, they might render the community an eminently valuable, and useful piece of service.'[19] Inspection was a gentleman's pastime.

The society began to receive substantial government funding in 1815. In 1816, it organized a teacher-training program and collected information from clergy throughout the country about the state of education. The master of the model school, Mr Veevers, was sent on a tour of the North of England, Scotland, and Ireland to ensure that the society's model school had adopted all educational 'improvements.' In the following year, the society decided to pay schoolmasters associating their schools with it and decided 'that for the purpose of checking and regulating the distribution of such remuneration, it is desirable to combine resident superintendence with periodical inspection.' The society urged all 'persons who feel interested in the cause of Education,' to visit the schools and to communicate with the committee. It also decided to engage 'a limited number of Inspectors.'[20]

The model-school master's inspectoral tour of 1819, which has been described as 'the first of its kind in Great Britain or Ireland,' included 112 schools and resulted in the creation of a standardized report form for the schools.[21] In the following year, the committee began to insist that subsidized schools keep a visitors' book and communicate regularly with the society. In either 1820 or 1821, a paid inspector was hired, two inspectoral circuits were established, and from then the inspectoral system grew rapidly. By 1823, the position of the society was sufficiently solid that the managing committee no longer found it necessary to fund private schools. There were about 1,000 schools under the society's direction, and henceforth it sought to have teachers it trained under its direct control, or under that of a local committee or patron. This system highlighted the necessity of effective inspection, for 'constant vigilance is required to enable a Committee, sitting in Dublin, to form a correct judgement of the actual condition and usefulness of each of the numerous Schools scattered over the whole surface of the Island.' Four new inspectors were hired in 1823. The society had 200 male teachers in training and began training female teachers. The inspectoral corps was provided with its own residence in Dublin. But the society faced a growing perception that it was engaged in Protestant propaganda.[22]

The Kildare Place committee members, inspectors, and model-school master were examined by the parliamentary commissioners of education in Ireland, who reported in 1825. The commissioners also examined the Catholic archbishops, who were opposed to the reading of the Scriptures in schools and who were incensed that the society channelled funds to the proselytist Association for Discountenancing Vice and the London Hibernian Society. The education commissioners themselves noted that, while the society had subsidized the construction of 431 schools, only 12 of these had been Catholic schools.

The education commissioners proposed the establishment of a system of public schools in the country, with, where attendance justified it, two lay teachers, one Catholic and one Protestant. Collective secular instruction was to be distinguished from separate religious instruction. All schools should be the property of a general board of education, which would also specify school rules and regulations and 'appoint Inspectors, who should be enabled to examine upon Oath.'[23] The commission recommended that the Kildare Place Society immediately cease grants to all other bodies and that its functions be replaced entirely by the General Board of Education.

Inspectors and Inspection

Of particular interest in the parliamentary commission's first report are detailed investigations of the operations of the inspectoral system and of the model school. J. Devonsher Jackson, a member of the management committee, was asked about the social position of the inspectors: 'Are those inspectors of the rank of gentlemen?' 'Yes,' he replied, 'for although one (Mr Mills) was in humble life, his conduct entitles him to that character ... all the rest are gentlemen by birth, one is a barrister.' Jackson explained that the society 'found it necessary to have persons intelligent and well informed, capable of holding communications with the resident gentry.' The educational plan was seen to depend upon the support of local élites, and hence inspectors had to be 'respectable.' They were paid the substantial sum (for Ireland) of £60 per annum with 15 shillings daily expenses while on the road, and were granted an initial £60 for the purchase of a gig and horse. Jackson insisted that a system of inspection was essential to a plan of national education, for there was no way without it that a body sitting in Dublin could keep itself informed about local conditions. The inspectors changed their circuits and were motivated primarily by a 'desire to be useful,' not by the salary their position offered.[24] Inspection was the work of 'gentlemen' interested in 'improvement.'

Matthew Donelan, the only Catholic inspector employed by the society, testified that each inspector left his comments on a given school in a travelling book kept for the information of his successor. According to Lewis Mills, the typical inspectoral visit lasted from 10:00 a.m. to 2:00 p.m. and involved an examination of all school classes, the school accounts, and the teacher's conduct. If the patron was nearby, Mills also spoke with him, and he reported all the information he collected on a standardized report form. To the question 'Are your visits unexpected?' Mills replied, 'They are,' but then said that schoolmasters communicated with one another, and he was often anticipated. Robert and Malachy Daly and William Fitzgerald provided similar information. Several of the inspectors reported opposition to the society's monitorial pedagogy.[25]

The committee of the Kildare Place Society responded to the commissioners' first report in its own annual report for 1826. It attempted to defend the reading of the Scriptures in school and insisted repeatedly upon the utility of its system of inspection that involved 'gentlemen of education and character.' While denying it was engaged in proselytism, the society announced it had severed its connection with all other societies. While this meant the loss of about 150 schools, 1,595 remained on its list. The society hired two additional inspectors in 1825 and divided the country into eight inspectoral districts.[26]

The Irish National Board of Education

The Kildare Place Society lost its share of Irish school funds in 1832, after the English ministry established a permanent body of commissioners for national education in Ireland.[27] However, its system of inspection was adopted and elaborated by the national commissioners. The national commissioners based their instructions to inspectors on those issued by the Kildare Place Society. Matthew Donelan, the society's only Catholic school inspector, joined the national body soon after its formation, and, in 1833, Mrs Campbell, the society's girls' model-school teacher, was hired by the national body as well.[28]

The commissioners of national education hired four inspectors at annual salaries of £250, including expenses. Messrs Hamell, Murray, Robertson, and Sullivan were engaged, assigned to provincial circuits – Robertson to Connaught – and advanced £50 towards their expenses. Four more inspectors were hired in 1833, salaries were raised, and the circuits subdivided.[29]

If Thomas Jaffray Robertson's experience was typical, candidates for inspectoral posts did not undergo 'strictly speaking, an Examination.' Robertson said they were subjected to 'an Inquiry to elucidate what Kind of Persons we were; what Station we had been living in, and what Habits we had been accustomed to.' Class position and moral character were the key elements in the development of professional expertise. Their salaries enabled the inspectors to maintain a social position comparable to that of the Irish gentry. Robertson himself revealed his concern with education as 'improvement,' a concern carried with him to Canada in 1847, in his first report to the commissioners. 'The Teachers at present in the country,' he commented, 'are all in general unacquaint-ed with School Discipline, and so identified with the People as to be more attentive to the Means of acquiring their Good Will than of deserving the Confidence of the Commissioners or their Officers. The former of these Faults is plainly in the highest Degree injurious, and it requires no Explanation to show how detrimental the latter must be to the Interests of Education.'[30] The 'Interests of Education' in Robertson's view were opposed to those of 'the People.'

The Board of National Commissioners acted from the outset to separate 'the interests of education' from partisan politics. When Robert Sullivan was found to have written a letter to the Belfast *Guardian* on educational matters, the board instructed its inspectors 'that they are not to publish any letter or document relating to' the proceedings of the commissioners, 'or to any theological or political subjects and that they are not to write any letter on the business of the Board unless to them or by their directions.' Inspectors were to root out from the teaching force those engaged in political activity, and teachers were told 'to abstain from all political Meetings whatever.'[31]

Early in 1835, the national board moved 'the expediency of making a complete arrangement within itself for the Statistics of the National Schools' and, by early 1836, it was able to use inspectors as special investigators of local complaints. Within five years of the appointment of inspectors, teachers were routinely being removed for violating various of the board's conditions for support.[32]

In February 1837, inspectors were assigned to new circuits, and the board ruled that the expense of a special inspection of a school missed on an inspector's regular circuit would be charged to him. However, after the resident commissioner, James Carlile, made his own tour of inspection late in 1836 (perhaps in his capacity as poor-law commissioner), and faced with mounting criticism in the Lords, the board moved for a system of county inspection. County model schools were to be established, partly to provide agricultural training; local committees were to supervise them; and resident superintendents for each school were to visit all district schools and receive monthly reports.[33]

Unfortunately, explicit documentary discussion of the necessity for this reorganization of inspection is lacking, and the second of the commissioners' minute books has been lost. But Irish educational organization was under intense criticism throughout the 1830s. The Presbyterian MP J.C. Colquhoun described the commission's inspections as a 'farce.' The inspector came to a school only once a year, supposedly 'stealing in upon the schools without notice,' but, in fact, his itinerary was well known in advance. 'School after school along his route can calculate, if not the hour, at least the day, at all events the week, of his arrival; and thus all wicked practices are discontinued, and all naughty books are hustled away; and the children, with clean faces and well combed hair, and the ''Scripture Extracts'' in their hands, are all marshalled in goodly row ... and when [the inspector] has made his tour, and turned his back, on the school, the school-master is safe till that day twelvemonth.' At the best of times, inspectors were kept ignorant of local educational practices, and hence the board was ignorant as well.

But Colquhoun also charged that 'the man who appoints the master commands the school,' and, in five-sixths of the cases in Ireland, that man was the priest. Hence, as far as Colquhoun was concerned, the Irish schools were centres for the spread of popery. His attacks were widely publicized, and other such attacks were increasingly common in the later 1830s.[34]

Coolahan has suggested that the increasing size of the school system led to the plan for county superintendence. But other attempts were also going forward at this time to reconstruct Irish administration through the creation of local governmental institutions. An industrial poor law was imposed upon the country, and inspectoral circuits may have been reorganized to coordinate more completely with poor-law unions. The commission appointed to investigate an Irish poor law included the educational commissioners Whately, Murray, Carlile, and Blake. The poor-law commission moved in favour of a comprehensive system of outdoor relief, on a plan closely resembling that of Poulett Scrope. The plan was rejected by Parliament (although soon after Poulett Scrope's brother secured a Canadian board of works).[35]

It is unlikely that the move to a county system of inspection was made in the interests of economy. The commissioners did complain in their report for 1837 of having 'eight inspectors, who, in consequence of the extraordinary expenses which they incur in travelling, receive a salary of £300 a year, and ... their services will be dispensed with when the superintendents are appointed,' but the resident superintendent for each county model school was to be paid £125 with lodging, which, given twenty-five schools, was a considerable increase. Some of this funding might have been secured locally, however.

In 1838, the commissioners announced that they had divided Ireland into twenty-five school districts, each with a superintendent who would visit the schools frequently, receive monthly reports from teachers, and make quarterly reports to the commissioners themselves. This superintendent was also to supply the commissioners 'with such local information as they may from time to time require from him, and to act as their agent in all matters in which they may employ him; but he is not invested with authority to decide upon any question affecting a national school, or the general business of the Commissioners, without their direction.'[36]

By the early 1840s, when Canadian reformers were debating educational inspection, the Irish commissioners had an elaborate system in place. Thirteen rules were printed for the direction of inspectors, and detailed reporting forms were distributed for their use. Three visits to each school were to be made annually, two of them at intervals kept secret from teachers, one of them, between 1 May and 31 August, to be the occasion of a public examination. In the course of these inspections, the superintendent was to attend to the general order and condition of the school, to examine the classes in succession, and the class rolls, register, and daily report book. He was also to report the average attendance and enrolment in each school. When applications were made for the establishment of new schools, superintendents were to consult with nearby clergy, and to collect any 'local information' that the commissioners might seek.

Superintendents were not to give orders, but to point out violations of regulations to the local conductors of the school. They were to write nothing in the visitors' book except the date and time of their visit and the number of students present. They were 'to avoid all discussions of a religious or political nature' and to 'exhibit a courteous and conciliatory demeanour towards all persons.' These regulations were included in the standard form of lease to schoolhouses whose construction was subsidized by the commissioners, and they were largely copied for Canadian inspectors.[37]

Perhaps because of the political contentiousness of religious instruction, the commissioners allowed a broader access to the schools than was the case in many jurisdictions. Thus they were compelled to devise and specify a distinction between 'visitors' and 'inspectors,' which also reappeared in Canadian legislation. Visitors were defined to include 'clergymen of all denominations residing in the neighbourhood of a school, or having any ecclesiastical connexion with the district in which it is situated,' as well as 'gentlemen of the neighbourhood.' These people were allowed free admission to the school and 'full liberty' to observe the students, books, lessons, apparatus, etc. However, teachers were by no means required 'to permit any person to interrupt the business of the school, by asking questions of children, calling for papers of any kind, or in any other way diverting the attention of either teachers or scholars from their usual business.' At the same time, a teacher was required 'to have his visitors' book lying open upon his desk, that visitors may, if they choose, enter remarks in it. Such remarks as may be made the teachers are by no means to alter or erase.' The admission of other visitors was at the discretion of the local management committee. However, a condition of the funding of schools was that the commissioners 'or their officers' be 'allowed to visit and examine the schools whenever they think fit.' Officers would be 'furnished with credentials under the [commissioners'] seal,' which they would show to teachers.[38] The admission of members of the 'respectable' classes to the schools of Canada West and the exclusion of others from 'interfering' was a contentious issue.

On the groundwork laid by the Kildare Place Society, the Irish educational system of the late 1830s had become the most organizationally sophisticated in the English-speaking world. Here inspectoral routine developed comparatively early. The experience of the Charter schools and of prison reform, in combination with the political isolation of élites surrounded by a hostile population, encouraged the development of practices linking central and local authorities and encouraged a central accumulation of knowledge. The exigencies of English colonial rule encouraged the development of ways of governing that were continuous with the cultural activities of men in the dominant classes and were later directed both towards the developing internal colony of the working class in England itself and towards colonists in other parts of the empire. Educational inspection involved the engagement of 'gentlemen': the right 'Kind of Persons' to lend prestige to the organization, people capable of social intercourse with the gentry: T. Finn, LLD, a former resident master of Trinity College; Robert Sullivan, holder of the MA from Trinity College; and the respectable Thomas Jaffray Robertson. The central authority's experience of inspection and inspectors led to the specification of procedures, which in time were detailed and codified, thus making it possible to routinize the wisdom of selected gentlemen as expertise and to displace inspectoral routine to lower-level, less prestigious officers. Selected members of the central inspectoral corps came to occupy other functions for the commissioners. Sullivan taught and supervised in the Normal School at Dublin, published a number of works used in the commissioners' schools (e.g., *The Spelling Book Superseded*) and publicized Irish practice. Robertson came to be known as the 'chief inspector' and likely supervised other officials.

The Irish experience embodied a pattern replicated in North America and in England as well; 'gentlemen' set in motion inspectoral systems, which were then entrusted to men of lesser social standing. Here was a translation of class culture into bureaucratic routine.

Scottish Precedents

The Principle of Locality

The work of the Scottish cleric Thomas Chalmers (1780–1847), a close friend and correspondent of the Canadian Anglican clergyman John Strachan, was especially attractive to Canadian educational activists from the 1820s. Particularly in *The Christian and Civic Economy of Large Towns*, Chalmers generalized plans for the supervision of working-class communities through what he called 'the local system' and the 'principle of locality.' Chalmers's plans were translated into educational practices by Scottish educational reformers like David Stow and John Wood.

Chalmers, an active evangelical educated at St Andrews University, held a rural parish until 1815 when he was transferred to the Tron parish in industrial Glasgow. Alarmed by the increasing gulf between social classes and by social unrest and generalized poverty, and imbued with a Malthusian political economy, Chalmers embarked on an experiment designed to reduce the dependence of the poor upon municipal rates. He attributed poverty to the moral degradation that stemmed from infidelity and the absence of religious education. Urban population growth and the declining social position of the clergy prevented effective religious work. But it was 'not to any violent demolition in the existing framework of society' that Chalmers looked for a remedy.[39] Moral education and clerical supervision could improve the poor.

Chalmers urged the creation of schools for the working classes and the establishment of regular contact between workers and 'those who are raised in circumstances above them.' Good schools would lay the lessons of moral decency, while fraternization with the superior classes would regulate popular behaviour and undercut tendencies to political discontent and radicalism. Direct contact between the ruling and working classes would produce political contentment, even where poor relief and direct repression failed; assuming, of course, that no real economic scarcity existed in working-class neighbourhoods and that poverty was simply a product of profligacy and moral degradation.

Chalmers's active philanthropy sought to place what he himself referred to as religious spies among working-class families.[40] In the new Glasgow parish of St John's, the 10,000 inhabitants were divided into 25 districts, each containing 80 to 100 families. Each district was put under an elder, charged with visitation, and a deacon, responsible for poor relief. No parish rates were accepted, and the poor were to be supported through their own efforts and voluntary contributions. Constant visitation by the elder and systematic educational efforts were to ensure that the poor learned moral habits while experiencing the goodwill of their social superiors.

Glasgow's poor-law expenditure declined for a time, at the expense of the poor themselves, but Chalmers's push for a national scheme failed, and it was abandoned in Glasgow in 1837.[41]

None the less, the plan was widely publicized and quite influential. Chalmers claimed systematic education combined with constant inspection was a sure antidote to revolution because it would break working-class unity and create a local corporate spirit in its place. As he put it,

it serves to divide and weaken the force of popular violence, when the vast and overgrown city is broken down into separate parochial jurisdictions – where each is isolated as much as possible from the other ... and where the people, instead of all looking one way, to the distant and general head, and forming into a combined array of hostile feeling and prejudice against it, are, in virtue of a local economy, which possesses interest enough to have formed a sort of *esprit de corps* among the inhabitants of every subordinate district, habituated to look several ways to that nearer and more interesting *regime* by which they are respectively surrounded.

There could be no equal of this plan for what was in effect local ecclesiastical government. No 'multiplication whatever of agents and office-bearers, on the part of the great city establishment' could take the place of 'the ecclesiastical police of a parish, whose *espionage* is the fruit of fair and frequent intercourse with the families and can carry no jealousies or heart-burnings along with it.'[42]

In North America, and increasingly in England, Scotland, and Wales, the possibility of a clerical police was in decline in the 1820s. Those interested in new forms of police thought increasingly in secular terms. Yet Scottish educational organization drew heavily upon Chalmers's reformed 'civic economy,' and it was taken as a model of the salutary effects of education on class relations by observers on both sides of the Atlantic. By the late 1830s, a stream of visitors passed through the Glasgow and Edinburgh schools, and these schools became very widely known. Inspection by active and morally select members of the dominant classes came to play a central role in experiments aimed at breaking working-class solidarity and at building a social consensus congenial to capitalist relations of production.[43]

European Precedents

Cousin's Reports

Among the most widely read and influential documents on educational organization in the first half of the nineteenth century were Victor Cousin's reports on Prussian and Dutch education.[44] They provided activists with contrasting models of educational organization and administration, one based upon detailed statutory regulation, the other upon the granting of broad and indefinite powers to administrative officials.

Cousin's *On the State of Public Instruction in Prussia* was published in 1831 and served as the basis of Guizot's Education Act of 1833. Education in Prussia was organized by the Ministry of the Interior until 1819, when a separate ministry of public instruction was formed. The scope of this ministry was broad, embracing 'everything relating to science, and consequently all schools, libraries, and kindred institutions – such as botanic gardens, museums, cabinets, the lower schools of surgery and medicine, academies of music, &c. ... The ministry of public instruction' covered 'everything of a moral and intellectual character.' The minister was surrounded by a council of public instruction, itself specialized according to branches of knowledge, and customarily the minister followed the council's advice. Special inspectors general sat on the council and could be dispatched to investigate 'if the minister learns from his correspondence that things are not going on well in any establishment.' Cousin stressed that all public servants in Prussia were salaried, came from different classes in society and were subject to 'the most rigorous examinations.' Thus they brought to the exercise of their functions 'the general spirit of the nation.' There were no Prussian placemen.[45]

The Prussian educational system was highly centralized and closely regulated by statute. The minister of public instruction was informed by inspectoral reports about the local operations of education and was thus enabled to direct the operations of the whole from the centre. Cousin regarded the central regulation of the size and the furniture of schools and of teachers' salaries with favour, the more so as it was combined with the legal requirement for local administrative units to maintain schools. All public authorities in Prussia were required by law to protect and advance the interests of schools.

Schoolmasters were public officers. Teachers passed through a three-year normal-school course and were certified after an examination before both lay and religious bodies. They were required to hold a brevet, subject to royal validation, specifying their duties and to take an oath of office. These duties were closely detailed by statute and 'gross violations of modesty, temperance & moderation or any open abuse of his authority as father, husband, or head of a family' was to be 'punished in a schoolmaster by the loss of his place.' Courts were required to communicate the appearance of schoolmasters before them to educational authorities. Inspectors examined teachers for promotion and encouraged teachers' associations.

Inspection was a key dimension of Prussian educational organization, and overlapping inspectoral circles existed. At the local commune or parish level, each school had a managing committee of clergymen, magistrates, and one or two elected householders approved by the intermediate school authority. Householders were elected for four-year terms, with no right of refusal. These committees controlled the internal organization of local schools and, in addition, the 'pastor or curate' served as 'inspector of the school of the village.' Larger towns were divided into districts, in each of which there was a managing committee, overseen by a town school commission composed of clerical and elected members as confirmed by the provincial consistories.

Each 'circle' (parish or commune) was to have a *Kreisschulaufseher* or *Kreisschulinspector* nominated by clerical authorities and confirmed by the minister of public instruction. Their duties were 'to examine into the interior of the schools, and the conduct of the committees and masters of such schools. The whole system of teaching and of education pursued in the schools' was to be 'submitted to their revision and their superior direction.'[46] These *Kreisschulinspectors* would normally be clergymen, all of whom were expected to study the theory of popular instruction and were subject to examination. Lower-level officials reported to provincial authorities called consistories, which could publish additional regulations for school organization. Inspectors general were attached to the Ministry of Public Instruction.

Cousin recommended the adoption of a similar system for France and urged the appointment of 'a special inspector of primary instruction for each department.'[47]

The Prussian system drew the admiration of many educational reformers, but provoked considerable uneasiness from some middle-class critics and from the workers' movement. Prussia was a despotic state, and Prussian education was held to be despotic education. By contrast, the Dutch system, which Cousin also publicized, seemed to middle-class observers to provide for flexible educational governance.

Holland

In *On the State of Education in Holland, As Regards Schools for the Working Classes and for the Poor*, Cousin retraced a path trod in 1811 by Georges Cuvier (1769–1832) and Jean-François-Michel Noël (1755–1841) and reproduced their earlier report.[48] Dutch education was based on a law of 1806 passed by the Batavian republic (itself declared in 1794). In this, as in the other French client states, educational organization was to be an important instrument for the spread of revolutionary ideas.

To Cousin, as to Cuvier and Noël before him, Dutch administrative organization was particularly appealing. Here public instruction was based on administrative regulation rather than on statute law. Schooling was organized through an interior ministry and supervised by a 'Referendaire' and an inspector of Latin and primary schools. The latter was described by Cousin as 'the mainspring of the public instruction.' In contrast to Prussia, there was no large corps of inspectors general in Holland. Rather, the provincial school inspectors were assembled from time to time at The Hague and formed into a council presided over by the minister of the interior. This council formulated all measures requisite for national education; that is, defined the 'interests of education.' Cousin emphasized that 'unity in national character can only be secured by unity in national education; and such unity can be obtained only by means of a permanent council, constituting as it were the high court of appeal in questions concerning public instruction.' If some such council did not exist, he continued, 'we must choose between the arbitrary will of the government, and the uncontrolled power of local magistracies. As a medium between these extremes ... the wisdom of Germany and the genius of Napoleon interposed a council with appropriate authority.'[49]

Through a council, the interests of education would be constituted by a group of experts independent of both legislative and judicial interference. In the Prussian system, all elements of the educational system were specified legally. Cousin pointed out that this was possible only because Prussia possessed no republican institutions; hence ordinance and law were indistinguishable. But Holland was a republic. Therefore, if education were regulated in detail by a law, 'the risk of having amendments inserted, during its discussion in a numerous assembly of men little conversant with such matters ... would utterly destroy the best devised schemes.' The interests of education had to be protected from popular and parliamentary interference if improvement were to proceed, a point that cannot be overemphasized, and a bitter lesson that Egerton Ryerson in Canada West later learned.[50]

In Holland, the education law specified only the nature of superintending authorities. The regulation of educational practice was left to the autonomous activities of these authorities. Regulation grew out of administration, not out of law. Thus *inspection* was the key element of the Dutch system, or as Cousin generalized, 'a superintending power is the main spring of all primary schools.' Cousin could not have been more explicit about the necessity of a bureaucratically controlled 'educational interest,' free from popular or legislative interference. '*This is the true kind of government for primary schools*, and to determine how the organization of that government shall be most skillfully contrived is, in my mind, the vital question in a system of popular education.'[51]

Professional inspection was the key to sound public instruction, and Cousin emphasized that 'it would be difficult to imagine a more efficient system of inspection than that in Holland.' In each Dutch district, a resident primary-school inspector visited each school at least twice a year. No one could teach in any kind of school or be promoted without his approval, and he chaired all educational meetings. District inspectors gathered three times a year in the provincial town for a lengthy conference with the provincial governor. Each inspector reported on his district, while a provincial educational board decided if inspectors had conformed to the provincial educational code. The results of provincial meetings were reported to the interior ministry. The national inspector general also periodically convened meetings with provincial inspectoral representatives. 'Thus,' Cousin pointed out, 'from the inspector general at The Hague down to the local inspector of the smallest district, the whole of the primary instruction is under the direction of inspection.'[52] In Holland, he concluded, 'the organization of the inspection is the entire law; and even that is not completed by the law, for many parts of it are contained in the general regulations ... Instead of attempting that precision, at once so easy and so deceptive, which looks so well on paper, but which in practice is always embarrassing, and leaves nothing for time and experience to do, the Dutch law is of a general nature and leaves a degree of latitude.'[53]

The Dutch Inspectoral Regulations

The Dutch ministry published 'Instructions for the School Inspectors, and for the Boards of Education' containing thirty-one articles. Inspectors were to make themselves personally acquainted with teachers and to be personally accessible to them. Their inspectoral duties were outlined: masters were to be required to teach so that the inspector could judge them, close enquiry into school organization was to be made, and teachers were to be advised discreetly about areas for improvement. Inspectors were to keep written notes of all visits. A district inspector could delegate his duties to others, but he was considered personally responsible for them. Monthly inspectoral reports were to be sent to the secretary of state for the Home department, to enable the central authority to publish, in a monthly periodical, relevant educational information, including vacant teaching posts. At the quarterly meetings of district boards of education, inspectors were to provide detailed reports in writing, outlining the number of schools visited and their general conditions, meetings held with schoolmasters, teacher examinations, and all other events having to do with the conduct of education, including books used and measures suggested for educational improvement. This material might be reprinted in the central government's monthly educational periodical and was to form the basis of an annual report that each inspector was to make to the district board meeting before Easter. Boards of education were to produce similar reports. These reports were then forwarded to the secretary of state for the Home department, who in turn would produce a general educational summary, copies of which would be distributed to district boards.

What appealed to foreign observers in the Dutch educational system was its *combination* of intense regulation and room for manoeuvre. Educational improvement was possible because inspectors and other 'friends of education' had independent powers to adopt regulations without these becoming the visible object of popular opposition or of entrenched authority. Educational governance was at once brought to the working class and the poor and protected from their interference, as from that of the legislature and the judiciary. The absence of detailed statutory limits to educational authority made the contours of the Dutch educational state difficult both to define and to oppose.

English Radicals were particularly impressed by this system. They saw in it a means of dealing not only with the increasingly radical workers' movement, but also with the rebellious Canadian colonies.

English School Inspection

Each of Cousin's two reports was translated into English by a major figure in Radical circles. The report on Prussia was translated in 1834 by Sarah Austin (1793–1867), a Germanophile who also wrote on educational subjects in her own right. Austin and her husband, John, shared a back garden with Bentham and the Mills (John Stuart is said to have called her *Mütter*). John Austin (1790–1859) held the first chair of jurisprudence in the University of London (1826) and sat on the Criminal Law Commission (1833) and on the commission to investigate the administration of Malta (1836). The Austins' London house was a social centre for many Radicals, frequently visited by Charles Buller and occasionally by Poulett Thomson. These two played central roles in Canadian educational reforms.

Cousin's report on Holland was translated and introduced in 1838 by Leonard Horner. Horner, best known as one of Her Majesty's inspectors of factories (his activity was much admired by Marx), was one of Brougham's schoolmates at the High School of Edinburgh. His older brother, Francis, was a founder of the *Edinburgh Review*. Horner was a fellow of the Geological Society from 1808 and of the Royal Society from 1813. He founded the Edinburgh School of Arts in 1821, the centre of a series of political meetings held between 1821 and 1826. He was influential in the formulation of the Combinations Act of 1825, corresponding on the subject with Peel. Horner was active in the foundation of the London University, serving as its first warden in 1828. He lived in Germany from 1831 to 1833, renewing ties established on a visit made in 1815. Horner sat on the Commission on the Employment of Children in Factories and served as an inspector from 1833 to 1856. The factory inspectors reported to the Board of Trade, whose president until 1838 was Poulett Thomson, the man later charged with reconstructing Canadian government. Horner's translation of Cousin's report was made in the context of plans for the formation of an English national education commission.[54]

That two visible Radicals, one of them at the same time an exceptionally busy state servant, should devote their energies to the translation of these reports is a measure of their importance to Radical and Whig views of educational organization and governance.

In his introduction to Cousin's *Education in Holland*, Horner argued that the imminent appointment of English educational commissioners demanded the bringing together of 'all the knowledge that can be collected from the best conducted schools already existing.' English observers could look to Prussia for examples of good normal schools and any good educational system demanded systematic inspection and regular reporting procedures. The Dutch system showed the Prussian system to be compatible with civil liberty.[55]

An official English school inspectorate was first organized in 1839, drawing upon practice on the continent and in Ireland. By this date there were already two salaried governmental inspectorates in England, one under the Factory Act of 1833 reporting to the Board of Trade, and the other under the Poor Law Amendment Act of 1834. Inspectors under the Factory Act possessed magisterial powers, examined factories in which children were employed, and attended to educational arrangements for them. The activities of the assistant poor-law commissioners were much broader in scope. These officers were charged not only with investigating workhouses, but also with all other matters that might affect the condition of the poor. Kay-Shuttleworth, the first secretary to the Privy Council Committee on Education, served as an assistant poor-law commissioner, and his investigation of workhouse schools fuelled his interest in public educational reform.[56]

Before the organization of a national school inspectorate, the two main voluntary societies, the British and Foreign School Society and the National Society, also conducted school inspections, but their inspectors were not paid, full-time officials. Parliament began to subsidize these two societies in 1833, with expenditures for buildings to be audited by the Treasury. When the audits proved haphazard, and faced with Brougham's 1837 Education Bill, Melbourne's Whig ministry moved to raise the parliamentary grant to £30,000 annually and to appoint a committee of Privy Council to administer it and to promote educational improvements. These plans were articulated by Lord John Russell, who proposed powers for the Committee of Council parallel to those of the national commissioners in Ireland. Opposition from the Tory party and from the established church led to modifications, but, in April 1839, the committee moved to appoint an educational inspectorate. The inspectors were 'to carry on an inspection of schools which have been or may be hereafter aided by grants of public money, and to convey to conductors and teachers of private schools in different parts of the country a knowledge of all improvements in the art of teaching, and likewise to report to this Committee the progress made in education from year to year.' Ball remarks that 'the scheme's similarities to the Irish system (unaccountably ignored by modern writers) were immediately noticed, and it was criticised by *The Times* as "a desperate attempt to introduce the Irish plan of education amongst us." '[57] It was *exactly* at this period that Poulett Thomson, in consultation with Russell, attempted to introduce a version of the Irish model to the Canadas.

In England, strenuous resistance on the part of the established church to secular inspection and similar objections on the part of the Scottish kirk led to the appointment of denominational inspectors and constrained the Privy Council committee to avoid interference with religious instruction in schools. Still, two inspectors were appointed in 1839, and a third for Scotland in 1840.

Any school applying for a building grant from the committee's funds was subject to inspection. The Committee of Council instructed inspectors to investigate such things as the site of the school from a sanitary point of view and the moral condition of the teacher. In cases of applications for extensive aid from 'poor and populous neighbourhoods,' the inspector was to investigate the general state of the poor and the condition of educational provision in the district. These instructions were amplified in an accompanying letter from Dr Kay, the secretary to the committee, where inspectors were told to encourage local efforts by publicizing educational 'improvements.' Ball suggests that these instructions may have been derived from Kay's own investigations of the Dutch educational system in 1838. In any case, the educational inspectors were not simply to enforce the law, but also to promote 'improvement' in educational matters through the collection of educational information and through the dissemination of plans.[58]

The English inspectors were gentlemen of considerable social standing and they were highly paid as well (£600 to begin, with travel expenses). They were university educated on the whole, and some of them had earlier been active in plans for social reform. Some of them were also personally acquainted with one another.

The publication of the first inspectoral reports allowed for the propagation of respectable middle-class views of 'what needed to be done.' Particularly important was the inspectors' insistence that low pay for teachers, and large numbers of students, led to poor educational practices. These were the grounds for a further intervention by the Committee in the subsidy of dwellings for schoolmasters, on condition of inspection, and in the subsidy of school apparatus, under a like condition. 'Apparatus' especially meant individual desks arranged in parallel rows, and hence this funding was a means whereby the committee could attack the prevailing monitorial pedagogy.

In turn, this expanded support multiplied the need for inspections and led to the hiring of four more school inspectors in 1844 (five including the replacement for Hugh Tremenheere, who resigned). At the same time, the council established five national inspectoral circuits, each of them subdivided into five sections containing at least twelve schools each. By 1844, many English schools were under a regular inspection, and from this period systematic national educational intelligence began to accumulate in the hands of the committee. Inspectors themselves began to agitate for the keeping of standardized forms of information by subsidized schools and argued for such reforms as the keeping of timetables.[59] The instrument of inspection enabled respectable men to push for the 'improvement' of the working class.

American Influences

European educational experiments, including inspectoral arrangements, early received the attention of American observers. The decline of clerical and community supervision of schools made many American activists receptive to European innovations in the early nineteenth century. The development of European social institutions was publicized in the popular genre of travel literature well before the appearance of Cousin's report.

John Griscom's *A year in Europe ... in 1818 and 1819* was particularly influential.[60] To a large audience, Griscom described the working of such European educational institutions as de Fellenberg's Hofwyl, Owen's New Lanark, Pestalozzi's school at Yverdon, the High School of Edinburgh conducted by Professor Pillans, the British and Foreign School Society's Borough Road School, and the Dublin schools of the Kildare Place Society. He encountered Sismondi in Milan and spent a considerable period with Thomas Chalmers, studying the 'local system.'

Griscom was particularly impressed by the schools of Holland. 'In no country of Europe,' he wrote, 'has the importance of education been more distinctly recognized by public regulations, or greater public liberality manifested in its support ... the Dutch schools are organized upon a plan which combined economy of expense, with certainty and expedition in the process of teaching. A mild and rational system of government is superadded to good literary and moral instruction.'

Griscom claimed that cheap education in Scotland gave 'a character of intelligence and thriftiness to its population' and he described Chalmer's local system as 'the least exceptionable' of all the schemes for reducing poverty. Finally, Griscom praised the Dublin model schools of the Kildare Place Society. 'The neatness and convenience of the buildings, and the good order and management which prevail in this school,' Griscom claimed, 'render it altogether, in my estimation, the first of the kind in Europe.' He praised the society's encouragement of emulation among teachers by awarding 'gratuities to the masters and mistresses of such schools, in all parts of the island, as appear, upon the inspection of an agent, who visits them under the appointment of the society, to be conducted with skill and fidelity.'[61]

In the following decade, the publication of Cousin's report on Prussian schools further stimulated American interest. An edition of Austin's translation of Cousin appeared in New York in 1835, introduced by J. Orville Taylor. While Taylor claimed that 'many parts of this system of public instruction are not adapted to the spirit and feelings of the American people, nor to their form of government,' he insisted none the less that, 'from the results of this great experiment in giving the *whole people* that *kind* and *degree* of instruction which they need, some of the most useful and practical lessons may be obtained.' A rash of books and papers followed the publication of the Cousin report. Calvin Stowe, later superintendent of education for Ohio (and married to Harriet Beecher Stowe), presented a series of lectures reprinted as *The Prussian System of Public Instruction and Its Applicability to the United States* in 1836. Stowe was then sent by the governor of Ohio to study the Prussian system. His favourable report was printed in Ohio in 1838 and reprinted in Massachusetts. George S. Hillard's *Lecture on Public Instruction in Prussia*, read to the American Institute of Instruction in 1835, derived largely from Cousin. Hillard argued that the system could not be adopted entirely in the United States, but its 'wise supervision' should be. Charles Brooks of Massachusetts used Cousin's report as propaganda in his agitations from 1834 for the establishment of a board of education and the first secretary of the board, Horace Mann, toured Europe himself in 1843. Mann's *Report of an Educational Tour* (1846), which so strongly influenced Egerton Ryerson in Canada West, largely restated the views of Stowe and of Alexander Bache. Bache, president of Girard College, praised Dutch and Prussian systems of inspection in a six-hundred-page report.[62]

Victor Cousin's 'report on education in Prussia,' a recent study of the roots of the American common school concludes, 'had a profound impact in the United States as well as in France and was quoted constantly. His subsequent report on the Netherlands was only relatively less influential.'[63]

Conclusion

Canadian activists frequently stressed the value of 'learning from abroad' – and went abroad to learn. They acknowledged their debts to foreign educational models, although not always in a disinterested manner. The Canada West School Act of 1846, for instance, was said by its author to come in 'law and government' from New York State and 'as a system of Instruction' from Ireland. But both of these systems were said to derive from Prussia in any case. The Education Office in Canada West planned to translate French manuals for inspectors, and when pushed, the chief superintendent maintained that Dutch administrative practice was his objective in education. When the Canadian Reformer Francis Hincks was accused by the opposition in 1850 of imposing American educational legislation on Canada West, he replied that his School Bill was 'not drawn from the United States any more than from any other country; it was in use in Scotland.' Canadian educational reformers viewed foreign experience in keeping with their own particular interests, but they were involved in a political process of an international character.[64]

The degree of consensus with which European educational developments were seen as guides in North America is particularly striking. These developments appeared as solutions to political and economic problems experienced or anticipated by the rising middle classes. Their generalization, at the same time, points to a process of state formation. But this was not an automatic process; different groups and classes drew different conclusions from their observation of European developments. The next two chapters discuss political conflict and debate over inspectoral organization in Canada West in the key decade of the 1840s.

3 Towards a Canadian Educational Inspectorate, 1835–1847

In her *Winter Studies and Summer Rambles in Canada*, written largely in 1837, Anna Brownell Jameson claimed that Upper Canadians were ignorant of educational systems in Europe and largely illiterate. 'It struck me,' she wrote, 'that if I could get the English preface to Victor Cousin's report (of which I had a copy) printed in a cheap form, and circulated with the newspapers, adding some of the statistical calculations, and some passages from Duppa's report on the education of the children of the poorer classes, it might do some good – it might assist the people to some general principles on which to form opinions,' for, she continued, 'nothing that had been promulgated in Europe on this momentous subject had yet reached them.' But her attempts were not encouraged: 'cold water was thrown upon me from every side – my interference in any way was so visibly distasteful, that I gave up my project with many a sigh.'[1]

Jameson was ignorant not only of the debates over educational organization that had preoccupied the colonial Parliament for a decade, but also of the fact that parts of Cousin's report, with J. Orville Taylor's preface to the American edition and Sarah Austin's introduction, had already been published in the Canadian colony, with a plan for the organization of educational inspection and draft legislation.

Plans for the organization of a system of common schools in the 1830s in Upper Canada foundered repeatedly not on popular ignorance, as Jameson suggested, but on the intransigent opposition of the Legislative Council to the extension of the powers of elected local government, and on that of colonial Reformers to the extension of the powers of centrally appointed justices of the peace. Until 1836, Reformers sought to place educational matters under the control of the representatives of male property holders in the locality. Tories in the Legislative Council, and to a lesser degree their allies in the House of Assembly, sought to strengthen the educational powers of appointed justices and to supervise these powers by centrally appointed boards of education. Despite sharp differences, both parties sought to organize systematic supervision and coordination of local educational efforts.

The political impasse was illustrated by reaction to the School Act of 1835, passed by a Reform Parliament and vetoed by the Legislative Council. This act would have provided for electoral representation on the appointed district boards of education, while easing access to the district grammar schools for boys. Archdeacon John Strachan and his fellow Tory legislative councillors did 'not find the principle of election applied in this manner in any country where Education is conserved, nor [could] they believe that a Town meeting is a proper place to select those who are to preside over the morals and intellectual development of the rising generation.' Strachan claimed that educational 'Superintendents ought to be persons of competent education and moral worth': in his view, 'qualifications which will not generally be found among the yeomanry of any country.'[2] The assumption that local proprietors were neither competent administrators nor worthy persons was a cornerstone of the ideology legitimating oligarchic government in the colony.

The Reform Assembly's reaction was expressed by William Lyon Mackenzie. 'It was objected to in the Bill,' Mackenzie observed, 'that the persons chosen at Town meetings would not be qualified to fill the office. But the people were beginning to choose better and better trustees every year; and the more power that was put into their hands, with regard to this matter, the more they would try to get proper persons, having the requisite abilities, to perform the duties assigned to them.'[3] Like the English Radicals with whom he was associated, Mackenzie argued that empowering 'the people' (male small proprietors) would make them more competent politically.

In his *Report upon the Subject of Education*, commissioned by the Reform Assembly in response to this educational impasse, Dr Charles Duncombe publicized Cousin's report on Prussia and proposed a detailed system of common schooling and inspection for Upper Canada. His plans were cut short by the election of a Tory majority in the Assembly in 1836. Several other attempts before 1840 to implement an Upper Canadian educational inspectorate came to nought.[4]

The Sydenham ministry acted in the first session of the united Parliament in 1841 to introduce an educational bill containing strong instruments of inspection. The bill proposed to allow the governor-in-council to appoint district school inspectors with extensive powers, aided by elected commissioners of common schools in each township. But the developing Reform opposition, seeing in central control of inspection a further attempt at imperial domination, undercut the clauses concerning an appointive rural inspectorate (centrally appointed boards of examiners remained in the towns). The School Act of 1841 proved a failure.[5]

The School Act of 1843

The Baldwin-Lafontaine ministry reorganized educational provision in Canada West through a revised School Act of 1843, drafted by the moderate Reformer and inspector general (finance minister) Francis Hincks. This act created the decade's most important Canadian state inspectorate.

Francis Hincks was a man 'highly qualified to bring the muddled finances of the Province into a state of order and security' and he was surrounded by men conversant, as he was himself, with Irish educational practice.[6] Hincks was the youngest son of the master of the élite Belfast Academical Institution, and some of his brothers became well-known scholars. His father was active in his support for the Irish National Board of Education. Hincks himself attended the Academical Institution and later Belfast University. In Toronto, he operated the Reform *Examiner*, where his editor was Hamilton Hunter, soon to be named inspector of the Home District under Hincks's School Act. Hunter was educated in Hincks's father's school and was well aware of Irish educational developments. Hincks's cousin, William Hutton, first inspector of the Victoria District and with whom he was in regular contact, was similarly conversant. In debate over his School Bill, Hincks drew parallels between his legislation and that in force in Prussia and the United States.[7]

The School Act of 1843 was organized around the Reform ministry's Municipal Bill of 1843, a plan for a county-based system of elected local government. The failure of the Municipal Bill disrupted the School Act's administrative organization.

In each school section under the School Act, property holders elected three school trustees who were to hire a licensed teacher and to organize the day-to-day management, furnishing, and supply of the schoolhouse.

All the schools in any town, city, or township were to be supervised by local superintendents of common schools, appointed and paid by town, city, or township councils. Local superintendents were to post a performance bond and were charged with dividing the town, city, or township into school districts (following council's directions), with visiting every school at least annually, and with distributing the parliamentary school grant. Local superintendents were empowered to examine and certify candidates for teaching posts within the township and to annul certificates with six weeks' written notice. Teachers could appeal to higher officials. Local superintendents were to collect from trustees and transmit to county superintendents information about the numbers of schools, school attendance, school monies raised and expended, and the size of the juvenile population. They were also required to account annually for all the monies they received. Local superintendents who failed or refused to account satisfactorily for school monies, or to pay over unspent balances when required to do so, were subject to a fine of £25, and the balances in question could be recovered from their sureties.[8]

The act made the clerk of the town, city, or township the local superintendent's clerk as well, charged with collecting and holding all books and papers, including trustees' reports, and with receiving and answering his correspondence. When the Municipal Bill failed, this labour devolved upon the township superintendents themselves.

The most important officials in this legislation were county school inspectors. All township, town, and city schools were to be visited at least annually by a bonded county superintendent of common schools, appointed and paid by the county council. This county inspector could license teachers and annul the certificates granted by local superintendents. While the certificates of the local superintendents were valid only for a year, those of the county superintendent were valid throughout the county until he saw fit to revoke them. The act required the county superintendent, at the direction of the chief superintendent, to re-examine teachers whenever either might find it expedient.

In his visits, the county superintendent was to 'examine into the state and condition of the Schools, both as respects the progress of the scholars in learning, and the good order of the Schools, and may give his advice and direction to the Trustees and Teachers thereof, and the course of studies to be pursued therein.' He was required by the act to provide annual reports and to furnish the chief superintendent with whatever additional information the latter might require. Failure to report on any occasion was punishable by a fine of £5.[9]

County, town, city, or township councils were empowered by the act of 1843 to levy a rate for the establishment of model schools for teacher training. At least until such time as a provincial normal school came into existence, the model schools were to be supervised by the county superintendents. The appointment of model-school teachers and all school rules and practices were subject to their approval.[10]

County councils were themselves to function as county boards of education, defining school districts, levying school taxes, supervising the county superintendent, and transmitting all school reports to the provincial assistant superintendent of education.[11]

Finally, the provincial assistant superintendent of education was to distribute the school grant to county superintendents on the basis of district population, to specify report forms for educational intelligence, to collect reports from county councils, and to promote educational 'improvements,' although the means at his disposal for so doing were extremely limited.

This scheme had to be modified in response to the failure of the Municipal Bill.

The duties of county and township councils devolved upon district councils, and the office of township superintendent (in the absence of township councils) became somewhat lame. District clerks found themselves charged with large amounts of administrative work. As the size of the now district superintendents' circuits increased (in most cases) to cover two counties, these men acquired a regional importance. The duties of town and village councils devolved upon the old boards of police.

The District Superintendents

District superintendents under the School Act of 1843 formed a pioneering Canadian state inspectorate. Inspectors were the central figures in this Reform educational plan, which itself embodied principles of regional educational autonomy. Superintendents were situated to oversee, regulate, and modify educational practice at the district level and, at first, they were largely independent. The legislation left much to administrative regulation, but the central Education Office was initially very poorly equipped, allowing a wide latitude to inspectors.

District superintendents were appointed by district councils and held office during pleasure. Where the office was lucrative and desired by the incumbent, a superintendent's activities were undoubtedly constrained. But district councils had no legislative power to specify superintendents' duties. Inspectors or superintendents (the terms are synonymous)[12] were legally empowered to make and enforce a broad range of judgments about educational matters, including teachers' qualifications and entitlement to pay, curriculum, pedagogy, and school management. Neither the School Act nor, at first, the Education Office specified the criteria according to which such judgments were to be made. Educational intelligence was centralized in the inspectors' hands. Their powers with respect to model schools gave them a further opportunity to define legitimate educational practice. The legislative requirement of a performance bond sharply limited access to the post, ensuring that incumbents would be either substantial men of property or men for whose probity substantial men of property were prepared to vouch.

The Reform education plan was quite in keeping with liberal views of Canadian governmental organization: governance was to be organized by respectable male proprietors, chosen more or less by their peers and exerting a strong measure of autonomy. The central authority was viewed largely as an agency to facilitate the activities of these men, while allowing for the formulation of views of general social conditions of interest to men of this class. Its functions were 'precisely organizational and connective.'

The Administration of the Act of 1843

The School Act of 1843 was greeted with confusion as recently appointed and largely inexperienced officers attempted to discover expected procedures from a poorly equipped central authority. Trustee elections held the second Monday in January as required by the act were invalid because most of the superintendents required to call them were not appointed until the district council sessions in February. The attorney general ruled to this effect, but refused permission to the assistant superintendent of education to publish his ruling.[13] Before setting to work, some superintendents waited for the Education Office to send them copies of the oath they expected school trustees to take, unaware that the reservation of the Secret Societies Bill invalidated this requirement in the School Act.[14]

All twenty district councils appointed superintendents of education in 1844, although many first appointed county superintendents and, then, with the failure of the Municipal Bill, were constrained to remove one of them, a process that generated controversy.[15] Many councils made no provision for the payment of superintendents' salaries, assuming that they would either serve gratuitously or be paid a percentage of the government grant. An attempt by one council to have the district treasurer perform the financial duties instead of appointing a superintendent was opposed by the Education Office. Debates surrounded the eligibility of other potential superintendents.[16]

As we shall see at greater length in chapter 5, most district councils appointed rising middle-class men to this new administrative position. But there was a considerable variety in the initial appointments, and several superintendents resigned the office upon discovering what it entailed. In six of the twenty districts, leading members of local élites were appointed, but five of these soon resigned.

Western District Council, to take one case, appointed Charles Eliot (?–1858) of Sandwich, an early settler in the district and one of its most prominent citizens. Eliot came to Canada as a half-pay lieutenant of the 43rd Regiment, likely in the 1820s, and, by the middle 1830s, his interests had spread across the Western District. He was named district judge in 1833 (at £225 per annum, the highest-paid district office), a trustee of the district grammar school in 1834, and by 1835 was commissioner of customs. A wealthy man, Eliot held stock in both the Commercial Bank of the Midland District and the Bank of Upper Canada. He claimed in 1836 that he personally guaranteed the finances of the district. His positions as judge and collector of customs, along with his army pension, earned him over £400 in 1835, eight to ten times the artisanal wage, and he held land and bank stock as well. Eliot ran unsuccessfully as a Reform candidate in the 1836 election.

Eliot was active in the defence of the frontier during the incursions of 1838–9.

He particularly distinguished himself during the Battle of Windsor by his attempts to prevent the summary executions of prisoners by Colonel John Prince, a political rival. These attempts earned him Prince's enmity and likely led to his retirement as district judge in the middle 1840s. He continued to draw an annual pension of £100 until his death in 1858.

Eliot was centrally involved in matters of social policy as chairman of the Quarter Sessions and as a member of the Western District Board of Education. He considered questions of jail reform, and the Board of Education called for the appointment of a provincial school inspectorate in 1839. As a school inspector himself, however, Eliot visited only a fraction of the district schools and resigned the position less than a year after being named to it, claiming that there was too much work involved.[17]

While a number of district councils appointed men of wealth and prestige, others, motivated by considerations of economy, appointed men in modest circumstances. As in the case of William Hynes, a private-venture schoolmaster appointed by Johnstown Council, an early resignation was often the reaction of these men was well. The inspectors who served for longer periods tended to be men of moderate means, many of whose fortunes were on the rise.

Severe retrenchment in the central Education Office in 1844 meant that no forms or instructions were printed for superintendents. Several district superintendents delayed inspectoral tours in the expectation of receiving such things, only to learn these were not forthcoming. The Education Office was urged to adopt the forms and instructions used in New York State, but superintendents were initially left to devise their own report forms and to apply their own standards in evaluating schools and teachers. Several adapted the report forms produced under the act of 1841.[18]

Financial matters were extremely confused. The payment of monies due under the act of 1841 in 1843 even to those districts that had not levied a tax created opposition to a school tax in many areas. 'An idea has become very prevelant [*sic*] in this District,' observed William Hutton of Victoria, 'that the Gov't Grants will be given to the several Towns & Townships for distribution amongst the Teachers *whether the tax be levied or not.*' This generated pressure on the council to repeal the assessment for 1844. The Board of Police in Belleville, and Huron and Dalhousie district councils, refused a school tax in 1844 and attempted none the less to draw the school monies. The confusion surrounding this question was not clarified by the suggestion of Robert Murray, the assistant superintendent, that the grant might be paid in relation to fees charged if no tax were levied.[19]

No reliable census existed in the colony, but school monies were to be distributed according to population density. The Education Office depended upon inspectors' reports of local population.[20] Superintendents were confused about how to assess ratepayers whose children crossed an administrative boundary to attend school. Robert Boyd of Prescott sought to include parts of the surrounding township in the town for assessment purposes. He also failed, despite Assistant Superintendent Murray's explicit instructions, to divide Prescott into school districts.[21]

The Education Office explored the contours of its own administrative authority. Robert Murray was instructed by the provincial secretary in April 1844 to act in educational matters as he thought 'the circumstances of the case render proper.' He was to consult with the ministry if he thought it necessary, but the secretary added, 'in all cases, let the drafts, or steps to be taken, be suggested by you, in the same manner as the business connected with the other Departments, are done by the Assistant Secretaries.'[22] In the same month, Murray was already dispatching district and township superintendents to investigate disputes over the payment of school monies and the qualifications of teachers.[23] Individual superintendents were advised about desirable courses of action in particular circumstances.[24]

Acting Assistant Superintendent McNab was alarmed to learn in the spring of 1845 that most district superintendents were paid a percentage of the school monies passing through their hands. This was in keeping with common administrative practice, but in violation of the School Act, which intended the grant for the payment of teachers. Superintendents were meant to be paid out of general district revenue. McNab acted, with mixed success, to end the practice of deducting salaries from the grant. His circular on this question was the first systematic investigation of educational administration throughout the colony, apart from the annual school reports. Responses to it revealed that, in many districts, the superintendency remained a partially venal office.[25]

Under the act, the district school monies were drawn in a lump sum by the inspectors, but paid out piecemeal to teachers, often only when they presented themselves for examination. For the inspectors, there was little clear distinction between personal and public finance in this formative period. There is no evidence that superintendents kept separate accounts of school monies, and many of them kept the grant in cash in their houses. The Education Office was compelled to depend upon their financial probity, with unfortunate consequences in at least two cases.[26]

In 1845, the office established its right to demand an accounting of school monies from superintendents. Alexander McNab was alarmed by accusations that Elias Burnham of the Colborne District was 'living in open concubinage,' had lost his barrister's gown, had committed perjury, and had loaned the school monies 'to Mr. Perry of Cobourg to purchase wheat at an exorbitant rate of interest for a few months say 10 per cent.' In response to McNab's queries about his powers, Attorney General Draper insisted that the assistant superintendent could demand an accounting in detail and at any time of any district superintendent. McNab was instructed to withhold the Colborne school monies for 1845 until Burnham delivered his accounts for 1843 and 1844, and he wrote to Burnham, demanding to know 'where you keep unexpended School Moneys, whether you employ them in any way for *your own* benefit, or otherwise, and if employed, how, on what conditions and when to be repaid.' Burnham apparently responded satisfactorily.[27]

Superintendents on the Act of 1843

On the whole, the inspectors themselves were satisfied with the School Act of 1843. While many of them suggested revisions, most of them felt that the act provided opportunities for educational 'improvement,' in pursuit of which, as we will see in more detail below, many of them were active. If anything, district superintendents thought too little power was accorded them by the act.

In the Newcastle District, in early 1845, a meeting of about fifty township superintendents and school trustees, chaired by the district superintendent, John Steele, expressed its general approval of the act of 1843. The meeting proposed twelve revisions to the act, all of them concerning 'housekeeping' matters: changes in the method of paying school monies, clear directions for the disposal of surplus monies, staggered trustee elections, and fines for non-performing trustees, among others. Steele himself pushed for uniform books, larger school sections, 'a more rigid and frequent inspection,' and the establishment of a 'County or District Model School.'[28]

Superintendents agitated for the payment of teachers more frequently than once a year. Where the government grant for the year was paid to a school after it had been open for the minimum three months required by law, some teachers immediately moved to another school. George Duck, Jr, claimed that, in this way, such teachers were able to take four schools in a year. To prevent this, the grant should be paid in quarterly instalments. John Strachan of the Midland District argued that the grant should be paid on 1 May instead of 1 August. 'This would be of great advantage to the Teachers by enabling the Trustees to settle up with them as at that time a great many female teachers are engaged especially in small districts.' Strachan also suggested that township superintendents be eliminated and that the grant for urban separate schools be paid according to population, rather than attendance.[29]

Again, Hamilton Hunter, a man with close connections to the Reformers, found the School Act 'good in principle' but in need of extension. He sought facilities for teacher training, better supplies, 'a good set of Common School books well adapted to the gradual progress of the children, and of such a character as to inspire them with interest in their studies and improve their minds,' as well as 'the establishment of District Libraries ... containing interesting and instructive works.' The latter particularly would provide people with the 'means of self-improvement.'[30]

Many superintendents shared these concerns, but most of them saw these as matters that could be organized within the framework of the 1843 act. There was no suggestion from any of them of the necessity of a major educational centralization, and Patrick Thornton of the Gore District later argued that the 1843 act accorded far more scope to inspectors to pursue educational improvement than did those that soon replaced it.

The Act of 1846

The Act of 1843 was in force for three years, from 1 January 1844 until 1 January 1847, when it was reconstructed by the School Act of 1846, authored by Egerton Ryerson and passed by the 'irresponsible' Tory administration. As I have shown elsewhere, the 1843 act posed a number of technical administrative difficulties with respect to such matters as the funding of new schools, methods of paying teachers, and the taxation powers of district councils.[31] As far as inspectoral organization was concerned, in the eyes of Ryerson and colonial Tories, the act did not confer sufficient authority upon the Education Office either to instruct superintendents or to enforce educational uniformity. These were *political* and by no means *technical* flaws.

The importance of inspectoral practice to educational administration was stressed in Ryerson's 1846 *Report on a System of Public Elementary Instruction for Upper Canada*, a document that began with a reaffirmation of Victor Cousin's praise of the value of 'learning from abroad' in matters of state. Ryerson insisted that successful educational systems were dependent upon the practical work of administration and claimed 'there is no class of officers in the whole machinery of elementary instruction on whom so much depends for its efficient and successful working, as upon the local Superintendents or Inspectors.' The role of government in educational administration lay in ensuring that grants were spent in the manner intended and that prescribed books and qualified teachers were in the schools, in 'discovering errors, and suggesting remedies, as to the organization, classification, and methods of teaching in the Schools,' and, finally, in 'animating' and 'imparting vigor by every available means to the whole system.' These were functions proper to the inspectorate, and Ryerson remarked, 'The proper selection of this class of agents is a matter of the greatest importance; they should make themselves theoretically and practically acquainted with every branch taught in the Schools, and the best modes of teaching, as well as with the whole subject of School organization and management. Where there is incompetency or negligence here, there is weakness in the very part where strength is most required.'

While he borrowed heavily from Irish educational practice, Ryerson took Holland, where inspection was the central administrative practice, as his model of an efficient inspectoral system. He insisted that inspection was especially important 'in the commencement of a system of Public Instruction' and emphasized that 'little hope of success can be entertained in this Province, wherever local Superintendents prove lax or careless in their ... exertions to carry every part of the law into effect, and to excite increased interest in the public mind in behalf of the education of the young. The establishment and maintenance of a School system [was] not like the digging of a Canal, or the building of a Railroad, where the work may be performed by strangers and foreigners.' The younger inhabitants were to be instructed by their parents and guardians, and, if public education were to succeed, the personal influence of the latter was of central importance. Ryerson conceived 'Government' as something that existed 'for the prosperity of the public family' and, by implication, inspectors were among the guardians of this public family. Moral regulatory forces, applied by familiar inspectors, were the central dimensions of governmental power in this paternalistic conception.[32]

The act of 1846 involved a major set of centralizing initiatives that, at least on paper, circumscribed, specified, and limited the extremely broad powers enjoyed by the school inspectors under earlier legislation. The formulation of school rules, pedagogical practice, and curriculum were now in the hands of the chief superintendent of education for Canada West and the newly appointed General Board of Education. The provisions for model schools remained largely unchanged, but the Education Office now moved towards the establishment of a provincial normal school, whose master would be empowered to regulate model schools. These two changes together undercut regional educational autonomy in teacher training under the direction of the district superintendents.

As under the act of 1843, district councils were to appoint district superintendents and to demand performance bonds from them. Ryerson's draft bill had intended the governor general to appoint the superintendent from a list of two candidates suggested by the district councils, with superintendents to hold office during pleasure. But Canadian education was not immune to parliamentary 'interference': the clause was lost in the House, and the act of 1846 authorized councils not only to appoint superintendents, but also to provide for their salaries by taxation.[33] Thus the superintendents became much more evidently district employees, rather than officials living off the provincial school monies (although many continued to do so). At the same time, the passage of amendments to the District Councils Act in 1846 allowed councils to elect their own wardens and clerks, officers formerly appointed by the governor-in-council. These amendments made no mention of district school superintendents, but there was a marked attempt by district councils after 1846 to regulate and specify the duties of their own employees. Several councils passed by-laws specifying the duties of district superintendents.

The School Act of 1846 defined the duties of inspectors in considerable detail. These included those involved under the act of 1843, with several important additions. Superintendents were to visit the schools at least once annually, but more frequent visits might now 'be deemed necessary' by the chief superintendent. While superintendents were to examine the schools and teachers as before, they were now not to license any person not a 'natural born, or naturalized, subject.' They were specifically instructed to 'prevent the use of all unauthorized foreign School Books in the English branches of education' and to decide all matters of educational dispute referred to them by any party, notwithstanding the chief superintendent's right to intervene on appeal.

The form and content of the inspectors' annual reports were now specified in much greater detail, and inspectors were required to report the frequency of their own visits. Additional items of intelligence were to allow the central authority to map existing alternatives to the state schools: the nature, number, location and condition of all libraries in the district, with the inspectors' suggestions for 'the improvement of the Schools and the diffusion of useful knowledge'; and the number of, attendance at, and subjects taught in private schools. Finally, an omnibus clause required the superintendents 'to act in accordance with the directions of the Superintendent of Schools, and to make an Annual Report to him, at such time and in such form as may be appointed by the said Superintendent of Schools; and to furnish the said Superintendent, from time to time, with such additional information as he may require.'[34]

The room for manoeuvre of the inspectors was limited by these developments, the more so as they were increasingly subject to regulation by two authorities whose interests were often at odds: the Education Office and the district councils. We shall see that superintendents were often constrained to ally themselves with one or the other.

The superintendents' condition was made more complex by school-visitors clauses in the act of 1846. The act eliminated township superintendents, but, anticipating criticism for this centralizing initiative and concerned to encourage clerical involvement in the schools (many local superintendents were clergymen), Ryerson had proposed to accord special powers of visitation to the clergy. 'I have not proposed to give *Visitors* any *authority* other than that of counsel,' Ryerson remarked on this clause in the draft bill. 'Perhaps *ultimately* it may be advisable to give them more authority, as experience may suggest, but the country would not bear it at present.' In the House, however, the definition of school visitor was broadened to include district court judges, justices of the peace, the district warden, and the relevant district councillor(s). These respectable men were accorded rather broad powers. Any two of them could examine and grant a licence to a schoolteacher to teach in a specific school for a year, and they could assemble at will to promote educational improvements. They were allowed to examine the schools and students on the occasion of quarterly school examinations and to send their remarks about any other school examination to the district superintendent for his information. 'I know not what greater power could be given to the Clergy, without destroying the School system,' Ryerson observed, 'positive control in the Schools ... cannot be severed from their Trustees and Provincial management.'[35]

In several instances in the ensuing period, inspectors found themselves in conflict with school visitors over conceptions of sound educational practice.

The reactions of district superintendents to this act and to its companion of 1847 came to the fore primarily in debate over the School Act of 1849 and are discussed below. But, even while plans for the bill were under discussion, some superintendents expressed their unease. Patrick Thornton's annual report for 1845, for instance, urged the necessity of a provincial normal school, but argued that such a school should differ from those in Dublin and Glasgow, especially in the attention paid to 'the philosophy of the human mind. ... This suggestion is dictated by careful study of the theory on which the training in each of these establishments is founded and confirmed by the Practice of those who have their Diplomas from these Seminaries – We have several teachers in this District bearing testimonials from said seminaries.'[36]

Ryerson claimed that his 1846 bill was anticipated and supported by William Elliott of the London District and he had circulated it in draft to three other superintendents: William Hutton, Dexter D'Everardo, and Hamnett Pinhey. The approval of Hamilton Hunter, 'a protégé of Messrs. Baldwin & Hincks,' was announced to the Tory Draper ministry, although Hunter's criticisms were not included.[37]

The Act of 1847

The School Act of 1847, which applied mainly to towns and cities, also reduced the scope of the district superintendency by severing urban and rural educational administration. While town and city superintendents had formerly been subjected to the authority of the district superintendent, an arrangement that, in some cases, had generated considerable conflict, the act of 1847 made urban superintendents responsible to the urban councils. Magistrates were not included in the lists of school visitors in towns and cities. At the same time, urban superintendents were accorded extensive, and heatedly contested powers to order municipal taxation.[38]

The Centrality of Inspection

The chief superintendent repeatedly insisted that inspection and finance lay at the heart of state power over education. In response to queries from the superintendent general of Indian affairs in 1847 about the best means of organizing schools, Ryerson wrote at length on this subject.

The interference or control of the Government should be confined to that which the Government can do with most effect and the least trouble – namely, to the right of inspecting the Schools from time to time by an agent or agents of its own – to the right of having detailed reports of the Schools as often as it shall think proper to require them, at least once or twice a year; and the right of continuing or withholding the grant made in aid of these Schools. It is in this power over the grant, the exercise of which will be determined by the inspections made and the reports given, that the paramount authority of the Government in respect to these Schools will be secured; while the endless difficulties arising from fruitless attempts to manage the Schools in detail will be avoided.[39]

The school law, Ryerson wrote to Dexter D'Everardo of the Niagara District, allowed 'the Government, through the superintendent of Schools, to interfere no further than to see that the conditions on which the Legislature has granted assistance to schools are complied with, and that the general spirit and objects of the law are not violated by any individual or local party.'[40] Again, in a letter outlining the nature of his office to William Millar, newly appointed Eastern District superintendent, Ryerson stressed that Millar's 'powers – though not extending to anything which properly belongs to the people themselves or their representatives, unless they appeal to you – extend to what is essential to the improvement of the Schools: – the object contemplated by the Legislative Grant.'[41] Of course, the 'improvement of the schools' was a political, not simply a technical, term. Ryerson saw control of the school grant as a lever under educational practice that could operate only on the fulcrum of inspection. And Ryerson, with many of those who opposed him on the *organization* of the inspectorate, recognized the charismatic potential of inspectors to 'animate' the people. Whose agent the inspector was to be was a key issue.

Public Opposition to the Acts

The Reform press was extremely critical of the act of 1846 from the outset. The act was seen as despotic, and there was a considerable amount of venom directed towards Ryerson for his perceived desertion of responsible government in 1844.

The *Examiner*, for instance, repeatedly denounced the 'Draper-Leonidas Scheme,' comparing it to the Prussian and Czarist systems: 'If this dark scheme, the joint concoction of Egerton Ryerson and Attorney-General Draper is to be carried out, it requries no prophet to foretell the consequences that must flow from it. A mistaught people, without independence or dignity of mind, prostrate in intellect, pusillanimous, imbecile, and the willing tools of corruption, present a spectacle on which unperverted humanity and true patriotism cannot look without weeping.' Despotic governments were said to be those compelled to rule by centralized educational systems. The *Mirror* similarly castigated the 'educational police system.' After the absconding of John Bignall with the Huron District school monies, the *Signal* described the district superintendents as 'an incubus' feeding on the 'energies' of the act and as 'worse than useless.'[42]

The act of 1847 replaced elected urban school trustees with boards appointed by municipal councils, and made property taxation the only mode of supporting urban schools. These changes provoked opposition from Reformers and some Tories and led to the closing of the schools of Toronto in 1848–9. Some sections of the press denounced the elimination of the electoral principle and claimed the government was seeking to impose a degrading pauper system on the working people of Toronto. The abolition of the rate-bill system in the towns and cities was claimed to deprive people of their main instrument of control over the conduct of schooling (their payment of fees) and to undercut their interests in the schools.[43]

Ryerson had initially argued for urban educational centralization as a means of providing graded central schools and secondary schools. These, he claimed, were generally lacking in the towns and cities of Canada West, 'except as they may in some instances be established and supported by private enterprise. But,' he continued, 'private schools are too expensive for a large class of the inhabitants of towns and cities; nor should the children of this large class of our fellow citizens be deprived of a good English education on account of the poverty of their parents, or be abandoned to the hazard of private enterprise.' 'Efficiency' demanded central management of such institutions, as in Germany and the United States.[44]

In the midst of the debate over taxation for the schools of Toronto, and in the wake of the disastrous Irish famine immigration, Ryerson defended property taxation for the schooling of the urban poor as both necessary and just: 'Had the property holders in Ireland for the last fifty years been responsible each according to his property for the Common School Education of all the children of Ireland, it would have been at this day a very different country from what it is. The most effectual means should be used to permit [*sic*] Canada from becoming a second Ireland – and especially in the ignorance and consequent pauperism of its cities and towns.'[45]

Opposition to the school acts also came from a number of churchmen. Some Free Church ministers were particularly alarmed by Ryerson's inclusion of the high churchman Hugh Scobie on the General Board of Education and by their belief that Ryerson had been writing in Scobie's Toronto *Colonist* in defence of the Prussian educational system. Dr Burns of the Toronto Free Church claimed this led him and his fellows 'to fear some foreboding as to the character of the public & government education which it may be the lot of this Province to receive under [Ryerson's] charge.' Burns was alarmed at the prospect of state control over religion leading, as in Ireland and Prussia, to a 'non-sectarian' Christianity that would exclude the Bible from the schools. He demanded some public statement from Ryerson on the question. 'For my own part,' Burns insisted, 'I would rather go along with the Examiner in *excluding religion in every shape* from our schools than introduce a system which annihilates the mysteries & miracles of the revelations of God. Better make *no pretence* to religion which is essentially not so.'

Ryerson responded to Burns that he had not written on Prussian pedagogy in the *Colonist*, although he thought the articles in question were excellent in their exposition of Prussian methods. It was also not his place to demand theological pronouncements from the editor of that paper, or from anyone else. 'I abhor German theology as much as you can do,' Ryerson closed, 'but as Superintendent of Schools, I am neither a Theologian nor a Politician.'[46] The 'interests of education' were above politics.

The Education Acts and the Local State

The act of 1846 attacked the autonomy of district councils in educational matters. Councils were compelled to tax to support schools, but now had little formal influence over educational policy. They were compelled to pay educational officials who were instructed by the central authority. Many opposed both the tax burdens and the threats to their autonomy, and several councils agitated against the act.

The Gore District Council sent a memorial against the school act to other district councils in the fall of 1847. Gore Council called for the act's repeal and for a return to the legislation of 1843, or even of 1816. Council argued that the act of 1846 was complicated and expensive, that the Normal School would train people for the professions at public expense, and that trustees and others were subjected to a large volume of useless forms and instructions. Gore Council urged making district councils district boards of education with powers of educational management. The council of the Eastern District supported this memorial in its entirety.[47]

Newcastle District Council circulated its own memorial on the act, calling for the removal of all superintendents, 'both Provincial and District,' leaving district clerks to organize educational reporting and trustees to negotiate with and hire teachers.[48] Both the Home and the Western district councils called for the subordination of the chief superintendent to the Board of Education, on the grounds that according so much power to a single individual was incompatible with free institutions. As far as the Western District councillors were concerned, the salaries of the inspectors were 'little better than a waste of money,' and the act created 'hatred and malice between neighbours.' Dalhousie District Council petitioned the Executive Council to call new district elections so that 'the people' could pronounce on the school act.[49]

Several councils, while critical of the School Act, none the less insisted upon the utility of inspection in educational administration. Their concerns lay with the question of whose agent the inspector was to be, and, in general, they took the position that the body paying the inspector should direct him as well. The education committee of Colborne Council, in the middle of debate over memorials on the act, wrote about the beneficial activities of the district superintendent of schools.

In the course of his visits to the schools, and his intercourse with Teachers, Trustees and Visitors, he has it in his power far above any other individual connected with local school management, to give a tone to public sentiment; to stimulate Teachers and pupils to more earnest and diligent application in their respective spheres; to exalt the standard of popular education; to originate and procure the adoption of plans for improving the internal structure and requisites of schools; to ally dissensions; to inculcate sound morality.[50]

'In short,' they concluded elsewhere, 'to enlighten, invigorate and control nearly all the Subordinate agencies employed in the wide range of the common School System.' Indeed, Colborne Council argued that 'most, if not all, of the defects complained of' by those critical of the act of 1846 were 'chargeable not so much on the law, as upon the administration of it; and this applies peculiarly to the office of District Superintendent.'[51]

Elsewhere, inspectors themselves intervened in council debates to prevent support for the Gore and Newcastle memorials.

Bathurst District Council

Of particular interest in this debate between central and local state bodies is the role of Bathurst Council. The district town, Perth, was founded by assisted migrant weavers from Paisley in the 1820s. 'Scotch' democracy was strongly entrenched here, and Bathurst Council drew upon the expertise of several experienced public educators. It was through Malcolm Cameron, a member for Lanark and proprietor of the *Bathurst Courier*, later a person close to the radical agrarian Clear Grit party, that the legislative challenge to the act of 1846 made it to Parliament. Cameron's School Act of 1849 was shaped by Murdoch McDonnell, who chaired Bathurst Council's education committee.

Bathurst Council's memorial claimed the colony's school laws had consistently failed because they were incapable of reaching the poor and those in areas of small population. The act of 1816 produced too many schools and funded unqualified teachers, and Bathurst Council rejected Gore Council's positive view of it. In Bathurst Council's view, the acts of 1841, 1843, and especially 1846 taxed the thinly settled regions to subsidize the rest. The act of 1846 was particularly obnoxious since it increased the level of school taxation while distributing monies according to population density rather than school attendance. Council was able to use the reports of its own superintendent of schools to demonstrate that Westmeath Township, a thinly settled area, had paid £32 in tax towards the district school fund, but had received only £10 from it. A similarly unequal distribution prevailed among school sections within townships.

Supporting schools according to attendance was the just principle, Council claimed. It argued that either school sections should be abolished entirely or the District Council itself should decide the placing of schoolhouses. In any case, schools should be established at convenient distances, and 'every man' allowed to choose the school he wished his children to attend. All details of educational management should be vested in the district council as a district board of education empowered to do 'all that is now transacted at an enormous expense, and most inefficiently and unsatisfactorily, by the Board of Education and the Education Office at Toronto.'

Bathurst Council rejected Gore Council's motion to abolish school superintendents and argued there must be '*a complete and efficient supervision.*' However, such a supervision was not one 'enthroned at Toronto, issuing its bulletin respecting what it can have no proper understanding and creating dissatisfaction, strife and disaffection in neighbourhoods which formerly were remarkably united and peaceable.' The supervision needed was 'a *local, itinerant* supervision that should extend to *every* school section,' and even in areas where there were no schools, visits should be made into people's houses, '*to their firesides,*' to awaken an interest in education. Good educational inspection involved the making of 'systematic and periodical appeals, to the inhabitants of each section, in the form of lectures, addresses,' and so forth. Council argued that the state of New York provided a model of decentralized supervision that Canada West should imitate.

The School Act of 1846 did not allow for the creation of adequate educational supervision. Bathurst Council claimed it was 'because the defective provisions of our School laws have prevented District Councillors from exacting of District Superintendents such supervision as is implied in the above, that the several Districts of the Province have received not adequate benefit from the services of Superintendents.' As we shall see in more detail below, Bathurst Council had appointed the Reverend Alexander Mann as district superintendent in 1844, only to discover two years later that he never visited the schools. As a Presbyterian clergyman supported out of the Reserves Fund, Mann was legally barred from paid public administrative activity. He performed only clerical operations as school superintendent and allied himself in contentious issues with the central authority against Council.[52]

Bathurst Council identified the same qualities in the ideal superintendent as did Ryerson in his report of 1846. But Council argued such superintendents could only be secured if district councils were themselves boards of education with broad powers. Finally, educational uniformity across the province was impossible, Council argued, because patterns of settlement were not themselves uniform; district councils could best deal with local variations.[53]

Three Views of Inspection

At least three major opposition positions to the act of 1846 were expressed by men of property, in addition to clerical attacks upon it. Some respectable men of property, those in the Dalhousie District, for instance, harkened back to an era in which bureaucratic structures of administration impinged little upon their powers of paternalistic governance. They opposed taxation as something that would interfere with private charity, and bureaucratic educational superintendence as an usurpation of the role of leading proprietors. Elsewhere, educational taxation was opposed as something that created a fund for despotic state officials, district superintendents among them, to apply for their own nefarious purposes. A third position, that of Bathurst Council, proposed a regularized and more or less bureaucratic educational administration, but one under the direct control of the regional representatives of 'social improvement.' Localized superintendence could exert more effective force on those in need of improvement, both through the status of and people's familiarity with the local superintendent, and because of the latter's more detailed knowledge of the locality itself. It was this analysis that propelled the legislative attack of 1849 on the Tory school acts of 1846 and 1847.

In a context of pauper immigration, economic restructuring, and resurgent agrarian radicalism, these divisions within the propertied classes in Canada West provoked a major educational crisis. Inspectors themselves played important roles in the ensuing struggles over educational organization, at the same time as they found themselves in the middle of struggles between the developing central and local states.

4   Inspection, Inspectors, and the Educational Crisis, 1848–1850

The accession of a Reform ministry to power in 1848, after the granting of 'responsible government' to the Canadas, the new ministry's revival of a plan for the organization of county municipalities and mounting criticism of the acts of 1846–7 led Egerton Ryerson to undertake revisions to the school acts in 1848 and again in 1849.

The Revisions of 1848

Ryerson maintained revisions were necessary because of earlier parliamentary interference. Key clauses in the acts of 1846–7, particularly those limiting the rate-bill system, had been defeated in the House.[1]

Ryerson claimed to have found general support for tax-supported schooling during his educational tour of the province in the fall of 1847. True, he admitted, 'in one or two instances the office and powers of the provincial Superintendent of Schools have been objected to, as also the office of District Superintendent.' But, with respect to the latter office, 'it cannot be supposed that all the District Councils have been equally fortunate in their elections or appointments to this office, and therefore its utility has not been equally exemplified in all the Districts.' As for his own office, it functioned simply as 'a kind of equity tribunal of appeal' for things done elsewhere in the system.

Ryerson claimed much of the difficulty surrounding the school acts stemmed from the fact that they aimed to elevate the 'ignorant and selfish' portions of the community and from general uncertainty with respect to the Reform ministry's educational intentions. 'All such laws' directed at the ignorant and selfish 'must be sustained for a time at least by the joint influence of the Government and the intelligent and enterprising portion of the community' if they were to succeed. But the uncertain policy of the present ministry made this sustenance difficult. 'The views and intentions of the present Government respecting the School law having been a matter of doubt and various representation, the difficulty of administering it during the current year has been increased, and persons opposed to its operations have not been wanting in their efforts to paralyze its authority and impede its success.' Who were these opponents? According to Ryerson, they included 'four classes or coteries of persons': ignorant schoolmasters, incompetent trustees, religious opponents, and the rather amorphous category of those 'opposed to any State system of Common School education.'

In his proposed revisions to the acts, Ryerson had consulted 'three intelligent and practical Educationists.' Not, one suspects, by accident, all three had links to the moderate wing of the Reform party. Dexter D'Everardo, Niagara District superintendent of education and Niagara District councillor, and provincial surveyor A.K. Scholefield were connected with W.H. Merritt. William Hutton, Victoria District superintendent of education, was Francis Hincks's cousin. Ryerson stressed that all three had read his draft bill, 'and they fully concur.'

The 1848 bill responded to some criticism directed at the earlier acts while strengthening the central authority. Two clauses addressed school finance, one making it optional, rather than obligatory, for urban councils to support teachers entirely by property taxation, the other giving rural trustees the option to impose a property tax, rather than depending entirely on fees. Trustees were accorded powers to tax for school books and apparatus, powers necessary, Ryerson claimed, because, under the existing act, 'any parent ... [could] defeat the object contemplated by the selection of a uniform series of Text-books, and prevent the classification of pupils in the School.' Trustees were to read their annual reports at the January school meeting and were to be able to appoint auditors: Ryerson's response to complaints about irresponsibility and mismanagement on the part of trustees. Finally, district councils were to decide disputes over school sites, the school-age population was redefined to include those up to age twenty-one, the alien-teacher clauses were repealed, and provisions were made for the establishment of separate schools for 'coloured children,' for libraries, and for teachers' institutes.

Ryerson also included the key reform demanded by Bathurst Council: educational grants would be distributed according to school attendance, rather than population, with penalities for false reporting.

Two clauses affected the operation of educational inspection. Pointing out that, in large districts like the Home, visitation of the schools by the district superintendent was practically impossible, Ryerson proposed to allow district councils to appoint a second inspector whenever there were more than 150 common schools. Again, because some inspectors complained that conducting teachers' examinations prevented them from visiting the schools, Ryerson proposed to create boards of examiners for this purpose. The General Board of Education and the chief superintendent would devise the program of examination and would create three distinct and uniform classes of teachers.[2]

This draft bill never made it to the House.

The 1849 Revisions

Ryerson redrafted his bill in February 1849 in light of proposals for a new municipal act, making a few additions and discussing at length the relative merits of a district as opposed to a township educational superintendence. Additional clauses allowed the chief superintendent and the General Board to certify Normal School graduates as teachers, provided for a second Education Office clerk, limited the powers of trustees to levy a rate-bill to the year in which the teacher's salary was due, and made them personally liable if they did not pay and appropriated funds for the establishment of a school of art and design.[3]

The bulk of Ryerson's draft bill of 1849 concerned the proposed shift from district to county municipal organization, and once again he made the argument that the effective operation of the school system depended upon the inspectorate. The key to educational 'improvement' was seen as leadership exerted by men drawn from the 'respectable' classes.

Ryerson claimed there was 'a great difference in the comparative efficiency of the School System in different Districts.' According to him, it was 'chiefly owing to the character of the local Superintendents.'

Where the District Superintendent is an *intelligent, practical, active, industrious* man, and *heartily alive to the great interests of the work in which he is engaged*, there the progress of the System is obvious and most gratifying, and the Municipal Council is disposed to carry out the judicious and various practical recommendations of the District Superintendent. As examples, I may refer to the Brock, Talbot, Niagara and indeed more than half of the Districts in Upper Canada.[4] But in other Districts where the local Superintendents are far from being efficient either from want of practical talent or diligence, the state of the School System and the interest of the people in the Schools are very different.

Any change in the organization of inspection in these last districts, in Ryerson's opinion, would be an improvement, and despite the reservations about township superintendence held by the superintendent of schools in the state of New York, he was prepared to suggest such a system for Canada West under a new municipal act. But legislation would have to overcome the limitations experienced under the act of 1843 with respect to township superintendence. Ryerson proposed two relevant clauses, one specifying a minimum salary to be paid superintendents by municipal councils, the other requiring superintendents to deliver lectures on educational improvement.

In support of this position, Ryerson discussed the superiority of more or less professional bureaucratic cadres over unpaid, voluntary administrators. This point was, at least implicitly, an attack upon the appointment of members of local compacts as school superintendents, an attempt to sever the 'interests of education' from control by entrenched élites.

Under the act of 1843, many people offered to serve as township superintendents without pay, and Ryerson claimed these offers were invariably accepted. However, 'gratuitous zeal soon subsided and as gratuitous service is irresponsible service, those who performed it, considered themselves entitled to gratitude for the little that they did, rather than liable to blame for the much that they did not.' In other areas, the office went to the person prepared to accept the lowest salary. 'When once in office,' however, such a person 'would proportion his work to his compensation.' In other instances the same system worked to ensure the appointment of 'many incompetent persons.'

Ryerson's proposals for a renewed township inspectorate sought to remedy these defects. The specification of a minimum salary would ensure that township councils could not resort to gratuitous inspection. But Ryerson also proposed to demand that superintendents deliver annual lectures in each school section on school subjects. As he put it, his bill 'would prevent the Councils from appointing persons who are not competent to prepare and deliver public lectures; and persons who are competent to do that will be most likely to be qualified to inspect and superintend the Schools – their qualifications for which will be necessarily increased by their obligations to prepare public lectures on such subjects.' Township superintendents would be required to visit each school section quarterly and to lecture in it annually. In contrast to the 3,000 'School visits' made by superintendents under the act of 1846, this would produce 12,000, 'besides 3,000 *public School lectures*, – one in each School Section in Upper Canada. The vast amount of good which will result from such an arrangement can scarcely be estimated.'

The draft bill required inspectors to attend any annual meeting called by the chief superintendent 'to confer on matters relating to the interests of Common Schools and the diffusion of useful knowledge.'

As in his draft bill of 1848, Ryerson proposed to vest the power to examine and license teachers in boards of examiners appointed by county councils.

This plan still left a considerable degree of autonomy to inspectors. They were not trained by the central authority, nor were the lectures they were to deliver produced by that authority. Ryerson's plan relied heavily on the cooperation of the local intelligentsia and upon its commitment to the educational project. His plan embodied the liberal political proposition that participation in government itself would train people to responsibility: in this case, inspectors would be constrained by the exigencies of their office to become knowledgeable and (Ryerson seems to have assumed) committed state servants. Ruling would school those who ruled.

Ryerson's proposals aimed to move inspection out of the hands of local élites into those of bureaucratic cadres. With the power to assemble inspectors for information sessions and with the resources to furnish them with materials from which to draw their school lectures, inspection might operate more directly as an adjunct to the central authority.

Ryerson insisted this inspectoral system would not be overly expensive. Many district superintendents already had the minimum £1 a year per school proposed for the township superintendents, and those who didn't, he insisted, were grossly underpaid.[5]

The Cameron School Act of 1849

By his own account, Ryerson expected these amendments to pass the House without controversy. He claimed to be completely surprised to learn in passing from W.H. Merritt that Malcolm Cameron, the Reform minister, had introduced and secured approval for a school bill quite different from his draft, although in fact his parliamentary allies had been warning him of this possibility.[6]

Cameron's educational bill was drafted in part by Murdoch McDonnell, a merchant from Perth, chair of Bathurst Council's education committee and author of Council's memorial on the School Act.[7] McDonnell was particularly conversant with the school system of New York State, and Bathurst Council was particularly strong in its opposition to provincial educational centralization. Cameron's School Act of 1849 was a decentralizing initiative in several respects. Cameron himself was leaning to the resurgent radical agrarian wing of the Reform party, and his act of 1849 was passed in the midst of a deep economic crisis by a Parliament distracted by street riots over the Rebellion Losses Bill.

Debate over the act began before the burning of the parliament buildings in the last week of April. Cameron outlined the main clauses in the House as 'provisions to enable the Trustees to establish a fund for the support of the weaker School Districts; to do away with District Superintendents, and to establish Township ones [the members cried 'hear'] which he believed would do better, as it had been found impossible for the Superintendents, in large Districts, to visit all the Schools properly.' He was asked explicitly if his bill affected the position of the chief superintendent, and replied, 'No. It did not affect his office at all.'[8]

While this was Cameron's response to queries on 13 April, the School Act, which passed on 26 May, a month after the Rebellion Losses riots, was of a different order. Cameron's School Act embodied many of the clauses of Ryerson's draft, but its general tenor was quite different. It began by eliminating the peculiarly autonomous position occupied in the colonial state by the chief superintendent of schools for Canada West. This official was neither a member responsible to the electorate, nor a permanent deputy-minister responsible to a parliamentary minister of education. In fact, he exercised ministerial prerogatives without ministerial responsibility (in the Reform sense of that term).

The Cameron bill turned the chief superintendent into a person of deputy-ministerial status, a chief inspector in fact as well as in name. This official was now required to post a performance bond, as were other inspectors, to be subject to the instructions of Cabinet and to be supervised by a board of directors to be appointed to oversee the Normal School. His salary and that of his clerk were specified and were to be accounted for. Ryerson claimed these clauses were the result of Cameron's personal animosity, but they embodied demands made by several district councils.[9]

In its other clauses, Cameron's bill gave county councils and county boards of examiners extensive discretionary powers over school finance and curriculum. Councils could distribute up to a quarter of the school monies in ways they thought appropriate, a measure intended to create a 'poor schools' fund. The model-school system, largely abandoned by Ryerson, was strengthened financially and again connected to the Normal School. Where township residents could not support a common school on a full-time basis, they were allowed to engage teachers part-time, or several school sections could share the services of a teacher in rotation. Ryerson's draft separate-school clauses for Catholics and 'coloured' residents were omitted.

The circuits of educational intelligence were also multiplied in this bill, and administrative knowledge, which Ryerson's bill kept secret, was to be published. Trustees were required to post a copy of the annual report of their schools in a public place. School reports were to go to the county clerk, who would assemble them and compile local statistics for the use of the county council before transmitting them to the central authority.

Cameron's bill did not include a minimum salary for township superintendents. Rather, they were to be paid by township councils by taxation, except in poor townships where they might be paid a percentage of discretionary school monies. Several other important changes were introduced in the operations of the inspectorate. No provision was made for the appointment of a single superintendent for a whole county, as Ryerson's draft legislation would have allowed. The visitation duties were to involve one official public examination a year, with a public lecture, in each school district, although the municipal council could require more frequent visits. More important, a superintendent was required 'to give notice to the Teacher of the School which he shall intend to visit, of his intention to visit and examine the same, at least three days before that on which he shall visit and examine the same, and the duty of the Teacher shall be to give public intimation of the notice, so that all having an interest in the School may have an opportunity to be present.' Cameron raised the fines for superintendents who did not perform adequately, or who did not hand over school records to their successors. The clause requiring superintendents to meet with the chief superintendent to confer on school matters was omitted, and the special powers granted to the clergy and other members of local élites as school visitors were also dropped.[10]

Cameron's bill did not attempt to eliminate educational superintendence, the gathering of detailed information in a standard form about schools and the reporting of this information to a central authority, or the implementation by local schools of centrally devised plans for educational improvement. It extended the powers of the boards of examiners contained in Ryerson's draft act.

It did attempt to make the central authority responsible to Parliament, to give local government more autonomy in educational finance and curriculum, to allow school supporters and local governmental bodies access to educational intelligence, to remove the special powers granted to clergymen and magistrates, to limit doctrinal religious teaching, to prevent discriminatory treatment of black residents, and to allow teachers and trustees to protect themselves from surprise visits by agents of the central authority.[11]

Ryerson's Response

After Cameron's bill received second reading, Ryerson sent a lengthy attack of it to Provincial Secretary Leslie. He called for the appointment of a commission before the acceptance of Cameron's bill to study and compare the organization of educational systems elsewhere. Ryerson claimed the bill was the result of personal venom and drew upon the educational intelligence generated by the district superintendents and upon educational practice abroad to attack some of its provisions.

Ryerson protested that Cameron's bill excluded clergy, magistrates, and district councillors as school visitors. These people, he claimed, exerted a positive influence on the schools, and their visits were conducive to local harmony in educational matters. Between 1847 and 1848, visits to the schools by clergy had increased from 1,823 to 2,254; by district councillors, from 882 to 959; and by magistrates, from 1,203 to 1,459 – clear evidence of the growing influence of the respectable classes in the schools.

Ryerson opposed the duplication of circuits of educational intelligence as wasteful and expensive. Allowing county clerks to collect and compile school reports was likely to fail, given that these officers had no interest in education and the central authority had no control over them. Ryerson maintained that the expenses of administering Cameron's bill would fall upon the school fund itself, rather than upon the general funds of the county, thereby reducing the amount of money reaching schools.

The proposed changes in the organization of inspection attracted Ryerson's particular attention and he was extremely critical of Cameron's proposal for advance notice of school inspections. His remarks bear quoting at length. This section of the bill was, according to Ryerson,

still more at variance with the very object of inspecting Schools, as well as the reverse of all instructions to School Inspectors on that subject in England, Ireland, and every other country where a thorough system of School inspection exists. The primary object[s] of inspecting a School are to enable the Superintendent to acquaint himself with the real state and character of the School – the condition of the School house – the discipline of the School – the habits of the Teacher, his mode of teaching, the studies and attainments and progress of the pupils, and to point out to the Teacher what is defective, and suggest to him what is necessary for his greatest success and usefulness. In order to do this two things are necessary. There should not be previous notice of each visit, or special preparations may be made for it by inefficient Teachers in the appearance and order of the house, the attendance of pupils etc., and then the Super- intendent cannot form an idea of the ordinary state and character of the School.

Second, the inspection should not be public. There was an important difference between an inspection and a public examination: 'The latter is a Show day; the former is a day of rigid investigation, of reproof, of counsel and encouragement, as may seem expedient.' Giving advance notice of school visits would be technically difficult in many instances, and failure to give notice would produce conflict and controversy.[12] While it might be useful to have school supporters and trustees present for superintendents' visits on some occasions, the sound principle of educational administration was 'in all such matters of detail as to modes of proceeding and where variety is admissable in some cases, to leave them to individual discretion and general instructions. Legislation on every detail of modes of procedure swells the law to an undue length, embarrasses action and gives birth to endless disputes.' Ryerson concluded his attack on the bill with the claim that 'the greater part of the disputes which have been brought under my own notice for the last three years have arisen from the possession of too little (and not too much) power by Council and Trustee Corporations, and by their being hedged about with too many forms and restrictions.'[13]

Ryerson proclaimed his loyalty, in these last passages, to the Dutch model of educational administration, in which the central authority specified a few general regulations, thereby allowing administrative officers room to manoeuvre in response to particular circumstances. Ironically, he criticized *Cameron's* bill as a 'Prussian' enactment, which attempted to spell out in law the detailed operations of the system. The Dutch model made the relatively autonomous activities of the inspectors absolutely central to the progress of the educational project and assumed a broadly common understanding and interest on the part of inspectors and the central authority. In it, the 'friends of education' were empowered to pursue educational improvement free from popular or parliamentary interference.

True, from one perspective, Cameron's bill did attempt to specify legislative limitations to the modes of action of educational administrators. But from the radical, Reform point of view, such limitations were necessary protections to local educational autonomy against the central authority. Cameron did not assume, and councillors in the Bathurst District had good reason not to assume, that the interests of the inspectors would necessarily accord with local educational interests. Why should a surprise school inspection be more conducive to educational improvement than one announced in advance? Surely teachers who expected the inspector would work to improve their schools; Ryerson admitted as much. The issues of surprise and secrecy were issues of central-against-local control of schools.

While it is true Ryerson experienced the lack of power on the part of local authorities as an impediment, the lack he complained of consisted of the power to impose unlimited property taxation for free schools, to tax for schoolhouse construction and furnishing and for other expenditures in harmony with the interests of the central authority. He did not find at all problematic the lack of power accorded under the act of 1846 to district councils over the determination of curriculum and school rules, which the Cameron bill attempted to accord to county councils.

Towards the Compromise of 1850

At first Ryerson's objections to Cameron's bill fell on deaf ears. He was not permitted to amend it before final reading, and his initial objections were ignored, despite the fact that he met personally with Francis Hincks and Malcolm Cameron at the end of April, apparently receiving Hincks's support.[14] It had been intended by the ministry to lay the School Bill over until the following parliamentary session, but, as W.H. Merritt wrote Ryerson on 26 May 1849, 'it appears at a Meeting this morn'g. the Members appeared desirous to passit, consequently it was brought in and will become a Law apparently without any opposition.'[15]

But internal struggles in the Reform party, brought to a head by reactions to the Rebellion Losses Bill and the Annexation crisis, quickly earned Ryerson a more receptive hearing from the party's moderates. After he threatened to resign unless the Cameron bill was amended, Ryerson was invited to outline his criticisms again, which he did at length to Robert Baldwin in July.

To the religious Baldwin, Ryerson denounced the abolition of clergy as school visitors. 'Under the new Bill, the Ministers of religion cannot visit the Schools as a matter of right, or in their character as Ministers, but as private individuals, and by the permission of the Teacher at his pleasure' – this while, in Lower Canada, the Catholic clergy were encouraged to visit the schools and to select all books relating to 'religion and morals,' something equivalent 'to an endowment of the Roman Catholic Church for educational purposes'!

More important, the exclusion of visitors kept the respectable members of society out of the schools and Ryerson remarked,

to the School Visiting feature of the present system I attach much importance, as a means of ultimately concentrating in behalf of the Schools the influence and sympathies of all religious persuasions, and the leading men of the country. The success of it thus far has exceeded my most sanguine expectations – the visits of Clergy alone during the last year being an average of more than *five visits* for *each* Clergyman in Upper Canada ... And who can estimate the benefit, religiously, socially, educationally, and even politically, of Ministers of various religious persuasions meeting together at Quarterly School Examinations, and other occasions on common and patriotic grounds – as has been witnessed in very many instances during the last year ...?

This was a promise of political and social stability from clerical intervention in education to a prime minister recently rocked by violent street demonstrations, as well as a plea to powerful landholders and their allies against the democratic tendencies represented by resurgent agrarian radicalism.

Again Ryerson pointed to international examples. In Ireland, the clause allowing clerics to be school visitors originated; in the north-eastern United States, public education was supervised by ministers of religion. No one complained of the Upper Canadian grammar schools, whose boards were largely clerical, and 'in the *five* vacancies which have occurred in the office of District Superintendent since last January, *five Clergymen* have succeeded *five laymen*, by the spontaneous appointment of as many District Councils.'[16] Ryerson repeated the substance of his early objections to the bill.

Baldwin appears to have been largely sympathetic. After a lengthy meeting with him in August, and just before departing for an educational conference in Rochester, Ryerson wrote that he felt able to 'renew my labours with fresh

confidence and prosecute my work as if nothing had [occurred] & as if nothing
would be done to impede it. I leave things to be righted quietly in the manner that
you have suggested.' Ryerson proposed to draft a new bill upon his return,
embodying the principles of both the 1846 and 1849 acts, 'and such additional
provisions as I conceive will remedy existing defects.' He added, 'I will submit
it *to you individually*.' These revisions were probably delivered to Baldwin in
September, but he proposed to await Hincks's return to Canada before pushing
ahead with school matters.[17]

But Hincks was confronted with the recently published Annexation Manifesto
on his return to Montreal at the end of September, a document that threatened the
financial negotiations he had just completed in London with Baring Brothers. To
reassure the bankers, and with Governor Elgin's support, Hincks purged
appointed officialdom of all voluntary signatories to the manifesto.[18] These
activities and others directed by moderate Reformers against both annexationist
and radical agrarian agitations delayed reconsideration of educational matters.

The Hayter Case

Meanwhile, demands for increased local control over school matters were made
in the Newcastle District, where Council fired Benjamin Hayter, its Tory school
inspector, in a debate over school finance. Hayter accumulated large balances of
unpaid school monies (as much as £400 in 1849) and, on one occasion, in
contravention of the School Act, paid surplus monies to the district treasurer. The
surplus monies were used for general district purposes. When he was again
instructed by Council to pay surplus monies to the treasurer in February 1849, he
refused. Some claimed that attempts to dislodge him were led by his predecessor
in office, the Reformer John Steele. The warden petitioned the governor to allow
a special meeting of Newcastle Council and, on 26 June, Hayter was officially
dismissed. A lengthy and heated debate among Council, Hayter, and the chief
superintendent ensued, and dragged on into 1850. Ryerson wrote Hayter about
the illegality of any superintendent paying monies intended for schooling for
any other purpose and published his letter in the district press.

Newcastle Council was incensed about the entire affair. A special committee
on Ryerson's communication denounced Hayter's performance as superintendent and claimed his negligence and incompetence were responsible for the
dispute. The committee said Hayter had no idea of the state of his accounts and
had never visited a large portion of the schools in the district. The surplus monies
in his hands rightly belonged to the district treasurer because Hayter had never
informed Council of the government grant as required, so an unnecessarily high
school tax had been levied. As well, a set of 'blunders' by the clerk of the peace

had caused an even higher school tax, and this surplus money should belong to Council, not to the district or chief superintendent. No one in the district felt any dissatisfaction with the expenditure of surplus school monies on roads because 'none of the School Acts which have been in operation for some years past have given satisfaction in this part of the Province, and rather than see so large a portion of the public money expended on the payment of useless officers, and keeping up an expensive machinery for the purpose of carrying out the provisions of a law, which is generally disapproved of, they would willingly pay a much larger share for local improvements.'

Ryerson praised Hayter's work in a public communication, but urged him not to resist his dismissal. 'I am well known to be thoroughly British,' Hayter had earlier claimed, 'which is in all likelihood the only objection there is against me.'[19] The central issue in this dispute was local governmental autonomy over finance. Ryerson's position, legally correct, did not earn the support of district Reformers.

In the meantime, other people active in Upper Canadian politics were organizing on Ryerson's behalf. J.W. Gamble, an influential Tory lawyer and lumber manufacturer from Vaughan Township, wrote Ryerson for his opinions on Cameron's bill and promised to carry these to the British American League 'Convention at Kingston' in the summer of 1849.[20] Richard Graham, a member of Niagara District Council, claimed that Robert Baldwin had told him in Montreal in May 1849 that the School Act would be laid over until the next session. Graham was alarmed to hear that a· new act had been passed and expressed his support for the act of 1846 and his opposition to tinkering with it.[21] Ryerson himself marshalled his forces, writing to the deputy superintendent of common schools in New York for information about the elimination of the county superintendents of education in that state.[22] Finally, Ryerson was invited to visit Hincks to discuss school matters on 3 December 1849, after internal struggles had lessened Malcolm Cameron's standing in the Reform party. Four days later, he resubmitted his observations on the Cameron act and, on 15 December, the ministry moved to suspend it. Ryerson was instructed to do whatever necessary to keep the act of 1847 in force in towns and cities until a new bill could be drafted.[23] On 18 December, he distributed a circular to superintendents and school trustees containing suggestions as to how to proceed, and soliciting information. Trustees were invited to read their annual reports at the school meeting, a measure contained both in Ryerson's draft 1849 act and his School Act of 1850, and to report as soon as possible to district superintendents. The superintendents, in turn, were asked to report as early in February as possible, that Ryerson might lay his annual report before the House in the current session. Superintendents were particularly asked to 'accompany their Statistical Reports with such remarks on the progress, condition and prospects of the Schools under their charge, as their own information and experience will enable them to make.' Ryerson's correspondence with Leslie was reprinted. Several inspectors interpreted this as a call for assistance and responded accordingly.[24]

William Hutton of the Victoria District was moved to a quick expression of support. Cameron's act, he wrote Ryerson, 'will never work – It subverts the *uniformity* of system so desirable & so much desired by you – It takes away all chance of your being furnished with proper materials for the nice & delicate work you have to perform. – It annihilates all hope of having a good national system.' Hutton particularly objected to distributing school monies according to attendance and assumed that the act would be changed.[25]

A vociferous campaign against Ryerson and his policies continued in the Reform press. The Toronto correspondent of the *Bathurst Courier* wrote of the 'benching' of the School Act by 'the Rev. traitor ... with his Prussian spectacles on.' Murdoch McDonnell, writing as 'Sandie Donaldson,' pilloried the revisions to the Cameron act throughout March and into April 1850.[26] Ryerson defended himself in print, at times with the assistance of active and former school inspectors. Samuel Ardagh, the rector of Barrie and a former superintendent of education, expressed his alarm at the exclusion both of the clergy and 'controverted theological dogmas or doctrines' from the schools by Cameron. Ryerson agreed with him that Cameron intended to ban the Bible from the schools and added that this was 'one reason why I expressed my preference to relinquish office rather then [*sic*] administer the new law.' Ardagh likely sent this correspondence to the Barrie *Magnet*.[27]

When Ryerson read in the Reform Toronto *Examiner* that the act of 1849 was 'a drop from which to close the career of this executive's political malefactor,' he wrote that he was pleased finally to see the purely political motives of the act announced. Ryerson denied that he had ever offered to resign over Cameron's bill, which had been promulgated without the party's knowledge by Cameron alone. Ryerson heatedly denounced the suggestion that he had ever attempted to promote 'arbitrary centralization' in education, having acted consistently, instead, to empower local government in school matters.[28]

Building 'Consensus'

While the debate raged, Francis Hincks organized the drafting and parliamentary defence of a replacement school bill and sustained Ryerson against attacks. As a preliminary step, his inspector general's office distributed a circular on official letterhead to district superintendents of education and a few others, soliciting views on the School Act of 1849. The replies were delivered to Ryerson. This 'testing' of public opinion produced a considerable diversity of views on educational organization, but at least revealed neither unambiguous support for the act of 1849, nor uniform opposition to the centralized principles of the act of 1846.

Hincks's enquiry was a propaganda campaign that he denied undertaking officially. District superintendents were invited to seek 'the views of the most intelligent Common School Teachers and Trustees regarding the Act of 1849.' Correspondents were invited to focus upon a few limited questions, rather than upon broad issues of educational politics and principles, and arguments in favour of Ryerson's positions were suggested. Correspondents were asked especially 'whether the control over school books &c should be vested in County Boards of Education or in the Central Board at Toronto. A strong argument in favour of the latter system is that it is calculated to produce that uniformity in the system which is so very desirable & without which it is urged that the Normal School system cannot be efficiently carried out.'[29] Hincks was clearly gathering political ammunition and the knowledge generated by inspectors was a political resource.

Inspectors' views were influenced by their own awareness of the political situation. Despite the publication of Ryerson's correspondence with Hincks about the act of 1849, several superintendents continued to suppose that plans for the repeal and redrafting of it were unknown to Ryerson.

William Fraser of the Eastern District wrote naïvely in early February 1850 that Ryerson would 'be happy to hear that the Government are going to reconsider the School Bill & have issued a printed circular for suggestion. I have answered strongly in favour of your objections & particularly Free Schools. In the Council & out of it over all the District I have pleaded for Free Schools & not one single man have [sic] opposed me yet in the main question.' Fraser concluded, 'this is the moment for action let all do what they can & we shall have it.'[30] Similarly, Benjamin Hayter, former Newcastle District superintendent, believed that Hincks's circular had been sent without Ryerson's knowledge and took the opportunity both to inform Ryerson directly and to defend Ryerson's position to Hincks.[31] Some superintendents pronounced on the act, but, after 'more mature reflection,' brought their views into line with Ryerson's proposed 1850 legislation.

Responses to Hincks's circular were simply sent to Ryerson for his information, and Hincks refused attempts by the opposition to have them published. Despite the fact that the circular was printed on letterhead of the inspector general's office, Hincks insisted that he 'did not send any official circulars to any one. He had certainly written to some of the District Superintendents, as he had done to other parties, but it was not officially, it was for his own information in drawing up the bill he intended to submit to the House' – this although it is also clear the bill was drafted by Ryerson and Hodgins. The ministry accepted Ryerson's proposed School Act of 1850 and, after some considerable debate in the House, the bill was passed and received royal assent on 24 July. Murdoch McDonnell was left to write bitterly and in private to Hincks,

I cannot help fearing, that you and your colleagues have been made, in some degree, the dupes of a '*party*' viz. of Dr. Ryerson; for whatever you or your colleagues may have been induced to believe, or whatever may have occurred between you and Mr. Cameron, the parties who drew up Mr. Cameron's Act had in view the public good only and no party purpose. Moreover, as one of the parties, I am prepared, in defence of that Act, to prove that Dr. Ryerson has, by *the most barefaced lying*, imposed upon the Ministry in regard to that Act.[32]

This letter was also sent to Ryerson.

District Superintendents on the Act of 1849

While disagreeing on many dimensions of the Cameron act, the school inspectors were clear that uncertainty surrounding educational policy made their own activities difficult. Trustees were described as confused and careless in their reporting practices because of the turmoil around the school law. The superintendents opposed repeated and major alterations in educational legislation: the interests of education should be protected from parliamentary interference and left to administrative regulation.

Central Control of School Books

With three exceptions, the superintendents supported central control over school books, some of them emphatically. Benjamin Hayter regarded posing the question as peculiar, since 'ninety-nine out of every hundred persons would decide for a uniformity of School Books selected by a Central Board.' 'All the intelligent Teachers and Trustees' with whom William Hutton had conversed supported central control over school books in the interests of economy and efficiency. 'The very excellence of the Irish National School Books,' Hutton wrote, 'shows the value of concentrating the knowledge of a few choice men for their compilation; and why not carry the principal [*sic*] out for their diffusion?' If this power were left to county boards, Chambers's books would be selected by Scots; Cobb's, Morse's, and Olney's books by Canadians and Americans; and so on. But, Hutton continued, 'the value of uniformity is too great to risque the choice to any but to competent chosen men who can judge without national, or early educational, prejudices.' This the central board of education could do.[33] Dexter D'Everardo of the Niagara District claimed that the vast majority of those 'competent to judge' in his district sought a return to the act of 1846, modified to suit new municipal institutions. D'Everardo was '*decidedly* in favour' of central control over books.[34] Most of the other superintendents took a similar position, reading this as a question of class and national dominance.

But there were opponents of central control. Charles Fletcher, Huron District superintendent, claimed central control over textbooks would be inefficient. The central board would have to produce an enormously long list of books to meet the needs of all districts in the province. No book dealer would be prepared to order all the list, and local school officials would have no reliable index as to which books would meet their particular needs. Fletcher had 'no sympathy with the fear, that the action of County Boards would, in any degree, disturb the uniformity necessary to the efficient carrying out of the Normal School System.' Teachers trained at that institution would themselves create a demand for one sort of books.[35] Fletcher clearly did not envision a single curriculum for the entire province.

In the Colborne District, Elias Burnham claimed 'the prevailing force of feeling, is in favour of a distribution of the power over School Books.'[36] In the Prince Edward District, Thomas Donnelly claimed most people supported central control over books, but he himself opposed it, feeling that really good school books would acquire a general circulation in any case.[37]

Three other questions are of particular interest with respect to inspectoral organization: the creation of a poor-schools fund, the existence of a school-visitors clause, and the proposals for a township superintendency in conjunction with the licensing of teachers by county boards of examiners.

Poor Schools

In the Cameron act, the poor-schools fund amounted to a quarter of local school monies and was intended to allow district or county councils to sustain schools in areas of low population or economic underdevelopment. At the same time, control over this fund might allow for a more forceful local regulation of educational practice. Several of the superintendents wrote in favour of the creation of such a fund, and none opposed it, although there were differences with respect to its organization. William Clarke of the Talbot District supported a poor-schools fund under the control of the county council. George Duck of the Western District argued that township councils would be best able to judge as to the distribution of these funds.[38] James Baird also supported some sort of poor-schools fund, claiming that, under the act of 1846, Newcastle Council had allowed him to make such grants in the amount of £5 out of surplus school monies.[39]

The payment of the school grant on the basis of average school attendance had long been a demand of critics of the School Act and Ryerson had already included such a mode of payment in his draft bills of 1848 and 1849. This principle, intended to encourage elementary schooling in poor townships, was continued by the Cameron act. But William Hutton objected. In poor townships, Hutton argued, many families did not have enough clothing to dress all their children for school, and hence the children attended in rotation. Funding schools according to attendance would work to the detriment of poor townships.[40]

School Visitors

Only William Clarke offered unqualified support of the school-visitors clauses in the School Act of 1846, clauses eliminated in Cameron's bill. Clarke wrote that the people he had consulted in his district 'especially desire[d] the continuance of school visitors.' The visitors had been 'productive of good' in the three years they had existed, and the clauses in the act placed respectable people 'under some obligation, to give their countenance and counsels to the Schools in their immediate vicinity.'[41]

James Padfield of Bathurst was rather more cautious. Padfield provided the views of 'persons deeply interested in Common School Education, and of considerable experience in the practical working of the Common School System' (Murdoch McDonnell apparently not among them). Padfield criticized the Cameron act for failing to provide an adequate mechanism for the settlement of disputes and supported the school visitors clauses in the 1846 act, with the exception of those parts 'authorizing any two School Visitors to give Certificates of Qualification to Teachers.'[42]

The proposal for county boards to license teachers was generally supported in the Newcastle District, according to James Baird who pointed out that under the act of 1846 'some persons disqualified, and many very poorly qualified, obtained Certificates from School Visitors and even from Superintendents.' It would be easier for a board to refuse such candidates.[43]

Patrick Thornton of the Gore District, the most systematic critic of existing and proposed educational organization, was particularly opposed to the school-visitors clause in the act of 1846, complaining that visitors had granted certificates to 'some of the most ignorant men, and some of the greatest drunkards' he had ever met.[44] Thornton himself had recently been embroiled with Ryerson in a bitter and protracted dispute over a certificate granted by a school visitor, and the Dumfries Teachers' Association, of which Thornton was first president, had agreed that only the district superintendent should certify teachers. Other inspectors had induced district councils to forbid school visitors to certify teachers.[45]

Township Superintendents

The discussion of the township superintendency allowed district superintendents to reflect upon the value and effectiveness of their own office. These were obviously not disinterested observations, given that both Cameron's bill and Ryerson's early draft amendments had proposed the elimination of what, for several superintendents, was a lucrative office. Many of the inspectors understood the organization of inspection to be a question of class privilege, with class frequently coded in terms of 'kind of person.' Henry Clifford's reaction to the Cameron act was shared by several others. 'Every day furnishes proof of the wish of the party in power,' he wrote, 'to sacrifice the best and most important interests of society for the sake of infusing as much democracy as possible into all our Institutions and adding to the influence of an uneducated mob.'[46]

Alexander Allan, the Wellington District superintendent, initially responded to Hincks's circular with a statement supporting the township superintendency but questioning the need for county boards of examiners. A month later, however, his opinion had changed. Now he argued that county superintendents should be retained, or, if there were to be township superintendents, it would be absolutely necessary to oversee their activities by a county board. This view was a product of his more mature consideration of the proposed act and of his 'seeing the class of persons likely to be appointed to the office of Township Superintendent.' It would be wise, Allan argued, 'to do away with Township Superintendents' because, in his earlier experience 'of that system, few of them were of much use unless in paying the Teachers salaries and making out the annual Township Report.'[47]

William Clarke, Talbot District superintendent, opposed the creation of a township superintendency, claiming 'the people generally' were 'well satisfied with the present arrangement for the supervision of their Schools.' If township councils appointed superintendents, they would look to their own constituents, and Clarke claimed there were many townships 'where a really competent person' could not be found. If the government did move to a township superintendency, the appointment should remain with the county councils.[48]

William Hutton opposed a township superintendency on the grounds that 'the materials for good Superintendents of Townships are not yet in the Country.' Most common-school students were more educated than potential township superintendents, and a delay of ten years was necessary before this defect would be remedied. Hutton supported a county superintendency, with inspectors visiting the schools twice yearly and lecturing in each for a salary of £1 per school per year.[49] Hutton, Allan, and Clarke were among those superintendents Ryerson described as particularly 'efficient.'

Both James Padfield and William Elliott also opposed a township superintendency, the former on the grounds that the act of 1846 generally worked well. Padfield held county boards of examiners to be unnecessary and supported a county superintendency.[50] Elliott suggested that money matters be taken out of the hands of the present district superintendents and that these men continue in office as county superintendents. 'It is easy to suppose,' he remarked, 'that one active intelligent person responsible for the educational interests of his County & co-operating with the Provincial Supt wd: be likely to prove of far more service than so many Township Supts having isolated powers.'[51]

In the Prince Edward District, Thomas Donnelly reported that a township superintendent was considered unnecessary. Since this officer would no longer examine and license teachers, 'little, therefore, [would] remain for him to do but to examine Schools and deliver his Lectures.' Without the power to license teachers, the superintendent would be unable to enforce any of his suggestions. In consequence, the office should be eliminated 'as there are comparatively few Townships in which are to be found men capable of delivering Lectures, which might be likely to be productive of much good, and, at the same time, who might be able and willing to do it.' Finally, Donnelly himself thought that county boards of education should be centrally appointed.[52]

Only James Baird of Newcastle, appointed after Reform councillors had fired his Tory predecessor, was unambiguous in his support for a township superintendency. Baird and those he consulted in this district, where opposition to central control was strong, favoured township superintendents because 'it was impossible that one person could examine One Hundred and Eighty Schools, dotted over a surface of Eighteen Hundred square miles, make himself familiar with the state and circumstances of the Schools, settle disputes, pay out the money, and answer the communications as he ought.' Some of those he consulted, however, thought that, like teachers, township superintendents should be required to be both morally and educationally qualified for the position.[53]

The only inspector to propose a markedly different approach to educational administration was Patrick Thornton of the Gore District. In his response to Hincks, Thornton supported the extension of the model-school system, which he claimed far superior to that of the normal school. He opposed a township superintendency, arguing that there should be county inspectors, and that these would be ineffective unless they had the power to certify teachers. If county boards were to examine teachers, the county superintendent should be a board member. Without the power of granting and annulling licences to teach, 'no Superintendent can be fully efficient. He has no power over the Teachers, – is reduced to the character of a spy, merely to report what he sees and hears.' Thornton also criticized the Normal School course.[54]

In his 1849 report to Gore District Council, Thornton again strenuously opposed the Cameron act, claiming it had disrupted educational organization. However, he was equally critical of the act of 1846. Thornton urged that all money matters be placed in the hands of district treasurers, that teachers be assured of their pay and trustees be secured from suits. As he put it, 'It is very seldom found, that the men best adapted for Superintending Education, are equally well qualified to manage the fiscal matters connected with it. Superintendents should have their whole care directed to the advancement of Education, and their business should be so regulated that the Schools may be visited, at least twice a year, as we have quite a different School population in Summer and Winter.'[55] Thornton also transmitted 'the ideas of two or three of our most intelligent Teachers' to Hincks. These teachers suggested the creation of several inspectoral circuits in each county, each supervised by a superintendent who would be a common school teacher and whose common-school would also serve as a model school. Thornton took this occasion again to remark that 'a Superintendent, to be efficient, should have his whole energies devoted to the improvement of the Schools. He should have no pecuniary business of any consequence to manage.'

The Gore District teachers proposed that councils be able to raise funds for teachers' salaries either by taxation or by rate-bill; that superintendents be appointed by township councils, but that only practical teachers be superintendents; that negligent trustees be personally liable; that a general board control books, but that practical teachers should sit on this board, which would have no power to interfere in the internal government of schools; that only superintendents be able to certify teachers; and finally, that, while a normal school was a laudable institution, detailed statistical information about the clientele, expenses of management, and destination of graduates should be collected and disseminated concerning this institution.[56] A similar communication from the Dumfries Teachers' Association was received by Hincks's office, and teachers in Middlesex County demanded that superintendents be practical teachers.[57] Little attention was paid to teachers' suggestions.

Other Reactions to Hincks's Circular

A considerable number of other people responded to Hincks's circular in anticipation of proposed changes in the school law. Gordon Buchannan of Colchester Township claimed that 'the most intelligent persons' in his township opposed central control over books; supported county boards in place of a central board of education; and proposed that township superintendents certify teachers, subject to the approval of county boards. Buchannan generally supported the act of 1849 and urged the abolition of the office of chief superintendent, or strict economy in its financial support.[58] But other correspondents took diametrically opposed positions. With respect to the inspectoral clauses, some correspondents favoured a county superintendency on the grounds of economy, others a township superintendency on the grounds of thoroughness. Some residents in Alexander Allan's inspectoral district supported the latter position, arguing that with township superintendents 'a greater supervision will be exercised over them now we have the benefit of a local Superintendent than formerly, when he did not visit us but once in the year and that only for a very short period.'[59] Hincks himself, in Parliament, claimed that the superintendents clause was the most contentious in the act of 1846 and proposed that to allow county councils to decide to appoint either township or county superintendents was 'the most certain way of giving general satisfaction.'[60]

At least two county councils opposed the power retained in the hands of the chief superintendent under the replacement act of 1850.[61]

The End of the District Superintendency

The School Act of 1850 was a compromise measure, but one that protected most aspects of the interests of education from parliamentary interference and laid the basis for a series of incursions by the central authority in the following decades. It owed its main propositions to Ryerson's draft bills of 1848 and 1849, but the climate of agrarian radicalism led to the inclusion of a number of significant concessions to popular pressure. The left wing of the Reform party had broken away to form the Clear Grit party, whose platform was a close copy of the demands of the English Chartists. Peter Perry, the radical democrat of the 1830s, re-entered Parliament, and the Canadas were still rocked by Annexationist agitation and by after shocks from the street riots of the preceding spring and summer. Men of small property were loudly demanding a larger share in government.

The powers accorded local élites under the School Act of 1846 were somewhat limited under the act of 1850. Local school meetings were no longer to be presided over by the senior magistrate, but by an elected chairman. School visitors were re-created and were given extensive powers to meet at will to consider educational improvement and to examine schools during the quarterly public examinations, giving advice and criticism to teachers if they saw fit. They were no longer allowed to license teachers.

Urban school trustees were once again to be elected and, in both urban and rural school finance, rate-bills and property taxation were made optional for the payment of teachers' salaries.

Rural municipalities could raise a poor-schools fund by property taxation, but this was to be above and beyond matching funds for the school grant.

Both school finance and the direct certification of teachers were removed from the revamped inspectorate. County and urban treasurers were now to hold all school monies, and superintendents were to issue cheques to teachers upon the treasurers. This move was conceived quite explicitly as a means of overcoming delays in the payment of teachers and the misuse of school funds by superintendents. Teachers were to be certified by county boards of public instruction, composed of local superintendents of schools and the trustees of the county grammar school. In the course of the following decade, the central authority specified the conditions for the certification of teachers.

County councils could appoint a county superintendent or one or more township superintendents under the act of 1850. For a minimum annual salary of £1 per school per year (to a maximum of 100 schools) to be paid out of general county funds, local superintendents were to visit each school within their jurisdiction at least four times a year and were to deliver an annual lecture on educational matters.[62] The kind of information to be collected by superintendents and transmitted to the central authority was specified in great detail, both in the act directly and in later administrative regulations.

The model-school system was largely abandoned. The act did allow townships to establish township model schools, subject to the publication of regulations by the Council of Public Instruction, but these institutions were not important until the 1870s.[63]

While at least one district superintendent continued to function as a county superintendent (William Fraser, for Bruce), the act of 1850 marked a shift to a decentralized inspectoral system. The clergy was particularly active in educational superintendence until the imposition of professional qualifications upon school inspectors under the School Act of 1871.[64] But the act of 1850 achieved considerably less than the Education Office sought in the domain of inspection. Conflicts between central and local state agencies prevented effective control over the appointment and training of inspectors by what became the Ministry of Education until the 1920s.

Still, the township school inspectors enjoyed far fewer discretionary powers than had their district predecessors. Their field of operation was quite circumscribed, and the central authority was increasingly well equipped to instruct them, to intervene to override their decisions, and to direct their efforts towards its own version of 'the interests of education.' Superintendents' ceasing to be leading regional figures represented a displacement of educational authority towards a central state bureaucracy.

While separate schooling continued to be a heated matter of parliamentary debate, the settlement reached under the School Act of 1850 largely freed the Education Office from parliamentary 'interference.' There was no parliamentary ministry of education in the province until 1876. The Education Office was able to make a number of bureaucratic incursions into schooling practices in the following decades, confronting persistent but localized resistance. Administrative practice came to substitute for statute law.

Through the experiments of the 1840s, male activists from the rising middle classes took charge of the domain of popular education, defined what 'needed to be done' to 'improve the people,' agitated for the entrenchment of this view of affairs, and, under the compromise of 1850, left the prosecution of educational 'improvement' to men of lesser social standing. The first group of men were implicated in an administrative dynamic in which their pioneering efforts, overseen and coordinated by a developing central authority, gave birth to ways of doing things that contributed to the institutionalization of bureaucratic routine. Their successful appropriation of educational governance was refined and enshrined as 'expertise.'

The tenure of office of district superintendents lasted six years at most, but this was a turning-point in the formation of the Canadian state, a period in which the groundwork for durable administrative structures was laid. Initially, the district superintendents were placed to make extensive determinations about educational matters, to put forward their own particular views of 'what needed to be done' as the truth about popular education. This truth was constituted by their own class positions, biographies, and cultural understandings. Who were these men? Elements of an answer to this question are presented in chapter 5.

5   The District Inspectoral Corps

Who were the district superintendents of education in Canada West between 1844 and 1850? Modern social categories are of little help in identifying these thirty-seven men, for, in the Canada West of the 1840s, few single occupations offered a sufficient livelihood. The means of commodity production and exchange were relatively little developed, and specialization in the social division of labour was very incomplete. At least a third of the colonial population depended primarily upon wage labour, but many wage workers had access to other marginal forms of subsistence. Conversely, many small landholders engaged in seasonal wage labour and were notorious for 'keeping one table,' that is, for eating with the hired help. Merchant capitalists, small masters, and artisans commonly accepted payment in kind. Large capitalist farmers often performed agricultural labour. Public officials and members of the clergy commonly owned land. Clerical salaries, especially in the sects not subsidized from the Clergy Reserves fund, were paid partly in kind. For some sects, clerical functions were entirely unpaid. For those who lived from wages, fees, and salaries, payment was irregular and often uncertain. Even relatively highly paid officials lived most of the time on credit.

The political economic reforms of the 1840s opened governmental structures to men on the rise and to the colonial intelligentsia, while creating new spheres of investment and encouraging capital accumulation. With stable wage rates in a period of rising land prices, these developments laid the foundation for an increasing differentiation of class relations in the 1850s and 1860s. But in the 1840s, the colonial class structure was still characterized by the existence of broadly overlapping class categories and by opportunities for social mobility. I am not saying everyone was 'middle class.' There were canal workers and chief justices, day labourers and lumber-mill owners, seamstresses and gentlewomen. But the stratum in the middle was large, if unstable.

While this reality makes the analysis of class relations at a high level of abstraction relatively useless, it points to the terrain on which educational superintendence operated. Inspection and its surrounding project of 'improvement' could draw together men of somewhat different means and social standing because of the fluidity of class relations. This fluidity provided the basis for the formation of an 'ideological-moral bloc': a dominant set of justifications for existing political economic relationships, in combination with conceptions of and standards for legitimate social criticism and change.[1] Educational inspectors participated in a political, moral, and religious culture that sought to repress perceived threats to the developing bourgeois political economy, while it 'pointed the way forward.' Educational inspectors, on the whole, worked to reform Canadian society in keeping with conceptions of representative government, security of property, and religious probity.

Expressed class interest does not correspond neatly to distinct class positions. Social class must be understood in both its objective and its subjective dimensions, as position and understanding. One may neither assume that class position will automatically determine cultural and political interests, nor that cultural understanding will make the constraints offered by class position unimportant. Class positions may limit cultural understandings and interests, but cultural understandings may transcend class barriers.

Class dominance depends upon both legitimation and leadership. Dominance contains an element of moral obligation between rulers and ruled, through which both make sense of and come to terms with relations of domination. This obligation does not imply simple acceptance, but rather offers a set of justifications for political relations and defines the limits to legitimate dominance. Successful political domination involves intellectual work by those who speak for the dominant class. This intellectual work typically involves attempts to anchor political relations in history and also to point the way forward under particular conditions of domination.

Those whom Gramsci calls 'organic' intellectuals may seem to be oriented to intellectual traditions (the love of learning, for instance) that transcend class interests and to be rendered independent by their material circumstances from identification with the dominant class. Yet intellectual culture is always grounded in political economic relations, and the success of an ideology of dominance is, in part, its ability to incorporate subordinate interests: to present the interests of the dominant class as the interests of society. The culture of 'improvement' and the 'interests of education' that inspectors formulated, defended, and sought to advance are to be understood in this light.

Inextricably bound up with the generalization of capitalist relations of production and exchange, with rational religion and bureaucratic administration, the culture of improvement and the interests of education offered an image of a natural and social world subordinate to human will. Material progress and cultural advance were tied to the internalization of a set of values and orientations by members of the body politic and to the creation of a new set of social and political institutions for their promulgation. Successful social governance in the largest sense was government of the self: moral regulation.[2]

Within the broadly common social-class position occupied by school inspectors, a range of cultural and political understandings was possible. To understand the operation of educational inspection as a real political force, one must combine an awareness of class position with a knowledge of the sense superintendents made of that position.[3]

Class Locations

One of the colony's leading industrial capitalists, Jacob Keefer of the Niagara District, served as a school inspector. Keefer's father, George, was president of the Welland Canal Company and a close associate of the ruling clique in the 1820s and 1830s. Jacob Keefer was granted water rights on the canal and constructed a complex of flour mills and grain elevators, which, by 1847, was the largest in the colony. In the early 1840s, the milling business alone yielded Keefer an annual profit in excess of £200. This enterprise was ruined almost at once by the repeal of the Corn Laws, and Keefer lost control of it. Still, in this decade, he was president of the Thorold Cotton Company, of the Erie and Ontario Railroad, and was a director of the Niagara District Mutual Fire Insurance Company. He chaired the grand jury, acted as a boundary commissioner, and was Thorold postmaster.[4]

Several other superintendents were capitalists. Richey Waugh of the Johnstown District owned flour and shingle mills on the south branch of the Rideau River and was a substantial storekeeper and informal banker.[5] Waugh's mills were valued at about £1,700 in the 1852 census, and produced a product valued at £300 annually. He employed fourteen men, a large number in this period of small local industry. Samuel Hart of Cornwall owned and operated a tannery and, by the middle 1850s, if not before, was a very wealthy man. He was closely associated with the wealthiest citizens of the town and district in the promotion of a mutual insurance company, was Crown Lands agent for the Eastern District and a contributor to local charities, as well as a town councillor and church warden (with S.Y. Chesley, of Trinity Anglican). In the 1850s, Hart donated 200 acres to the maintenance fund of the Anglican church and held £2,800 worth of stock in the Bank of Montreal.[6] In the 1860s, he was one of the guarantors of the debentures for the new Strachan Memorial Church.

John Steele of the Newcastle District chaired the Quarter Sessions and held considerable investments in the lumber trade and in brewing in the 1830s, but, by the mid-1840s, was bankrupt. He engaged in a number of speculative mercantile and other ventures.[7] Dexter D'Everardo, who succeeded Keefer in Niagara, was also a wealthy man. D'Everardo's fortune stemmed mainly from finance, and he was reported to have had large sums out 'at interest' in the neighbourhood of his home in Fonthill. In the early 1860s, the £3,000 he had at loan and his other activities were earning D'Everardo about £1,250 a year.

In addition to these merchant/industrial capitalists, several members of the inspectoral corps owned large amounts of capital in land. The most visible of these were Hamnett Pinhey, William Hutton, William Elliott, and Thomas Higginson. Pinhey, from the Dalhousie District, owned 2,000 acres and had milling interests, in addition to serving as an informal banker. Pinhey brought property valued at £1,100, much of it in gold, when he immigrated in 1820. His mills were on a small scale, employing three men full-time and two part-time in the 1820s, and an unknown number of wage labourers were employed on his land. Pinhey was a very wealthy man. He was able to afford the £55 tuition fee for his son to attend Upper Canada College in the 1830s and held at least £1,500 in bank stock in the early 1850s. He was one of the promoters of the Montreal-Bytown railway company.[8]

William Hutton, the Victoria District superintendent, was an improving gentleman farmer who distinguished himself sharply from the mere 'farmers' around him. Hutton employed wage labour on his land, although he, and more especially his wife and children, were actively engaged in farm labour. Hutton's farm never paid off the debts he incurred in the 1830s in acquiring it, and, until he gained access to lucrative public offices in the 1840s, his circumstances were somewhat straitened. Still, in colonial terms, he was extremely prosperous, land-rich if cash-poor.

The father of William Elliott of the London District bought a substantial farm in London Township in the late 1830s. After his father's death about 1841, Elliott left the farm in the hands of a manager. It was valued at about £1,000 in the mid-1840s and supported Elliott and his mother.[9]

Thomas Higginson of the Ottawa District also owned property in land on a more modest scale and loaned money at interest. He was one of the promoters of the Ottawa-Bytown railway in the early 1850s.[10] Henry Clifford of the Simcoe District speculated in land. A shrewd man (and somewhat of a jack of all trades), Clifford ran a store and extended credit to local farmers, which enabled him to accumulate a number of farms.[11]

This group of substantial landholders, merchants, and small financiers also included John Bignall of the Huron District. By virtue of his close connections to the directors of the Canada Company and his Tory party loyalties, Bignall held a substantial land grant in addition to highly paid public office. George Duck's father was a substantial capitalist farmer.

Several inspectors occupied key positions in the judicial branches of the state system. John Wilson of the London District and Charles Eliot of the Western District were both district-court judges, a position of wealth and high prestige in the colony. Both of these men had other economic interests and sources of income. In the 1850s, Wilson held £1,800 in shares of the Bank of Upper Canada, was a shareholder in the British American Fire and Life Assurance Company, and sat on the Board of Directors of the London and Lake Huron Railway Company.[12] As we have seen, Eliot was earning about £400 a year from his public offices and pension and may also have owned a substantial farm.[13] Elias Burnham of Peterborough was the senior practising lawyer in the Colborne District. He was also a railway-company director in the early 1850s.[14] Alexander Allan of the Wellington District, the son of a brick and tile manufacturer and son-in-law to a thread manufacturer, held a degree from Aberdeen University and was a retired senior member of the Society of Advocates and burgess from that city.[15] He was probably connected by blood or marriage to the directors of the Canada Company. George Duck, Jr, attended law school in Toronto during the latter part of his inspectorate, and William Elliott served a legal apprenticeship, finishing his career as a senior judge (from the 1860s).

The Clergy

Of the thirty-seven superintendents active in the 1840s, eleven held clerical occupations: S.B. Ardagh (Episcopalian); James Baird (Church of Ireland); Newton Bosworth (Baptist); William Clarke Sr (Congregationalist); Charles Fletcher (Church of Scotland); John Flood (Episcopalian); William Fraser (Baptist); Colin Gregor (Church of Scotland); William Landon (Baptist); Alexander Mann (Church of Scotland); and James Padfield (Episcopalian). However, the clerical contingent was stratified. Some of the men described as clerics subsidized their religious vocations by farming, schoolteaching, or some other activity, while others were men of means. The mere fact of a clerical occupation tells one a limited amount about its incumbent.[16]

For the clerics, a key distinction was between those subsidized from the Clergy Reserves fund and those not. Samuel Ardagh, John Flood, Alexander Mann, and James Padfield were supported out of the Reserves fund. But Presbyterians like Mann were subject to deductions from their shares of the fund of an amount equal to their non-clerical income after 1847, while Episcopalians were not.

It is challenging to reconstruct salaries even for these 'established' clerics, given fluctuating sources of church revenues. John Flood, who was supported entirely out of the Reserves fund, with no contributions from his congregation, earned £100 a year in the 1840s. He complained repeatedly of his inability to survive on this amount, although it was about twice the annual wage for an artisan.

Parliamentary reports reveal that Alexander Mann earned £153.13.4 from the Reserves fund in 1846, and about £175 in 1847. Both these amounts were likely in addition to donations from his congregation.[17]

James Padfield would have earned £175 from the Society for the Propagation of the Gospel as a missionary in the 1830s, less than the £191 he had earned at Upper Canada College before 1833. Parliamentary returns suggest he was paid £100 annually from the Reserves fund in the 1840s, but he likely had other sources of income. His parish was endowed with two Rideau River–front lots, and he owned a town lot on Richmond Street in Toronto. Padfield also earned £100 a year as district superintendent, all of which made him a prosperous man.[18]

Samuel Ardagh's Barrie rectory paid only £70 per annum, in addition to contributions from parishioners, but Ardagh came from a very wealthy family. At his departure from Ireland, his parishioners presented him with a purse containing £130 in gold. Ardagh's entire household immigrated in 1842, including a number of domestic servants.

Colin Gregor had no clerical charge while he served as district superintendent, but may have earned as much as £200 as master of the Ottawa District Grammar School.[19] No information has survived about income for Charles Fletcher or James Baird.

In terms of the population they supervised, these representatives of what Westfall has called the 'religion of order' were men of economic substance. The economic condition of the members of other sects, representatives of the 'religion of experience,' was rather less comfortable. At one extreme was William Fraser, an evangelical Baptist preacher who survived by small-scale agriculture and schoolteaching and who complained bitterly of the £7 of his own money he was required to spend as superintendent. Still, after he moved from the eastern to the western part of the province, Fraser had sufficient wealth and leisure to travel to Scotland and to write a travel book.[20]

Far better off were William Clarke and William Landon. The indications are that Clarke, a Congregationalist, was well-to-do. He was able to subsidize a medical education for his second son, Charles, and a religious education for William Clarke, Jr, to educate at least one of his daughters at the Burlington Ladies' Academy, and to support a large family in a respectable condition.[21]

The circumstances of William Landon are particularly instructive with respect to the relationship between religious vocation and the political-economic project of 'improvement.' An 'open communion' Baptist, Landon covenanted with his neighbours and joined small masters and artisans in the formation of the Woodstock Reading Society, owned a substantial three-storey brick house in Woodstock village, and entertained Lord Elgin on his visit to Landon's village in 1849. But, while Landon was commonly addressed as 'the Reverend,' he was, in fact, an elected elder, a position for which he did not consistently receive pay. Throughout the 1840s and 1850s Landon scrambled to make a living, running a boarding school in his house, briefly editing a newspaper, serving as county clerk, census enumerator, and, in the 1850s, hawking dubious railway shares around the county.[22]

Landon's Baptist colleague Newton Bosworth owned a forty-seven–acre farm on the outskirts of Woodstock and was a published author.[23]

By denominational affiliation, the thirty-one members of the inspectoral corps for whom information exists included eleven Presbyterians, nine members of the Church of England, four Baptists, three Wesleyan Methodists, two Unitarians, a Congregationalist, and a Quaker. Unity among the superintendents was not based on common sectarian identification.

Speaking of the formalization of nineteenth-century Protestant religion, William Westfall has argued that, 'in much the same way that Victorians took education out of life and put it into schools, so they took religion out of the world and put it safely away in churches, temperance societies, and missionary organizations.' Yet, in the 1840s, clerical activities overlapped very much with civil administration and with schemes for capitalist development. These clergymen were directly implicated in ongoing debates about the place of the church in government and, like Landon, some were directly involved in the colony's nascent capitalist economy.[24]

The Teachers

Three teachers – John Strachan of the Midland District, Thomas Donnelly of the Prince Edward District and Patrick Thornton of the Gore District – served throughout the period under study, and two other teachers were inspectors for shorter periods: William Hynes in the Johnstown District (1844–5) and William Millar in the Eastern District (1847–9). With the possible exception of Donnelly, these men occupied a class position comparable to that of the respectable artisanal worker, with all its uncertainties. Four of them had been active as teachers of private-venture schools before the beginning of state schooling. Hynes had taught for thirty-five years when appointed inspector, having begun at the age of fourteen in 1808. His school was the largest in the Johnstown District in the 1830s, with about fifty students, and he was mainly dependent upon student fees. He was a founding member and vice-president of the Johnstown District Teachers' Association in 1842.

John Strachan, the son of an artisan, also taught in the Johnstown District, in the village of Gananoque, after emigrating from Scotland in 1835. His school was also large but unable to support his family. Before 1840, he moved to Ernestown in the Midland District, where he taught school and likely farmed.

William Millar was conducting a private classical academy in Cornwall when he was appointed superintendent, and claimed the £80 he made from the latter position was not sufficient to support his family.

Patrick Thornton of Hamilton was one of only four teachers considered competent by the town board of examiners in 1843. Thornton complained that his initial superintendent's salary of £100 did not permit him to live as well as many of the teachers he examined.

With the exception of Thomas Donnelly, these teachers were respectable men of modest means. They were certainly not 'strictly speaking, gentlemen,' but they were men with whom gentlemen would have been prepared to associate in public. Donnelly, by contrast, seems to have used teaching as a temporary occupation while looking for something more lucrative. While an inspector, he became a newspaper editor, and later a substantial grocer in the town of Picton. By 1861, Donnelly and his wife occupied a three-storey brick house, kept two carriages, and had $20,000 invested in their business.[25]

Many of the other superintendents had had some direct experience of teaching: John Wilson and Dexter D'Everardo taught school as young men, and William Hutton attempted to supplement the income from his farm by teaching at times as well.[26] William Elliott elaborated a plan to teach in London in the 1840s, although it seems not to have succeeded.

Several of the clerics had been teachers before or were teachers after taking orders. James Padfield was Johnstown District Grammar School master in the 1820s and a teacher in Upper Canada College in the early 1830s. John Flood taught or attempted to teach the Richmond Grammar School, James Baird offered classical instruction in his house, William Fraser eked out his meagre clerical income by farming and teaching school, and Colin Gregor was principal of the L'Orignal Grammar School from 1833.[27] William Landon ran a private school in Woodstock. On the whole, these men met the criterion that a sound inspector should have a practical knowledge of teaching methods.

Other Occupations

Information about the class position of several superintendents is less complete. Hamilton Hunter, the superintendent of the Home District, the most populous in the colony, edited the Reform Toronto *Examiner* at the time of his appointment. Like William Hutton, Hunter was a Unitarian in religion, and their parents were acquainted. In a move designed to counter the rising tide of democracy represented by the organization of free schooling in London in 1850, Hunter was recruited as principal of the new Union School.

Benjamin Hayter was a half-pay former naval lieutenant who held land in the Newcastle District and who claimed to have been employed at Victoria College when appointed superintendent of schools. Hayter had been in the English diplomatic corps at Caen in France in the 1820s, profiting from the French he had learned as a prisoner of war in 1805.[28]

Francis Allan, who died soon after appointment as Bathurst District superintendent in 1844, was the Perth postmaster and Crown Lands agent. The post office paid Allan £89 in 1843, while the agency was worth £117 in 1842 and £96.10.11. in 1843. Allan was district auditor and likely ran a book and stationery store.[29]

George Hendry, the Brock District superintendent (1846–7), and his partner John Bain ran a cabinet-making business that worked to order in the Woodstock area. Hendry was popularly described as a 'mechanic,' and the fact of his appointment was raised in the legislature by a Tory member as proof positive that the act of 1846 could not produce men of adequate social standing as school superintendents.[30]

Some obscurity surrounds the identity of the Western District superintendent for 1847, Robert Reynolds. There were two Robert Reynoldses living in the vicinity of Amherstburgh at the time of the 1861 census, either in the same or in adjacent houses: Robert J., a medical doctor, aged forty-two, and Robert, a farmer aged eighty. The elder Robert Reynolds was a man of regional importance in the 1830s, acting as commissioner for the Hartley's Point Light House and as an investigating commissioner of the Bois Blanc Light House. He was likely a relative of the Western District sheriff, Ebenezer Reynolds. One of the two Robert Reynolds was a land dealer, whether on his own account or as a broker is unknown, and a justice of the peace. Dr Reynolds was appointed to the Amherstburgh Board of Health, and was one of the two men who organized the incorporation of Amherstburgh as a town. Given that regional competition characterized the appointment of the superintendent in the Western District, with George Duck, Sr, of Howard engineering the appointment of his son in 1845 and again in 1848, an informed guess would suggest the younger Robert Reynolds was superintendent of schools.[31]

In terms of social class, the personnel of the inspectoral corps ranged from a few occupants of positions comparable to those of respectable artisans, to members of the rising capitalist class and large landed proprietors with pretensions to gentility. The majority of superintendents were at the upper end of this range, while there were no workers or small farmers (and, of course, no women or people of colour) included. The presence of one small master among the superintendents was a matter of considerable controversy. The appointments of the men of more modest standing were vetted by members of local élites. William Hynes had been the schoolmaster for George Sherwood, later MPP, and the Reverend Mr Smart testified to Hynes's lifelong 'character for respectability and usefulness.'[32] John Strachan's appointment in the Midland District was supported by J.S. Cartwright.

Class position does not mechanically determine activity. In practice, inspectors differed substantially, both in the energy with which they inspected schools and in their attitudes to the educational capacities of members of other classes. Newton Bosworth and Alexander Mann, for instance, occupied a similar class position and had similar educations. Bosworth lauded the attempts of parents and teachers at self-improvement in the Brock District, while Mann refused to give any teacher a certificate and spoke contemptuously of parents' capacities. These questions of style cannot be addressed in terms of a class-positional analysis, and are difficult to capture at a high level of abstraction. But these were variations within a common class position.

Education

In colonial terms, the inspectors were remarkably well educated. Seven of these men had attended university, and many others attended advanced private schools. Alexander Allan held an MA from Mareschal College; Alexander Mann an MA from King's College, Aberdeen University; and Samuel Ardagh an MA from Trinity College, Dublin. Colin Gregor held a BA from Glasgow; and James Baird a BA from Belfast College (he was one of the first graduates). Newton Bosworth, a Fellow of the Royal Society, studied at Cambridge, although it is not clear that he graduated. John Strachan finished two years of the classical course at the University of St Andrews, taking the prize in French both years and excelling at Latin and Greek.[33] William Clarke attended Hackney Academy, and Hamnett Pinhey Christ's Hospital. William Hutton's father held a degree from Trinity College, Dublin, and provided his son with a superior classical education. Hamilton Hunter held a diploma from the Belfast Academical Institution. By their numbers, these men constituted a quarter of the inspectoral corps, but five of them served throughout the period 1844–50.[34]

About the education of others we know less, but most of them had a 'classical education': an education including Latin and Greek. William Millar offered to teach these subjects. Henry Clifford had a 'good education,' which probably meant the same thing, and James Padfield was at least as well educated. In the 1820s, when he was master of the preparatory school at Upper Canada College, Padfield was described as considerably less well educated than the other masters (all of them university graduates), but he was none the less qualified to serve as master of the 'prep.'

Jacob Keefer was apprenticed to a pharmacist as a young man (which probably involved his learning Latin). Elias Burnham and John Wilson served legal apprenticeships before acting as superintendents, and William Elliott did so afterwards. Elliott taught himself Euclidean geometry. Wilson attended grammar school in Perth, Upper Canada, as a youth. George Duck, Jr, was admitted to Osgoode Hall in 1848. All of the men who passed the law board exams would have had Latin and perhaps Greek and some mathematics.

How well-educated the clerics who did not attend university were is unclear. John Flood had the reputation of possessing a remarkable love of reading, and William Fraser wrote a travel book in his later life. William Landon received his early education in New York State.

George Hendry was described as someone who was clearly not a classical scholar, although his cultural activities show a love of self-improvement. Patrick Thornton was notorious for his love of the natural sciences, particularly astronomy, which he demonstrated to students by means of apparatus. Thomas Higginson was probably educated at home, but was an amateur astronomer and poet. Richey Waugh arrived in Canada at the age of ten, and so was likely educated either at home or in the local grammar school. Benjamin Hayter was enrolled in the navy by the time he was thirteen, which suggests a limited education, but one can assume that the newspaper editor Thomas Donnelly was quite literate.

We know little about the education of the remaining superintendents: Robert Reynolds, John Steele, William Hynes, Samuel Hart, Charles Fletcher, Dexter D'Everardo, and John Bignall. All of these men wrote a clear hand, and were involved in public offices that required literary skills. Fletcher was on the examining committee of John Nairn's private academy in Goderich. Hynes was vice-president of the Johnstown District Teachers' Association. John Steele was elected to the management committee of Queen's College. Furthermore, Ardagh, Clarke, Eliot, Flood, Gregor, Hart, Higginson, and Wilson, all served as district grammar-school trustees, and Wilson was a member of the London Board of Examiners.[35]

While levels of literacy in Canada West in the 1840s were quite high, it was very unusual for a person to have been educated beyond the local common school. Most of the inspectors had done so. Their relative social wealth was paralleled by high educational standing.

The Press

Several of the superintendents had close connections to newspapers. In addition to Hunter of the *Examiner*, Thomas Donnelly edited the *Prince Edward Gazette* from 1846, John Steele and his brother started the Port Hope *Pilot* in the 1850s, one of William Clarke's sons edited and published the Long Point *Advocate* and later the *Canada Farmer*, and Benjamin Hayter's son the Port Hope *Messenger*. William Landon, who described himself as an editor in the 1852 census, co-edited the *Western Progress and County of Oxford General Advertiser* for a short period.

Public Office

As a group, the inspectors were heavily involved in political and civil administration. Five served as district wardens at some point in their careers, and three of these were appointed directly by the governor-in-council.[36] Two of those who held the wardenship did so at the time of their own appointments as district superintendent. Two other inspectors were district councillors, as were the fathers of George Duck, Jr, and Jacob Keefer. A third superintendent was a town councillor, a fourth a town clerk, a fifth a county clerk. Three served as members of Parliament, and a fourth ran unsuccessfully, while two of the elected members were later appointed to the Legislative Council.[37]

Nine of the superintendents were justices of the peace, four chaired grand juries, several were grand-jurymen, and three served as postmasters. Samuel Hart and Francis Allan acted as district land agents, George Duck, Jr, worked as a Clergy Reserves inspector, while William Hutton was a part-time arbitrator for the Board of Works. Hutton and John Wilson worked as district returning officers, while Patrick Thornton was the assessor for one of the Hamilton wards. Benjamin Hayter was a district licence inspector. Hart, Hutton, Hendry, and Francis Allan were district auditors. Duck, Reynolds, and Landon served on local boards of health. Alexander Allan, D'Everardo, Duck, Keefer, and Pinhey were notaries public. Wilson and Steele were Rebellion Losses commissioners. Charles Eliot, George Duck, Jr, William Hutton, and John Wilson were active in county militia units. Thomas Donnelly claimed to have fought in the Rebellion, as did one of Thomas Higginson's sons. John Bignall was the Canada Company's elections manager for the Huron tract, and both Alexander Allan and Hamnett Pinhey were connected to this private land company. In addition to these visible public offices, several superintendents were active at the district level in schemes for economic 'improvement.' These included mutual insurance companies and building societies and railway, macadam road, and harbour companies. Their names commonly appeared on the lists of contributors to popular charities, such as the

Irish-Scottish relief funds. Educational inspection was combined with local moral, judicial, administrative, and economic leadership.

Age and Life Cycle

Twenty-two of the thirty-three inspectors for whom information exists were between thirty-two and fifty years of age at appointment, and fourteen of these were in their forties. Five of the superintendents were in their twenties, eight in their thirties, four in their fifties, and three in their sixties.

The youngest superintendents were George Duck, Jr, who was twenty-four in 1845, and Richey Waugh, who was twenty-five. Duck's youth was the source of complaints on the part of teachers who refused to accept the authority of one not much older than many of their students, and his father's influence was key in his appointment. Like Duck, Waugh was appointed after Council's first choice proved unable or unwilling to act. James Baird was only twenty-six when appointed Newcastle superintendent in 1849, but his appointment was made in the midst of serious local conflict over the conduct of his predecessor, Benjamin Hayter. Thomas Donnelly was also appointed in his twenties.

The superintendents who were in their sixties on taking office were well-established men of standing. Alexander Allan, the oldest inspector, at sixty-nine (and on horseback at seventy-five in 1850!), and Newton Bosworth were at the end of lengthy careers, and Hamnett Pinhey was well-advanced. It was their high social standing that led to the appointment for these three. Pinhey and Bosworth subsidized the office out of their own incomes.

Of the thirty-four inspectors for whom information about marital status exists, one was single and the rest were married. George Duck, Jr, the unmarried inspector, married in 1854.

Three inspectors married while holding office: Hamilton Hunter in 1846, Colin Gregor in 1847, and William Elliot in 1848. Hunter's marriage coincided with a salary increase from the Home District Council. Charles Fletcher had been married for about a year when he took the Huron District superintendency. Two others, Patrick Thornton and James Padfield, had children who married while their fathers were district superintendents.

Many of the inspectors were supporting young families. Samuel Ardagh had seven children from his marriage of 1828 by 1844. Thomas Donnelly, John Flood (who married in 1842), Alexander Mann, and Richey Waugh also had small children in their households. One of John Strachan's children was nine years old in 1844, and Samuel Hart's household included a daughter born in 1841. Patrick and Janet Thornton had children born in 1845 and 1846, in addition to an adult son and daughter. Hamilton Hunter had a child born in 1847. James Padfield's household contained eleven children in 1852, Thomas Higginson's seven, and William Clarke's household included six children, not to mention his son John, a doctor, who lived in the same village. William Landon and his wife, Emory (ten years his junior), had no children.[38]

All of these households seem to have been well within the bounds of contemporary middle-class convention, with the exception of that of Dexter D'Everardo. D'Everardo's one-and-a-half-storey frame house was described by the 1852 census enumerator as 'a sort of Public Office at which much of the Township business is done.' In addition to D'Everardo's wife, Eliza, the household contained six other people. D'Everardo had adopted two female children sometime earlier, and gossip had it that these had been kidnapped.[39]

Most inspectors lived in households that supported dependants. For most of them, the inspectorate was a vital source of income, and this fact undoubtedly shaped their appreciation of their position in the developing project of social improvement, as well as in conflicts between central and local authorities. But one cannot draw any uniform conclusions in this matter. Patrick Thornton was entirely dependent upon his salary as superintendent, yet opposed official policy bitterly on several occasions and defied the direct orders of the chief superintendent. The wealthy Hamnett Pinhey was not even paid as superintendent, but he also opposed official policy.

The information necessary to investigate the place of the office of inspector in household economies is not generally available. The considerable difficulties involved in reconstructing the biographies of these important men are much magnified where their mothers, wives, sisters, and daughters are concerned. It is clear that men's relations with women, and with other men through women, were basic elements in the social organization of rule, but the overwhelmingly male-centred orientation of record-keeping systems tends to restrict one to glimpses of this reality. The women to whom the inspectors were married are almost impossible to identify, and relatively little can be recovered about family economy. A great deal has been written, for example, about the Keefer men, especially Samuel and Thomas, but their sisters are identified only in terms of their marriage partners.[40]

Still, the domestic situation of William Hutton is informative. While Hutton took some interest in and pleasure from it, educational inspection was important to him largely as a supplement to the income generated by his farm. After serving an apprenticeship as a farmer in Ireland, Hutton, the sixth son in a family of eight children, had come to Canada in 1833 when he was thirty-two years old. Frances McCrea Hutton and five young children (the eldest seven years old, the youngest in her arms) followed in 1834 after Hutton had purchased a farm on the outskirts of the village of Belleville for £750 in currency borrowed from his father. The

Huttons were subsidizing an advanced education for their son when William became district superintendent, and their four daughters were still at home. The eldest child was eighteen in 1844, the youngest eleven.

Despite the energetic efforts of William, Frances, and the children, and despite William's 'improved' methods, the farm could not be made to pay their debts. In 1840, for instance, the farm produce was sold for £95, but costs were £45 for labour, £10 for blacksmithing, £10 for implements, £15 interest, and £2.10 in taxes. Hutton complained this left 'less than would buy us a cup of tea.'[41] The household did not lack food or clothing, but cash was quite scarce, and the success of the farm depended upon the prodigious amounts of fruit-picking, canning, preserving, baking, spinning, weaving, sewing, haying, and dairy work performed by Frances Hutton and her daughters, especially after a back injury limited William's farm activity and Joseph was sent off to school. The women's efforts freed William to pursue public employment and provided the resources for Joseph's education.

While William Hutton took an active intellectual interest in public improvement, especially in the domain of agriculture, he struggled to maintain a genteel style of life. The pursuit of this goal led him to hold a variety of other offices while he was superintendent of schools. Hutton was named warden of the newly created Victoria District in 1842 and held this position until it became elective in 1846. He had hoped to earn £60 to £100 in it, but he seems to have been paid only £30. He earned £2.10 as a returning officer in 1843 and £40 in 1844 and 1845 as superintendent of schools, an amount that was increased in 1847 to £70 on condition that he deliver lectures in the schools, which he seems not to have done.

After the accession of the Reform ministry strengthened the hand of his cousin Francis Hincks, Hutton's fortunes improved. In 1848 he was appointed an arbitrator for the Board of Works, which earned him 10 shillings in expenses while travelling and 30 shillings a day. This yielded £73 in 1848, more than the school superintendency. In the same year, his son Joseph was appointed a clerk in Hincks's inspector general's office, initially at £150, but later reduced to £125. By the end of his superintendence, Hutton had the means to live the style of life that his class background had led him to expect and, as secretary of the Bureau of Agriculture after 1853, he was one of the colony's highest paid civil servants.[42]

One consequence of Hutton's activities was that inspection was a part-time occupation to him. There were 113 schools in Hutton's district in 1849, the last year of his superintendence. He seems to have made one annual tour of school inspection, usually in the winter, which lasted about six weeks. It is extremely improbable that he actually visited many of the schools, for he would have had to have seen almost three a day, including Sundays, to inspect them all in six

District Superintendents' Salaries (£)

Superintendent	Year 1844	1845	1846	1847	1848	1849	No. of schools (year)
A. Allan	?	?	?	?	?	?	113 (49)
F. Allan	died before acting						117 (46)
S. Ardagh	25	25	–	–	–	–	78 (46)
J. Baird	–	–	–	–	–	?	184 (49)
J. Bignall	130	130	130	130	?	–	41 (47)
N. Bosworth	50	50	–	–	–	–	122 (46)
E. Burnham	50	50	50	50	50	50	148 (47)
W. Clarke	00	00	?	?	?	?	109 (47)
H. Clifford	–	–	70	70	70	70	93 (49)
D. D'Everardo	–	–	?	200	125	175	180 (49)
T. Donnelly	50	50	50	50	50	50	98 (47)
G. Duck	–	?	50	–	125	125	146 (49)
C. Eliot	75	–	–	–	–	–	139 (46)
W. Elliot	–	100	100	100	?	?	220 (49)
C. Fletcher	–	–	–	–	–	100	64 (49)
J. Flood	–	–	–	–	–	15	68 (49)
W. Fraser	–	–	–	–	minus	7	161 (49)
C. Gregor	4%	4%	?	?	–	–	39 (46)
S. Hart	4%	4%	–	–	–	–	174 (46)
B. Hayter	–	–	125	125	125	?	171 (47)
G. Hendry	–	–	100	100	–	–	148 (47)
T. Higginson	–	–	–	–	?	?	45 (49)
H. Hunter	150	150	175	175	175	175	300 (47)
W. Hutton	40	40	50	70	70	70	113 (49)
W. Hynes	75	–	–	–	–	–	217 (46)
J. Keefer	?	?	–	–	–	–	191 (46)
W. Landon	–	–	–	–	100	100	136 (49)
A. Mann	50	50	50	–	–	–	120 (47)
W. Millar	–	–	–	80	80	–	178 (47)
J. Padfield	–	–	–	100	100	100	117 (49)
H. Pinhey	00	00	00	00	00	–	83 (46)
R. Reynolds	–	–	–	125	–	–	134 (47)
J. Steele	75	?	–	–	–	–	177 (46)
J. Strachan	60	100	100	100	100	100	176 (49)
P. Thornton	100	100	100	150	150	150	178 (47)
R. Waugh	–	?	100	150	150	150	204 (49)
J. Wilson	?	–	–	–	–	–	190 (46)[43]

weeks. Hutton was criticized in Council in 1850 for having neglected to deliver school lectures as expected when his salary was increased in 1847.

In addition to this tour of inspection, Hutton examined and certified teachers, but his examinations, like those of his contemporaries, were brief, to say the least. W.R. Biggs was examined by Hutton sometime before 1846 while Hutton ploughed in his field. With Biggs walking alongside, Hutton turned the plough towards the house and asked Biggs to spell 'One fox's head,' 'Two foxes' heads,' 'One lady's bonnet,' and 'Two ladies' bonnets.' Biggs was then required to parse the phrase 'The lady said in speaking of the word that, that that that, that that gentleman parsed was not that that that she requested him to analyze,' at which he succeeded. When they reached the house, Hutton wrote out the certificate.[44]

Party Politics

Given that the office of superintendent was a district appointment, the party complexion of the district council commonly influenced the selection of candidates. Several inspectors had clear party connections. In the Huron District, John Bignall owed his appointment to his function as Tory party hack and elections manager for the Canada Company. The Tory warden William Chalk opposed the reappointment of Charles Fletcher in February 1849 because Fletcher was initially named by the Reform ministry after Bignall absconded. Hamnett Pinhey was a high or 'compact' Tory of long standing, and his party views were largely shared by Thomas Higginson of the Ottawa District. John Wilson was elected a Conservative member of Parliament in the later 1840s, although he abandoned the party after the Rebellion Losses riots, and Richey Waugh held moderate Tory views. It is likely that Samuel Hart was a Tory in politics, and the same is probably true of Alexander Mann, Samuel Ardagh, and James Padfield. After the burning of the parliament buildings in Montreal, Thomas Donnelly spoke at length in a public meeting in Picton against the Rebellion Losses Bill and attacked the Reform politicians present. Donnelly also attended a public dinner for one of the Prince Edward Tory members. William Millar signed a public letter calling upon J.H. Cameron to offer himself as a candidate in the Eastern District.

Three superintendents had particularly close links to the Reformers. Hamilton Hunter edited the Reform *Examiner* and was described by Ryerson as very close to Francis Hincks and Robert Baldwin. Hunter had been educated at the Belfast Royal Academical Institution, where Hincks's father was master. George Hendry organized a large public Reform dinner for Hincks in Woodstock in 1846 and spoke at length in support of him. William Hutton was Hincks's cousin. Both Jacob Keefer and Dexter D'Everardo were moderate Reformers with links to W.H. Merritt. Charles Eliot's politics were of the moderate Reform variety, and both William Clarke and William Landon supported the second Baldwin-Lafontaine ministry.

In practice, the experience of the inspectors in office was sharply influenced by relations between the district council and the Education Office. Superintendents tended to orient themselves from political conviction towards either the central or the local authority. These orientations were relatively independent of party politics, and at least two superintendents lost their positions because of them.

Common Culture

The ideological-moral bloc in which these men participated centred upon a discourse of social improvement through the diffusion of useful knowledge. The education of the population by the state was seen to place the means of self-improvement within the reach of all people in the colony. In a period of relatively underdeveloped class antagonisms, the ideology of self-improvement could contain an apparently viable form of moral leadership. Many of the inspectors took pleasure in adopting 'improving' habits and pastimes in their own lives.

Political hegemony depends upon the dominant class in society presenting its interests as the general interest of all classes. Thus cultural forms capable of mediating social antagonisms are required. The culture of improvement could speak to the interests of artisans, small masters, and farmers concerned with social advance and political democracy, as it spoke to the interests of capitalists and large landed proprietors in the generalization of respect for property relations. The language of social betterment could be understood by different speakers in terms of social liberation or social domination; of bettering the social situation of wage workers, small farmers, or women, or of bettering the hold of power relations upon them. The concept of improvement carried many other connotations, from cold-water temperance to general reciprocity with the United States.

The superintendents shared an interest in improvement. Eleven of them were involved in some way with libraries or mechanics' institutes. Thomas Higginson was first president of the Vankleek Hill Mechanics' Institute; Jacob Keefer was vice-president of the Thorold Mechanics' Institute; and Patrick Thornton was librarian of the Hamilton and Gore Mechanics' Institute, from its first formation in the 1830s. William Elliott was an active member of the London Mechanics' Institute, lecturing there in 1845 on intellectual culture.[45] His predecessor as district superintendent, John Wilson, was vice-president of the London Institute, and gave a series of lectures on electricity, illustrated by scientific apparatus.[46] Hamilton Hunter was a member of the London Institute, at least, in 1852. The three Brock District superintendents were all involved in the Woodstock Reading

Society, and two of them in the Woodstock Mechanics' Institute. George Hendry served as the Mechanics' Institute's first president and organized a series of lectures on scientific subjects. The third, Newton Bosworth, interested himself in the Paris Mechanics' Institute. In the two years before his death in 1848, Bosworth gave lectures titled 'The Nature and Property of Matter' at the Paris Mutual Society and Circulating Library and 'The Progress of Discovery in the Sciences and Arts, and their Influence Upon the Mental and Moral Condition of Society' to the Mechanics' Institute. Francis Allan was a founding member of the Perth Mechanics' Institute and was involved in the local library as well. Elias Burnham attempted to secure a government land grant for the construction of a central school and public library in Peterborough, which he proposed to subsidize with his salary as district superintendent.

In various media, the superintendents promoted social improvement. As grand-jury foremen or chairmen of the Quarter Sessions, Charles Eliot, Keefer, Pinhey, and Steele wrote reports on jail conditions and prison reform. William Elliott published caricatures on similar subjects.[47]

Charles Fletcher was particularly active in the temperance movement before taking office, lecturing frequently on this subject at various places in Goderich. William Clarke, Jacob Keefer, Alexander Mann, Newton Bosworth, George Hendry and William Landon were also involved in temperance activities.[48]

Several of the clerics were active members of Bible societies. After his transfer to Guelph from L'Orignal in 1848, Colin Gregor joined the local branch of the Bible society and delivered a public lecture titled 'Argument for Christianity, deduced from the Word and Works of God, especially consonance of Revelation and Benediction.' James Baird was active in Bible and missionary societies in Port Hope.

Local or county agricultural societies provided a further outlet for social interests in improvement, and their meetings provided occasions for substantial proprietors to exhibit their leadership. John Steele was a central figure in the Northumberland County Agricultural Society, and Thomas Donnelly participated in the parallel body in Prince Edward County. William Hutton was a founding member of the Victoria District Agricultural Society and was zealous in his pursuit of agricultural improvement, both through agitation among his neighbours and in print. Hutton wrote prize essays on this subject before joining the Bureau of Agriculture in the 1850s. William Elliott was corresponding secretary of the London District Agricultural Society in the mid-1840s.

In a somewhat different way, Henry Clifford of the Simcoe District participated in the same moral culture. Clifford used the leisure available to the man of moderate means and intellectual interests to develop his own capacities. Clifford, among other things, was a bookbinder, carpenter, wheelwright, shoemaker, and, later, amateur photographer. Inspectors could choose to cultivate their intellectual and creative interests.

John Flood enjoyed a local celebrity as a man who loved to read. Patrick Thornton was celebrated in Hamilton for his love of astronomy, which he demonstrated to his students by means of apparatus. Thomas Higginson shared this interest in astronomy, using the tower of the Anglican church in Vankleek Hill, whose construction he subsidized, as an observatory. Several of the inspectors shared a fascination with phrenology, holding this in common with Egerton Ryerson, who considered phrenology a serious subject for common-school education.

These kinds of cultural activities exposed the superintendents of rather modest social status to men of political and economic power. As librarian of the Gore District Mechanics' Institute, Patrick Thornton was in personal contact with the mayor of Hamilton and the local members of Parliament, as well as with several district councillors. On the examining committee of the Burlington Ladies' Academy, Thornton associated with other members of the élite in the Gore District (as well as with Egerton and John Ryerson). Several inspectors also participated in the ethnic organizations present in most towns, especially the St Andrew's, St Patrick's, and St George's societies. 'Social improvement' was an ideology that cut across class boundaries to a certain extent.

A stronger case for common culture can be made through a prosopographical investigation of the inspectorate. The population of Canada West was only about 450,000 in 1841, and about 950,000 by 1852. Men of means and advanced education were few and likely to be in contact, even if communication by land was difficult.

The relations among inspectors in the Brock District will be outlined below. These three – Bosworth, Hendry, and Landon – were well acquainted. In the Eastern District, Samuel Hart dealt with William Fraser when the former was district and the latter township superintendent. Hart's fellow churchwarden Solomon Chesley was town superintendent for Cornwall and would have visited William Millar's school. Some of Jacob Keefer's relatives moved to Cornwall. James Padfield travelled with the pastor of Hart's church to clerical association meetings and can be expected to have encountered Hart through their common religious activity. Padfield had been Pinhey's curate in the early 1830s, and Pinhey and Hart signed the retirement application of at least one teacher. The retirement application of the controversial Johnston Neilson (see chapter 6) was signed by James Padfield, Richey Waugh, and Alexander Mann. The application also included a testimonial signed by Francis Hincks's father. Pinhey and Thomas Higginson were involved in promoting the Montreal-Bytown Railroad Company, and Higginson had encountered Keefer's brother Thomas while the latter was involved in an Ottawa District survey. Jacob Keefer, John Wilson and Robert Reynolds were implicated in a Huron District Crown Lands scam.[49]

Hamilton Hunter corresponded with Jacob Keefer in November 1845 about the desirability of a common-school journal in the colony and may have contacted all his fellow superintendents.[50] William Hutton visited Hunter in Toronto while they were both inspectors, and these two were joined by common religion (Unitarianism), national origins, and politics. The Board of Trustees for the London Central School, which recruited Hunter as principal in 1851, included John Wilson and William Elliott. Moreover, W.F. Clarke (Jr?) was the London superintendent of schools while Hunter was principal.

Before setting out on his first inspectoral tour, Dexter D'Everardo called on Jacob Keefer to discuss school matters. Dr Ironside, who assisted at the birth of Christina Keefer's younger children, earlier sat with Robert Reynolds on the Amherstburg Board of Health. Both Patrick Thornton of the Gore District and William Clarke of the Talbot District were members of the examining committee of the Burlington Ladies' Academy, an institution attended by one of Clarke's daughters and visited frequently by Egerton Ryerson and his brother. Clarke's daughter's poetry was reprinted in the *Journal of Education*. William Elliott of the London District was in regular contact with John Wilson of the same district and frequently sought career advice from him. In the first week of January 1846, Elliott spent several days with Patrick Thornton, discussing educational matters and touring schools. R.H. Thornton of Oshawa, who was likely Patrick's brother, corresponded with the teacher to whom John Strachan of the Midland District sent students for training. The school books authored by the Thornton brothers were distributed through the network of Presbyterian book dealers, which included Francis Allan's son James in Perth. Many other kinds of connections existed and continued in the following generation.

The inspectors did not have regular information sessions with the central educational authority because of the failure of a clause in Ryerson's draft 1848 bill. They had little official face-to-face contact with the chief superintendent, although several of them had occasion to correspond or meet with him over other matters: William Hutton's son, for instance, briefly attended the Normal School in 1849. Ryerson conducted a general provincial tour in the fall of 1847, and this was the first time, in many cases, he actually met his field officers.[51] But while there were no regular meetings, and while, unlike their Irish counterparts, the Canadian inspectors never had common training or common meeting rooms, they participated actively in a common culture focused on social, political, and, to a lesser extent, economic improvement, which led many of them to a degree of personal acquaintance. Class dominance is not a theoretical abstraction, but rather something based on a network of social and cultural relations and practices.

Continuity

A common criticism levelled by conservatives against the Common School Act of 1841 was that adequate educational supervision was not secured by it. Particular criticism was directed at the elected township commissioners of common schools, charged with managing and inspecting the schools. Elected commissioners were frequently denounced as ignorant and incompetent.[52]

But several district superintendents had themselves served as township school commissioners. Francis Allan, Jacob Keefer, Thomas Higginson, Alexander Mann, John Flood, George Duck's father, and George Hendry had all acted under the act of 1841 as members of township school commissions. Samuel Hart was active on the Cornwall Board of Police for schools, and D'Everardo, in addition to serving on the Pelham School Commission, acted in Niagara District Council on school matters.

After the transition to a system of township or county superintendents in 1850, many of those active in the 1840s continued to serve, some of them consistently until the imposition of educational qualifications on the inspectorate in 1871. Twelve of the thirty-four surviving men who served as district superintendent were named town or township superintendents in 1850, and between 1850 and 1871 at least seventeen of those active in the 1840s, half the survivors, served again at some point.[53] Some superintendents were geographically mobile: William Fraser superintended schools in the extreme east and extreme west of the province. The schools of London were supervised at times between 1850 and 1862 by William F. Clarke, Hamilton Hunter, and John Wilson.[54] Several former superintendents joined county boards of examiners, continuing in this capacity to examine teachers.

Three of the five men who were teachers before superintending returned to the schoolroom: William Hynes taught in Brockville, and, when pensioned off, acted as Prescott town superintendent. Patrick Thornton taught in one of the Dundas schools and was appointed Barton Township superintendent in 1850, before becoming Dundas postmaster. John Strachan and his seventeen-year-old son taught in the Consecon Union School for five years in the 1850s (it bankrupted Strachan), and Strachan was principal of the small Uxbridge Union School in 1858. He taught in Clarke Township until his retirement in 1865. In addition, Hamilton Hunter was principal of the London Central School from 1851 to 1855, and then taught in the same school from 1858 until 1868, when he took a position in the federal Inland Revenue department.

Other former superintendents continued to visit schools and to lecture on educational questions at quarterly examinations. Educational administration was characterized by an important degree of continuity. Furthermore, educational administration and the personal relations it fostered overlapped with other activities in the state system. Many former superintendents encountered one another in later years in other areas.

Conclusion

Far-above-average wealth, direct access to the means of production, advanced education, extensive activity in the state system and in the religious sphere, common culture, personal acquaintance, continuity in activity: these characterized the inspectors as a group. They were men joined by bonds of property and propriety, culture and Christianity, in a collective project aimed at the moral, political, and, in some cases, economic improvement of their social inferiors and dependants: farmers and workers, women and children, Indians and blacks. Within a broadly common class culture, these men reacted in their own ways to the educational conditions, debates, and conflicts they encountered. Some stressed the civilizing and liberating possibilities presented by capitalist economic development and representative government. Others focused their energies on attempting to counter the threats posed by such social currents to their social dominance. The following chapters undertake an examination of their activities as inspectors and of the practice of educational inspection.

6   A Fledgling Bureaucracy at Work

Educational inspectors engaged in varied and wide-ranging initiatives under the school acts of 1843, 1846, and 1847. The acts allowed these men to exercise a broad and initially little-defined 'inspective function.' The acts created a political and financial basis for the pursuit of social improvement. Educational administrators conceived the practical work of inspection as the real centre of efforts at public instruction. This chapter investigates some of the working conditions of the district superintendents in Canada West and documents some of their preoccupations.

Social Mapping

The first school inspections were primarily attempts at identifying and locating schools. Effective educational administration from the centre depended upon intelligence about the geopolitical condition of popular education. The central authority could not govern schools about which it knew nothing. But how to know schools that were as yet imperfectly contained in an administrative grid? The first superintendents transcribed information about prior educational organization onto the new coordinates provided by the central authority.

Maps of any description, let alone reliable ones, were not available for most colonial districts, and no central register of schools or school districts existed in 1844.[1] Plans for the geographical mapping of the province were pursued with energy by speculators and publishers in many parts of the colony. A key dimension of the initial work of the inspectors was the attempt to discover schoolhouses and to create some general record of where they were located. While the limits of the agricultural frontier in the southern part of Canada West were reached by about 1850, many areas were not settled until the 1840s. Overland communication remained difficult and dangerous.

In their mapping exercise, superintendents were dependent upon their own local knowledge and social connections to find schools. Itinerant clergymen were among the few people travelling a regular, regional circuit and, given that the same building frequently did double duty as school and church, clergymen enjoyed a practical advantage as school inspectors. Samuel Ardagh, the Simcoe District superintendent during 1844–6, travelled throughout his district and frequently held religious services in schoolhouses. He took the occasion of church service to act educationally, as he indicated in his diary in February 1844. 'Held Divine Service at Nigers' School house, quite full. After service spoke to them about schools & gave some advice as I was lately appt'd – by the unanimous vote of Mun. Council – Supt. of Schools for the whole County.'[2] George Duck, Jr, may have had a knowledge of his district parallel to that of the itinerant clerics by virtue of his work as a Clergy Reserves inspector, and Benjamin Hayter served as an inspector of licences, but most lay superintendents would have been dependent upon the knowledge of others to find schools.

Even where school districts were reported to the district council, it might be difficult for a superintendent to discover them. William Elliott was given conflicting information from neighbours about the location of schools in the London District.[3] Alexander Allan, in response to complaints that he had not visited the school in section 2 of Derby and Sydenham, wrote: 'On arriving at the house occupied in 1848 as the School house it was occupied as a Carpenters Shop and there was no person on the premises to give any information. I expected to meet with it along the road to the village & made enquiry of several people on the road but without success.' No one in nearby Sydenham village knew of the school either, so Allan assumed it had ceased operations.[4] School trustees complained many schools were missed in this way in the 1840s. Benjamin Hayter, charged with failing to visit many Newcastle District schools in 1848, defended himself by remarking that 'the very last time I was out on my tour – I passed six schools – in Haldimand ... *all vacant* – indeed whilst they may be legally closed six months in the year, the Dist Sup. has no chance of extricating himself from calumny.'[5] While schools could qualify for government subsidy by remaining open only six months a year, no inspector could be sure of visiting them while they were in operation.

The superintendents were often dependent upon local residents for food and accommodation, especially in the 'back' townships where inns and taverns were rare. John Strachan of the Midland District was initially accorded only £60 for his inspectoral duties because 'the Council did not consider that the Superintendent would be at much expense in travelling, for he would be cheerfully entertained by the farmers wherever he went.'[6] William Hutton was somewhat surprised after his first tour of inspection that 'during the whole month that I was absent my expenses did not amount to 5 shillings.' This, he wrote to his mother, was because 'no one would accept of any remuneration, and [all] expressed great gratification in having an opportunity of seeing me at their houses. I did not calculate on such *warmth* of hospitality, but I did not wonder upon seeing the state of their schools that they were anxious for a supervision of them by one whom they esteem competent to guide and direct in their management.'[7] However, the quality of the accommodation on offer offended the sensibilities of young William Elliott. After spending the night in a one-room log cabin, Elliott recorded in his diary: 'This promiscuous lodging is the *greatest* most unpleasant part connected w/ my office,' and some of the beds he slept in were flea-ridden.[8]

Jacob Keefer toured some of the schools in his Niagara District from 14 and 24 October and from 25 November to 5 December 1845. He visited forty-eight active schools in fifteen different townships, went to twenty-four vacant ones, and heard about nine others from third parties. He travelled on horseback and stayed frequently with friends or business associates.

Keefer kept rough notes of the geographical situation of schools and drew himself at least one map to aid in locating them again. Some schools were built on bits of waste ground and would have been impossible for a casual visitor to find. Mr Chalmers, the district councillor for Sherbrooke Township, took Keefer to the union schoolhouse with Moulton Township, a log building situated below the high-water mark on Lake Erie.

Even with his close connections to local proprietors, Keefer wandered. On 20 October 1845, he left Dunnville in the morning and 'started to visit the School on Forkroad about 6 miles from Dunville,' but, en route, he 'learnt that the female who taught the School had quit about 2 weeks since.' The following day, he 'came from Furry's,' where he had spent the night, 'down the road north of the Beach for the purpose of visiting a Branch of No 2 in the Township of *Wainfleet* at *Daly's Ditch* and found it had been closed since 1st Septr – No. 2 *Wainfleet*, Miner's Settlement, near Sugar Loaf, is closed; found the Menonists holding meeting there.' Keefer returned home on the morning of Friday, 23 October, passing through the village of Ireland 'down to the mouth of Black Creek,' but, as he wrote, 'thinking that Dist. No. 1 in Willoughby was below the mouth of Black Creek, I mist the opportunity of seeing it. – A new school house farther down the River was not in operation.' Keefer returned to Thorold by way of Chippewa village, a remarkable day's journey on horseback.

Keefer was an energetic inspector, but even he managed to visit only 140 of the 227 schools in his district in 1845, not venturing at all into some townships. Given that he saw as many as nine schools a day, his inspection can only have been of the most cursory sort. The fact that he went to so many vacant schools points both to the paucity of secondary sources of information about schooling and to the importance of inspection for a central authority concerned to estimate educational conditions.[9]

Conditions of overland travel were relatively primitive, although the Niagara, Gore, and Home districts were more densely settled than most. Extensive travel in the 1840s was physically dangerous, and the two or three superintendents who toured in horse and buggy were no safer than the majority who rode. Benjamin Hayter was thrown out of his buggy while on tour in June 1848, an accident that left him 'seriously hurt, having three or four ribs broken on his left side.'[10] Hayter's successor, James Baird, was on tour in the winter of 1850 when his horse 'became frightened ran off and broke two of [Baird's] ribs.' Baird attempted to continue his school examinations, but caught 'a severe cold.'[11] In the Colborne District, illness prevented Elias Burnham from visiting any schools in 1848, and James Padfield of Bathurst was prevented by a like cause from visiting many in 1847.[12] Several other superintendents had similar experiences.

Relations with City and Township Superintendents

Township superintendents were poorly paid, which limited candidates for the office. There were so few in the Huron District that township councillors individually appointed 'such Parties as they thought best qualified ... at a salary of £2:10 pr. annum.'[13] In at least one district, no person would serve, and elsewhere others found the appointment daunting.[14] No systematic investigation of the township superintendency has yet been undertaken, but those appointed were men able to post a substantial performance bond. The district superintendents were dependent upon them for the payment of money and the making of reports until 1847.[15]

Still, many district superintendents complained of the incapacity or inaction of township inspectors. Samuel Ardagh, no democrat, repeatedly denounced these officials. 'You will understand the trouble I have in part of the County,' he wrote to Robert Murray in 1844, 'where I inform you that some of the Township Superintendents cannot spell the word "School." ' His report for 1844 was late 'in consequence of the Township Superintendents not receiving any Salary' which meant Ardagh had 'little or no control over them.' He continued in a similar vein: 'the Trustees are generally illiterate persons and incompetent altogether to manage the Schools, and draw up a report ... Also the Superintendents themselves are in many instances inefficient, from a like cause, and those who are competent take little pains owing to not receiving remuneration for their time and labour.'[16] Many district superintendents opposed the office of township superintendent, and some of the latter officials agreed.[17] The labour involved in township superintendence was 'immense' and, in the Johnstown District, a superintendent wrote:

'the people are averse to paying a salary in proportion to the services required. Your humble servants gets £5 per annum.' This person had to post a £700 performance bond.[18] The Education Office was seriously considering the abolition of township officials in 1845 and sought advice from district superintendents.[19]

Popular reaction to educational superintendence remains obscure. The superintendents themselves reported that they were generally welcomed in the countryside, but there were frequent complaints that the office was expensive and ineffective. A public meeting in section 9 of Adelaide Township resolved, in February 1845,

that there are too many Superintendents with an unlimited power to raise their salary's to whatever they please and of no service whatever to the Children attending School If the Parents or Guardians of children, combined with the Trustees and School Master, who are always on the spot, do not look to their Interests, it cannot be done by a Superintendent residing at a distance, occasionally paying them the compliment of a Dollar and a half's visit, and as the Township Clerk has to make out all the returns, and to keep the Book Accompts the returns could as well be forwarded by him to the Education Office, which would be a considerable saving of the school fund which might be appropriated to the defraying of Teachers Wages.[20]

It is clear that officials in this fledgling bureaucracy themselves struggled to define spheres of jurisdiction, appropriate qualifications, and modes of procedure.

In the Gore District, Patrick Thornton, the district superintendent, had travelled a voluntary inspectoral circuit in the late 1830s, had been instrumental in the organization of the Dumfries' Teachers' Association, whose first president he was, and agitated for the examination of teachers by the district superintendent alone as a means to male teachers' professional self-improvement. Thornton's activities smack of empire-building, given his attempts to have his own series of school books adopted by teachers in the district.

Thornton was persistent in his efforts to make the Education Office specify limits to and procedures for the office of township superintendent and attempted to extend the discretion accorded his own office. Thornton wondered if he was required to recognize the appointment of a non-resident clergyman as superintendent for Dumfries Township.[21] He asked the Education Office at least three times about the certification powers of township and district superintendents in his first year in office, claiming that conflicts over their relative powers reigned. On each occasion he was informed that both superintendents could examine teachers, preferably with the township superintendent examining first, and then the district superintendent on his inspectoral tour doing so again. Alexander McNab assured Thornton that the district superintendent could annul the certificates granted by township superintendents, agreed that township superintendents were not all well-qualified, and suggested that, if Thornton wished to rid his district of incompetent teachers, he should 'visit every School in [his] District once a quarter.'[22]

Thornton took quite an assertive stance with respect to teacher certification. During his tours in 1844, he disqualified several people who had been teaching for quite some time. One of these, he claimed, 'had gone to the trustees and offered to keep school if the people would give him his board and the Government money. On this condition he was engaged without any reference to his qualifications.' Cases like this, it seemed to Thornton, were 'calculated to mar the end of this Government' in educational policy. The Education Office supported him in not paying such teachers if they did not have certificates, arguing 'it is the duty of Teachers to apply for their certificates, & if they do not do so, they must bear the consequences.'[23]

But there was another version of these events presented by the township superintendent for Esquissing, W.G. Stewart. In parts of this poor township, Stewart had granted temporary certificates and allowed trustees to hire inferior teachers. When Stewart visited these schools, he wasn't particularly impressed with the quality of teaching, but he saw some teaching as better than none. However, when Thornton visited the schools after they had been in operation for eight months, he claimed the teachers were completely unqualified and refused to pay them. Stewart thought Thornton's examination 'fair, mild and moderate,' but insisted that, where people could only pay £20, qualified teachers could not be had. The Education Office gave quite a different response to Stewart than Thornton had received: 'A Township Superintendent is as competent in the eye of the law to grant certificates of qualification as the County Superintendent and they are just as good to the Teacher until such time as they are annulled. In my opinion the certificate of a Township Superintendent should never be set aside without the strongest reasons by a County Superintendent.'[24]

The superintendents occupied an ambiguous position in a governmental system moving towards bureaucratic administration (a point I pursue in a later chapter). Their idiosyncratic intellectual and moral qualifications were central to their activities. High moral character, intelligence, diligence, public spirit, and a concern for social improvement – laden terms all – were personal qualities sought of superintendents by the central authority: attributes members of local oligarchies had arrogated to themselves. But educational administration was tending towards rational bureaucratic organization, calling into question an earlier oligarchic cultural, moral, and economic dominance. Class power in the developing state was being transformed into bureaucratic administration. In practical terms, inspectors had a great deal of discretion at first and were able to make and enforce educational determinations. The central office, following policy interests outlined in legislation and other documents, but often without clear plans or instruments to translate policy into practice, reacted, haphazardly at first, to reduce the more blatantly autocratic activities of superintendents. District superintendents sometimes policed township superintendents in a like manner.

Could the teacher of the district school be a township superintendent of schools? wondered a resident from Hornby. If such were allowed, 'it would be useless to urge a complaint against such a Teacher, as he would be the person to whom the complaint must be made.' The Education Office noticed that such a posting was not prohibited under the School Act, but 'there is something anomalous in such appointments.'[25]

John Strachan was sent to investigate the claims of a teacher in Napanee that the township superintendent had withheld some of his pay and had given the money instead to the superintendent's own daughter.[26] In the Simcoe District, Henry Clifford for Oro found no schools in his township conducted according to the School Act and proposed to spend the school grant on books and supplies. The Vespra Township superintendent, John Chanter, reported that he had paid what he thought was 'a sufficient remuneration to the Teachers who taught.'

Township superintendents had no discretion in matters of paying teachers, the Education Office insisted. The grant was intended entirely for the teachers and superintendents could neither withhold part of it nor decide themselves what was sufficient payment for teachers. They were not 'to take the hard earned potatoe out of the Teacher's mouth and give it to the Farmer's sons who have bread to eat & to spare.'[27] William Williams, a teacher in Marmora Township, complained that 'Mr Campion thinks now being, Justice of peace, Councillor and Superintendent that he can do as he likes and give me what he thinks proper.' The Education Office again specified the proper mode of payment of the school monies.[28] George Barber, Toronto city superintendent, received a rebuke from the Education Office when it was reported he corrected his overpayment of monies to a teacher in one school district by underpaying his successor in the same district the following year.[29]

The district superintendents undertook their own ideological initiatives. John Wilson of the London District wrote and sent circulars to township superintendents (10 April 1844) and to trustees and teachers of common schools (1 and 4 June 1844), instructing them as to how they should act in educational matters. Wilson described in great detail what he personally considered to be desirable schoolhouse architecture, sound curriculum, teaching methods, and so forth.[30]

At the same time, the limits of the office of district superintendent were being tested. Patrick Thornton's attempts to refuse recognition of a Catholic separate school on the grounds that 'sectarianism' motivated its supporters more 'than a love of education' were opposed by the Education Office.[31] Colin Gregor told a

Protestant teacher working in a Catholic school not to teach the catechism, despite the insistence of the local priest, 'in order to prevent the imputation of partiality.' But Robert Murray claimed 'the law gives no power to the District or Chief Supt. to interfere in the matter' and insisted that Gregor had no authority over the books used in the schools.[32] Others who complained against Gregor's certification of an illiterate teacher were told that the trustees were at fault for hiring such a person, and 'the people have the power to remedy the evil of which you complain, once a year, by the removal of such officers.'[33] The Education Office defended the fact of bureaucratic authority, while attempting to regulate its exercise.

District superintendents supervised cities and towns under the act of 1843 and stood in the same position to city and town superintendents as they did to township superintendents. Close relations often prevailed between the two kinds of officials: both the Eastern superintendent, Samuel Hart, and the Cornwall superintendent, Solomon Chesley, were wardens of the Anglican church, for example. But the potential for conflict was real. In Toronto, the city superintendent was George Barber, a Tory, former treasurer of Upper Canada College, proprietor of the *Herald* newspaper, as well as an active cricketeer. The Home District superintendent was the Reformer Hamilton Hunter, a former student of Francis Hincks's father and for a time editor of Hincks's *Examiner*. Conflict between these two was frequent, with Hunter refusing to recognize certificates granted by Barber and certifying people Barber had disqualified. A similar situation existed in Belleville, where the moderate Reformer William Hutton confronted George Benjamin as town superintendent, a Tory rival. The School Act did not come into effect in that town in 1844.[34]

Under the Act of 1846

With the abolition of the township superintendents, the entire work of examining, licensing, and paying teachers, and most of the work of inspecting schools and composing annual reports, devolved upon the district superintendents. The act of 1846 was perceived in many districts to demand a full-time inspector. Its implementation was followed by salary increases for inspectors and by district by-laws specifying their duties. George Duck, Jr, in the Western District, resigned the office in 1846, feeling he would not have the time or energy to devote to it under the new act. Duck had been paid £50 in 1846, but the salary of Robert Reynolds, his successor, was £125. Reynolds attempted to perform only the clerical functions of the office, and Western Council was inundated with complaints from local school sections. Council perceived the utility of a full-time inspector and Duck, Jr, was rehired, with much controversy and a lower salary, in 1848.[35]

Ryerson himself urged councils to hire full-time superintendents in his circular to wardens of districts, issued in October 1846:

The importance of this office can hardly be overrated. It requires not only a man of rare qualities and qualifications – a man of sound judgment whose heart is penetrated with the benevolent work of training up a youthful generation and who is thoroughly acquainted with the nature and best methods of that training; – but it requires the entire time and energies of such a man ... The excellent system of elementary instruction in Holland derives its unsurpassed efficiency from its local superintendence and inspection ... on this point, the greatest economy has been found in the greatest efficiency of the office.[36]

Yet the amount of work for full-time inspectors was very large, even in the smaller districts. In the most populous, it was overwhelming. Patrick Thornton claimed he worked twelve-hour days, spent four nights a week away from home, and travelled 3,000 miles a year. Thornton's district contained 178 schools in 1847.[37]

In the Home District superintended by Hamilton Hunter, there remained 300 schools even after the act of 1846 removed those in Toronto. When the 1846 legislation was still in draft, Hunter complained about the labour it would entail. 'In such an extensive District as this,' he wrote, 'I am afraid no one man can perform it. He cannot be in his office to pay Teachers and visiting schools at the same time.' Hunter protested the form of reporting proposed by the Education Office. The operation of separating the funds in each school section derived from the school grant from those derived from the local tax demanded '736 calculations,' and 'any person who has an idea of the sort of materials that will be furnished by the Trustees from which to make a Report and the difficulty of putting them into some respectable shape would guard against imposing any unnecessary labour upon the Supt.'[38] Two years later, Home District Council's Education Committee complained of 'no supervision whatsoever having taken place in many parts of the district during the last two years.' The committee recommended a by-law stating 'certain fixed times during the whole year in which [the superintendent] will be absent in visiting the Common Schools in the country, or be in the City of Toronto, in his office, to attend to his stationary duties.'[39] The heavy demands of the office limited the capacity of its occupants to visit schools regularly and repeatedly.

The Education Office continued to limit the exercise and the appearance of arbitrary or excessive authority on the part of the inspectors and to push for an administrative style that would contain educational conflicts. 'Give intimation to the trustees ... in *writing*,' Ryerson instructed Colin Gregor with respect to his decisions, 'for what is stated verbally is not considered official.' 'In such cases where it is impossible for us to judge safely,' he wrote to Benjamin Hayter, 'I think it better to leave the parties to act upon their own responsibility. Trustees are a corporation, and it will not do for us to interfere except with great caution in what legally belongs to them.' In a later communication to Hayter, Ryerson supported his suspension of a teacher's certificate on grounds of immorality, but added, 'it would be better for you in cases of a charge as to unfaithfulness, immorality, &c, against a Teacher, to give him an opportunity to speak for himself, before you decide officially – however well satisfied you may be in your own mind as to the respectability of the parties and the justness of the complaints. It leaves the guilty man without the shadow of plea or excuse or complaint.' Ryerson did not oppose the substance of Hayter's judgment or question his capacity to judge; his suggestion of a standardized procedure was a method of rendering such judgments effective and defensible, of formalizing and making them 'efficient.'[40]

The Education Office objected to inspectors who examined teachers only when they presented themselves to be paid, instead of while they were actually teaching. The office opposed teachers who hired substitutes and instructed superintendents not to pay school monies to any but teachers themselves.[41]

In January 1847, Hamilton Hunter set aside a trustee election in section 1 of York Township, on the grounds that the chairman of the school meeting had exercised favouritism, and called for a new election. The trustees complained to Ryerson, who secured the solicitor general's opinion that Hunter had exceeded his authority. This was a serious matter, Ryerson warned Hunter, because 'in the exercise of a newly conferred power great caution is necessary, especially in the highest exercise of it.' Setting aside a trustee election was like setting aside the election of a member of Parliament, and if party spirit was not to be allowed to pervade school matters, all trustee elections should be final. Ryerson again stated his belief that practical experience in local government would overcome electoral corruption. 'Experience and increasing intelligence are, in my opinion, a better remedy for their irregularities than any sort of encouragement to a litigious and party spirit by *public meeting investigations* and adjudications.'[42] Administration should be immune to public interference, and officials should have faith in its educative capacity.

Superintendents and School Visitors

Many of the superintendents worked to limit or circumvent the force of the school-visitors clause in the act of 1846. Even Dexter D'Everardo, Ryerson's staunch ally, expressed concern about visitors and wondered how he was to know who had granted certificates to whom. Ryerson responded that 'the number of Certificates given by School Visitors in your District must become known to you by your own visits,' and added that he hoped 'ere long to see the giving of certificates of qualification by Visitors discontinued. This provision of the act was intended to be temporary – to smooth the transition from the Township to the District system.'[43]

Colin Gregor in the Ottawa District was engaged in disputes with school visitors shortly after the act of 1846 came into effect. In April 1847, he sought advice from Ryerson with respect to his powers of annulling certificates granted by them. The Education Office had specified a minimum standard for the certification of teachers, and Gregor was told to lower it only in cases where parents were extremely poor. The books of forms and regulations printed by the Education Office contained advice both as to the granting and annulling of teachers' certificates.[44]

The trustees of school section 9 in West Hawkesbury complained that Gregor had annulled the certificate granted to their teacher by the Anglican minister, Mr Tramayne, and by Thomas Higginson, a justice of the peace and soon Gregor's successor as inspector of schools. The trustees claimed that Gregor 'came to the School house on a Saturday in April last, for the purpose of creating a special visit without giving any previous notice and for the express purpose of annulling the Teacher's certificate.' The trustees complained this was done 'without ever Seeing that person as there was no School that day and Setting at defence [sic] the certificate given by Two of the most respectable gentlemen of the County.' Thomas Higginson, who had replaced Gregor as inspector by the time these complaints reached the Education Office, supported this account and claimed that a dispute between Scottish and Irish settlers was involved. Ryerson, however, supported Gregor's actions, pointing out that the teacher could not meet the lowest standard of qualification and appeared to have refused to meet the district superintendent to be examined. Higginson was instructed not to pay this teacher.[45]

Again in June 1849, William Elliott in the London District declared a person morally unfit to teach and denied him a teaching certificate. This person got one anyway from two school visitors and was hired by a set of school trustees. When the trustees discovered his character, they attempted to fire him, but the teacher refused to leave the school and demanded to be paid. Ryerson instructed Elliott to annul this person's certificate, to refuse to pay him, and to keep his share of the school monies for some other qualified teacher.[46] There were undoubtedly similar cases.

Some superintendents worked simply to nullify the visitors clauses. In the Johnstown District, Richey Waugh maintained to Council as early as February 1847 that the teachers certified by school visitors were generally incapable of teaching such things as grammar and algebra. Council resolved to investigate and published a lengthy list of items of information to be sought by the district superintendent in his school inspections, including a detailed description of the schoolhouse and its appendages, the subjects taught and method of instruction, and the teacher's salary. Council was especially concerned to identify those schools where 'Grammar and the higher Branches of Arithmetic' were, or could be, offered. This enquiry (which Waugh himself conducted) supported Waugh's views. In February 1848, Council accepted his report that most problems in the schools could be resolved by hiring qualified teachers and moved that school visitors should no longer certify teachers, but rather refer candidates to the district superintendent.[47]

In the Gore District, Patrick Thornton, in his double capacity as president of the Dumfries Teachers' Association and district superintendent of education, secured a resolution from the teachers that only his certificates should be considered valid in the district. A bitter and very protracted dispute raged between Thornton and Ryerson in 1848 and 1849 over Thornton's refusal to pay the widowed Mrs Merry, a woman with a large family who took over her husband's school at his death, on the strength of a school visitor's certificate. Ryerson paid this woman out of his own pocket while he attempted to make Thornton pay her, and appeals and counter-appeals were directed to the governor general. In the midst of his battle to retain his own position as chief superintendent, Ryerson earned a stiff rebuke from the ministry, 'that the discretionary power of the District Superintendent, ought, as a general rule, to be left unfettered.' Nothing in this case warranted Ryerson's interference. In the meantime, however, Ryerson had convinced Gore Council to order Thornton to pay Mrs Merry.[48]

Thomas Donnelly of the Prince Edward District reported to Council in May 1848 that the chief superintendent had instructed him 'not to grant certificates to common school teachers not possessed of the amount of qualifications laid down in the Book of Forms and Regulations.' This meant that such teachers – 'by far the greatest number' in the district – had to be examined and certified by school visitors. Donnelly argued this procedure did not work well, did not give 'satisfaction to the people, or add to the efficiency of the schools.' He stated his strong opposition to it and added 'the tenth clause of the 17th Section of the School Act makes it my duty to "act in accordance with the directions of the Superintendent of Schools," but if sustained by you I should be strongly disposed to depart from his directions in this particular.' A committee of Council recommended Donnelly proceed as he had in the past, and Council as a whole agreed.[49]

In effect, like Thornton and Waugh, Donnelly arrogated the powers of school visitors to himself and, in this way, these inspectors worked to increase their own jurisdiction and, indirectly, that of the educational bureaucracy. At times there was an explicit conflict between the central and local authorities in these matters, out of which came pressure to specify more clearly the duties and to regulate the autonomy of inspectors.

The District Model Schools

Under both the acts of 1843 and 1846, district councils could tax to support model schools and, for a minimum levy, could receive matching funds from the central government. The schools were to be supervised by the district superintendent, although, after the establishment of the Toronto Normal School in 1847, they were to be regulated by the master of that institution as well. Several superintendents were actively involved in the organization and management of such schools, although exactly how many came into existence and with what influence on educational development remains obscure.

Fragmentary information about model schools in four districts survives. It is not clear if there were others, and this topic has been largely ignored in the literature. The early operations of such schools convinced Ryerson that a normal school 'must be the precursor of *good* Model Schools,' and little place was accorded them in his educational legislation of 1850. These institutions were revived in the late 1870s and, from then until well into the twentieth century, provided the bulk of initial teacher training.

In the Dalhousie District, Hamnett Pinhey organized a model school at Bytown, engaging a teacher named James FitzWilliam Briedon Healy as master. Healy was trained in the Dublin Model School of the Kildare Place Society. It was said that £110 was levied by the district council in 1844 for this institution, and it received a government grant of £37.7.6 in 1845. Pinhey used the institution as a venue for his examinations of teachers, but it operated sporadically, and its teacher sought alternative employment in 1846.[50]

The London District Model School opened at St Thomas in February 1845, and Council levied a tax of £80 towards its support. The matching grant from Parliament was slightly more than £32 for 1845. This school was a source of conflict in the district and of debate between the district superintendent, William Elliott, and the district council. As early as June 1845, a dispute between the model-school master and supporters of a local common school demanded Elliott's intervention. To end competition between the two schools, Elliott joined them together. The model-school master, Duncan Campbell, was paid the enormous salary of £160 a year, with £100 for his assistant, a Mr Holt. Elliott was convinced, however, that Campbell was incompetent, despite his boasts of extensive experience in a (apparently fictitious) model school in Cobourg.

By mid-August, Elliott had decided that Campbell should be fired and notified him of his dismissal. But Campbell refused to leave or to accept the portion of his salary offered him and insisted upon teaching the remainder of the year. When Elliott arrived at the school on 19 September, he found the students outside and Campbell 'walking backwards w/ his hands behind his back' and refusing to give up the key of the school as 'it was not time.' Elliott had a letter of dismissal addressed to Campbell from the trustees of the school, but Campbell refused to read it. He eventually surrendered the key when the trustees themselves arrived, but then entered the school and refused to leave. Finally, Elliott noted, 'Dr. [?] opened the sch. door and [told] Mr. Campbell to walk out. This he wd not do so the Dr. took him by the collar & walked him out & this is the close of Mr C's rule in the Model Sch.' Campbell's assistant was hired as master, with a Mr Nichol as his assistant. Part of what was at issue in this dispute was a conflict between residents of American and English origin for control of the school, and Elliott's national preferences were clear: 'The putting of an old country man of experience like M. Nichol on the Sch wd. show that I was determined not to yield [to] the American feeling which seems to prevail to a surprising extent.'

But the matter did not end here. Council requested Elliott to appear before it to address questions surrounding the model school, and he initially refused. He agreed to answer questions in writing, but felt that to appear in person would create a precedent for Council members to interrogate him about other school matters. He did appear, none the less, before a council committee formed to enquire into the school in November 1845 and there expressed his view that the institution had been opened prematurely. Elliott elaborated these views in a letter to Acting Assistant Superintendent McNab, commenting that model schools were needed to improve teachers, but the London District Model School did not work because its master was incompetent, and it was difficult to find a qualified replacement. It was not possible to 'bring one out' from England, unless that person knew the Canadian curriculum. Elliott wondered if the normal school was in operation and revealed his temptation to advise the discontinuation of the model school. While McNab replied that model schools were needed, nothing more was heard of a London District model school until June 1846. Campbell, the displaced master, brought a suit against Elliott for wrongful dismissal. A jury decided in Campbell's favour to the amount of £132.15.[51]

Matters were different in the Midland District inspected by John Strachan, himself a university-educated teacher. There are mentions of three model schools in this district, at Kingston, Newburgh, and Camden East. The Newburgh Model School was awarded £25 in 1850 at least, the Camden East Model School £20 in 1847, and Midland Council voted money for a Kingston model school in February 1846.[52]

The Newburgh Model School, the most important of the three, was conducted either in or in close association with the Newburgh Academy, a private secondary school of some repute whose principal in the middle 1840s was the Methodist Dr Nelles, later principal of Victoria College. The academy was founded about 1841, and the model school at Strachan's suggestion early in 1844. Strachan advertised his visits to the model school in the district press and urged 'Teachers not sufficiently qualified for the duties of their situation, to attend the *Model School* of Newburgh for a few months.' He informed Council in his annual report that 'spending a few days in the most central schools and having a number of teachers present' was 'attended with beneficial effect.'

Strachan held progressive educational views and toured extensively in his district, suggesting improved methods to teachers and announcing these in the press. Teachers, he stressed, should treat students as intelligent beings and should use familiar objects to make them understand their lessons. This would make schooling pleasant to students and reduce the need for the rod, the regular use of which Strachan took as a sign of incapacity in a teacher. 'Two of the best teachers in the Midland District,' he wrote, 'who maintain first rate order in their schools, told me that they had sometimes been six months without using the rod; instead of flogging, they explain every thing their pupils are studying and by that means render them fond of study.' Strachan also urged trustees to hold regular quarterly examinations of the schools with parents.

This did not exhaust Strachan's activities, for he also organized less formal methods of teacher training. He sent a beginning teacher in 1845 to board with and to learn grammar from William A. Pringle, a teacher in Fredericksburgh whose school Strachan described as 'the best I have seen.' At least one other teacher was sent by Strachan to observe Pringle's school.[53]

In the Johnstown District, Richey Waugh attempted to organize a system of teacher training on the Irish Kildare Place Society model. There is no mention of contact between Waugh and members of an earlier Johnstown District Teachers' Association, whose vice-president, William Hynes, had preceded Waugh as inspector. Waugh found the district teachers a poor lot. In his first official correspondence with the Education Office, he claimed, 'there is a great number of very poor Teachers in this District and the Trustees appear to be unwilling to pay such Salaries as will reimburse competent Teachers.'[54]

Waugh established a district model school, which opened officially on 1 January 1846 (actually on 12 February) in the hamlet of Frankville in Kitley Township. The master was Johnston Neilson (1797–?), a visible and controversial teacher in this and the adjoining districts, assisted initially by William Carroll. Both of these men had been trained at the Kildare Place Society's school in Dublin. Neilson had begun teaching in 1813 and included a testimonial from T.D. Hincks, DD, among his credentials. These two proposed to train teachers in the society's monitorial school system, using the school books of the Irish National Board of Education. Free instruction was offered for those having taught or intending to teach, provided they had a recommendation from one of the district councillors.[55]

Administrative difficulties and public controversy surrounded the school from the outset. While Council passed a by-law in 1846 regulating the relations between the model school and the district superintendent, no assessment for the support of the school was levied until February 1847. Council neglected to appoint trustees for the school, leaving Neilson uncertified, and thus unpaid.[56]

Attacks on Waugh and the school soon appeared in the press. 'A Friend to Justice' complained that Waugh had earlier granted certificates to unqualified teachers on the grounds that the opening of the model school would improve the supply of good ones. But the school was open, and Waugh continued to certify unqualified teachers and, worse, to withhold certificates from qualified teachers who refused to attend the model school. Waugh was said to have given 'a certificate to an individual in a large and populous Division, who was not qualified to teach Geography, when at the same time it was required to be taught in the School.' He was guilty of 'impositions' on the district.

Johnston Neilson leaped to the defence of one 'of the friends of British Connexion and of Monarchy, as the County Superintendent is and ought to be,' only to earn the riposte that the model school was unpopular, that Neilson himself had only about a dozen pupils, some of whom spent their time studying Latin, and 'for what? for Common School Teachers? or for some other profession?' The model school was no model worth imitating. This critic claimed a normal school like that at Albany, New York, was what was needed for teacher training, not a model school where dead languages predominated.

The assistant master then defended Waugh, Neilson, and the school. The institution was 'based upon the national system of education adopted by the Kildare Place Society' and was the best of its kind anywhere. Carroll insisted he had 'been present upon more than one occasion when the District Superintendent held examinations of pupils for certificates, and although some had been attending the Model School for several months, and none less than two, yet they were rejected by him.' But a 'Friend to Justice' again replied that no one in the district knew what the Kildare Place system actually was, and Neilson only had four pupils. Later a 'Schoolmaster' wondered whether dead languages should be taught in a model school and whether 'Teachers addicted to intemperance will be permitted to instruct in Model Schools.' After this, the public debate around the school subsided.[57]

Waugh commented publicly on none of this. He sought the school's government subsidy in September 1846 and was urged by Ryerson to ensure the school delivered a good report because 'a *Model* School to which a grant was made last year proved a failure and was actually discontinued before the end of the year.'[58] The model school report for 1846 claimed that forty-three teachers had been trained between January and November and that 'the systematic course adopted in this School is Bell's.' As for the curriculum, 'Foreign Books, as far as practicable, have been excluded from the School. The Books of the Irish National Board of Education have been introduced, and, as far as they will supply the wants of the pupils, are altogether used.' The warden remarked that 'the popular clamour, which arose upon' the school's 'establishment is now hushed.' Neilson had been paid £87.17 as master.[59]

Waugh claimed in his annual report to Council that the school worked well and that model-school graduates received 'from 14 to 20 dollars a month which are maximum rates of wages in this District,' unlike most other teachers, who were hired only for so long as the school grant would support them.[60] As we have seen above, Waugh also succeeded in having Council oppose the certification powers of school visitors.

The adoption of the Kildare Place system reveals Waugh's low estimate of popular intelligence and capacity, but his model school was not successful. Johnston Neilson had lost the services of his assistant by May 1847, and it seems that the school itinerated with him, to Ryerson's surprise and dismay, until it was abandoned in October 1848. By this time, Ryerson had announced his intention to reduce the subsidies offered model schools in the future.[61] Waugh had obviously not been presenting Ryerson with a particularly accurate account of the Johnstown school. Still, it is significant, in light of Ryerson's institutionalization of much of the Irish system in Canada West after 1846, that some inspectors were working in a similar direction at the local level.

Several of the other superintendents attempted to provide teacher training on a more or less formal basis and agitated for a good system of local model schools, but the failure of model schooling in at least three of the four districts where it was attempted tended to discredit this dimension of district educational autonomy.

School Books

With rare exceptions, district superintendents advocated and promoted uniformity in the books used in common schools. The superintendents regarded the paucity of school books as an obstacle to educational improvement and favoured collective instruction over the kinds of individual tutelage that predominated in the schools. Unlike the township commissioners under the act of 1841, of whom the central office complained that they had left the teachers 'to name their own, or rather to teach such books as the Parents chose to send,' the district superintendents attempted to place ample supplies of what they considered good books in the schools.[62] They did this, at first, quite independently, with the means at their disposal and at a pace dictated by local circumstances and their own positions.

'The selection of Schools books being placed in the power of the Trustees, has been an impediment to my superintendence,' wrote Samuel Ardagh, 'as books published in the united states owing to their cheapness have been adopted, which are for many reasons totally unsuited to the British constitution.' 'The greatest evil under which we labor in our Common Schools in this [Victoria] district,' echoed William Hutton, 'is decidedly the want of a universal adoption of a uniform set of School Books.'[63]

With varying degrees of enthusiasm, the inspectors regarded the Irish National school books as the best series available. William Hutton waxed lyrical about the magic and beauty of these texts, while Newton Bosworth was prepared to support them if the texts of the British and Foreign School Society were not available. But this was an area in which inspectors were particularly active. Bosworth arranged for the importation of the British and Foreign School Society books for use in the Brock District.[64] Henry Clifford, while still Oro Township superintendent, and Benjamin Hayter in the Newcastle District, both devised elaborate plans for the supply of books to the schools.[65]

Most inspectors regarded the Irish series as deficient in grammar, history, and geography, and various plans were elaborated for dealing with these short-comings.[66] At least one superintendent had an interest in other books. Before the act of 1846 vested control over books in the General Board of Education and sought the generalization of the Irish texts, Patrick Thornton set out to produce his own series of books, beginning with a geography text. Thornton's 'Canadian Progressive System' was in circulation at least in the Gore and Home districts in the 1840s. Indeed, Hamilton Hunter remarked that the schools in Whitby were far more advanced than others in the Home District in 1845, in part because of 'the general introduction and use of Thornton's Series of Common School Books.'[67]

With the formation of the General Board in 1846, the secretary of the Gore District Teachers' Association recommended the general adoption of Thornton's books. But a Hamilton teacher complained that most teachers actually wanted the Irish series, adding 'as many of the teachers in this county were trained at the Model School, Dublin, a set of the reading and spelling Tablets could be used by them to greater advantage.' At a meeting of teachers held by Thornton, 'one of the principal objects the Superintendent had in view, was to get the teachers to use a uniform set of books, and those to be *his own* publications'! Thornton reputedly made 'unjust and envious remarks' about the Irish readers.[68]

Thornton himself enquired of Ryerson late in 1846 if it were true that the General Board intended to publish the Irish books, commenting 'if so, it is of no use for me to strive further to improve the Canadian Progressive System, though it is now nearly completed so far as the Reading books and the Geographical Text-book.' And while Ryerson pointed out that government policy did not exclude any Canadian books from the schools, the Irish books had 'been prepared, not by a private individual, or as a private speculation, but by a *Board* consisting of both Protestants and Catholics – *have* stood the test of the severest scrutiny – are the most popular and the most extensively used and the cheapest series of School Books in the British Empire.'[69]

Some of the opposition to the act of 1846 surrounded the 'arbitrary' textbook clauses, opposition that the inspectors were left to manage in many cases. While most of them supported central control over and uniformity in school books, several advised the central office against a complete ban on foreign books. William Elliott pointed out that many foreign books in his district 'seem to have been introduced because British or Provincial works of the same kind were not to be had at anything like the same price.' 'Perhaps,' Elliott suggested, 'it would be better not to preclude the use of these books abruptly.' Kirkham's *Grammar* and geographies by Mitchell and Olney were extensively used in the London District, although Elliott reported having taken 'a good deal of pains to have the reading books published by the Irish Board of Education introduced' and having 'the satisfaction of seeing them fast superseding the *English Reader* which was universally in use – & which was extremely ill adapted for interrogation in nine Schools out of ten.'[70] An American geography and Kirkham's grammar book were both included on the list of authorized texts.

Similar views were expressed by Dexter D'Everardo. D'Everardo took the trouble to discuss Ryerson's textbook proposals with 'several gentlemen' who were 'deeply interested in educational matters' and reported that 'they were entirely approved of.'[71] Ryerson himself worked to justify the policy to other superintendents, although, on the matter of eliminating spelling books, he was intransigent.[72]

It is improbable that most inspectors were able, even if willing, rigidly to enforce official opposition to American textbooks. The editor of the Brockville *Recorder*, reflecting on the 'Beauties of the School Act' of 1846, paid particular attention to what he saw as the General Board's objectionable powers over books. The American Cobb's *Speller* and Olney's *Geography* had been disallowed, while everyone knew they were the best books available. But the superintendent of schools allowed these books to continue in use in the district, because, if he followed his instructions to the letter, all the schools would be forced to close. 'That class of officers which are chosen by our District Councils,' the editor observed, 'will be very careful how they obey the political Parson to the prejudice of their own interests.'[73]

Still, most of the superintendents worked to generalize the Irish texts. Even the lax John Bignall persuaded Huron Council to appropriate £100 for the purchase of Irish books. His successor, Charles Fletcher, ordered four sets of object lessons from the Education Office and proposed to do all he could 'to draw the attention of Trustees and Teachers to the system.'[74]

In the same vein, superintendents were active in attempting to increase the circulation of the *Journal of Education*, published by the Education Office from 1848 but made the official medium for government educational communications only after 1850. As early as November 1845, before the Education Office acted in this matter, Hamilton Hunter had sent what he called a 'Prospectus of my Contemplated School Journal' at least to Jacob Keefer and had attempted to interest acting Assistant Superintendent McNab.[75] When the official *Journal of Education* did appear, most superintendents subscribed themselves and attempted to secure subscriptions from others.[76]

Social Harmony

Many of the inspectors worked to eliminate local conflicts over schooling. Most of them attempted to limit the formation of separate schools for Catholics and Protestants, aided by official policy, which sought to fund separate schools at a lower rate.[77] They worked to 'calm down' disputes, to replace incompetent teachers with ones they considered better, and to ensure an equitable distribution of school monies. They surveyed the national origins and political loyalties of teachers, and some proposed teachers' associations for mutual improvement. They attempted to launch circulating libraries.[78] Most of them perceived the domain of schooling as one in which all citizens would be equally subject to or have equal access to possibilities of 'improvement.' Many of them supported the claims of women teachers.[79]

Only fragmentary information survives about the superintendents' attitudes on issues of racial equality. Jacob Keefer was titillated by, but not openly condemnatory of, reports of a white woman living as a wife to a 'coloured' man and having 'yellow' children.[80] William Clarke was active in the French and Indian missions and opposed attempts by school trustees to exclude a black child from one of the Simcoe common schools. His son was a militant anti-slavery campaigner.[81] The position of the Education Office under Ryerson was at best ambivalent in these matters. Ryerson at times supported the right of Indian and black children to attend common schools, but he believed that Indians and workers generally were far less reasonable beings than members of the middle classes and, albeit reluctantly, introduced separate-schooling clauses for 'coloured' residents into legislation in 1848.[82]

Several inspectors attempted to defend the rights of Indian and black children and, except under the tenure of Alexander McNab, were supported by the Education Office. Robert Murray sustained Patrick Thornton against a township superintendent who refused to pay a teacher until the teacher expelled Indian children from his school in Onondaga Township. But Alexander McNab, Ryerson's deputy in 1844–5, promoted separate schooling for black children.

Patrick Thornton sought direction from McNab in the case of 'a coloured man, whose boy, though active and cleanly, and I may add well behaved, has been denied equal privileges with the white children in the same school. The trustees allow him to attend school, but they peremptorily forbid the teacher to let him either sit or read with the other children. He is ordered to sit in a corner by himself and also to read by himself – by this means he is quite discouraged.' McNab argued that trustees would lose the school fund if they excluded any person from access to the school, but instructed Thornton, 'in regard to any arrangement that may be made by the Trustees, relating to coloured children, as to where they shall sit in the Schoolhouse; or when they shall recite their lessons; it will not be necessary to interfere.' The act of 1843, it should be recalled, did give the chief superintendent authority to propose regulations for the internal organization of schools.[83]

McNab went farther than this in communications with John Cowan, the clerk of the Western District. Cowan complained that schools in his district were being broken up because whites would not allow their children to attend schools with black children and because many township superintendents refused to pay teachers who excluded black children. Cowan reported that the district council had attempted to address the problem by creating separate school sections for black ratepayers, 'but, learning that a certain clause of the Act went to forbid *any class* of children from being denied admission to Common Schools – and probably urged on by designing people, hostile to the present act,' black ratepayers would 'not avail themselves of the means put in their power, but insist upon mixing with the Whites.' Cowan wondered if the council could exclude blacks from white schools.

McNab read the cause of this dispute as black ratepayers' 'being determined to force their children into the same schools attended by those of the' whites. If the council had set off separate school sections for blacks, Cowan had 'the remedy of the evil complained of, it appears to me, in your own hands, for Trustees and Teachers are not obliged to receive children, from another School district.'[84] George Duck, Jr, whose father was a leading figure in the Western District Council, called for separate schools in Chatham for black children in his annual report for 1845, and Council itself sent a stream of racist petitions to Parliament.[85]

For his part, Ryerson regarded the exclusion of black children from the common schools as 'at variance with the principles and spirit of British Institutions which deprive no human being of any benefit which they can confer on account of the color of the skin.' But while he instructed the Western District superintendent to investigate cases of exclusion, and to refuse to pay school monies to those involved, Ryerson concluded that 'prejudice – especially the prejudice of caste, however unchristian and absurd – is stronger than law itself.' Ryerson's draft 1848 and 1849 legislation and the School Act of 1850 included separate schools for blacks, and inspectors were encouraged to fund 'coloured schools' out of discretionary school funds.[86]

A Regulated Autonomy

Although their contribution to the establishment of state schooling has received relatively little attention, district inspectors played a significant role both directly and indirectly. The school acts gave them a political position and a set of instruments from and with which to work in a relatively autonomous manner in the pursuit of 'improvement.' They worked to put in place educational practices in the colony, modelled most frequently upon state schooling in Ireland and New York. At the same time, much of the social mapping necessary to the successful regulation of state schooling by a central authority was performed by them. It was these officials who located schools; investigated them; scrutinized teachers, texts, and pedagogies. They identified educational 'problems' and attempted solutions. And even where their experiments at educational improvement failed, these proved instructive to the educational authority. Their efforts led to clearer definitions of bureaucratic jurisdictions, of the administrative hierarchy, and of proper procedure.

But the educational autonomy enjoyed by superintendents was under attack virtually from the outset. District councils attempted to specify their duties, the central office to lend a regular form to their activities. Chapter 7 investigates the experience of inspectors in three colonial districts.

7   The Local State and Educational Inspection: Three Cases

The creation of representative local state agencies in Canada West under the District Councils Act of 1841 changed the dynamics of political rule in the colony, despite continuity in the personnel of local 'compacts' and district councils. The councils tended to engage a wider spectrum of men of property in political governance, rather than to transform radically its class, ethnic, or gendered character. But the very existence of local state structures created the potential for new differences of interest between centre and locality. In educational administration, such conflicts shaped the experience and activities of inspectors. The central authority attempted to use local government as a subordinate management agency, while local government agencies pushed for effective control over many aspects of educational policy. Superintendents often played key roles in the fate of central educational initiatives in the locality. These points are illustrated through an examination of educational superintendence in the Bathurst, Brock, and Dalhousie districts. In the Bathurst District, Council was strongly opposed to central control over public education. In the Dalhousie District, Council was opposed to public education itself. The Brock District Council presents a middle point between these extremes.

The Bathurst District

Three men held the office of district superintendent of education in the Bathurst District, although the first, Francis Allan (1793–1844), died before he could act. Allan was the Perth postmaster, the Crown Lands agent, a district auditor, grand-juryman, and, in 1844, a trustee for one of the Perth schools. He was active in attempting to get a model school for the village. His son James, who succeeded him as postmaster, was Perth's main bookseller and a contributing member of the Perth Library and Mechanics' Institute.[1]

Allan was closely connected with Murdoch McDonnell, an author of the Cameron School Act of 1849, who, in 1844, was already proposing major alterations to the school laws. While members of the Drummond Township school commission, Allan and McDonnell formulated a plan to unite the Perth village school sections and to hire a classical scholar. After Allan's death, McDonnell, now superintendent for Perth, went ahead with the plan, to the anger of a teacher whose common school was threatened with extinction by it.[2]

The appointment of a school inspector was hotly debated in Bathurst. At the 14 February 1844 meeting of the district council, several candidates were rejected in turn: J.G. Malloch, who was about to be appointed district judge; Murdoch McDonnell; Rev. Robert Dick of Lanark; Robert Bell, the Reformer and councillor, who refused to act; Robert Lee who lost on a vote; and William Sommerville, a schoolmaster, whose name was put forward but later withdrawn. These were all respectable men of standing in the district. The next day, the councillors settled on Allan, but he died within the week.[3]

The prospect of a further appointment exercised 'a McNab Settler' who argued that the superintendent should be a long-time resident, well familiar with the district, someone whose 'interest should be known to be identified with the people's. In every sense, he should be so much *one with the people* that his services will not be those of a hireling, but of a man superintending a business in which he will have as great a stake as anyone who will be interested in it.' 'Settler' insisted that the inspector should be a full-time official.

There were again four candidates for the position: Murdoch McDonnell, Rev. Robert Dick, Mr McIntyre, and Captain Douglass. McDonnell was identified as a man with considerable expertise in educational matters, someone whose educational works had been cited and praised by J. Orville Taylor. However, 'Settler' felt that McDonnell's business interests in Perth would overly preoccupy him. Captain Douglass and McIntyre were dismissed as place seekers, and this observer urged the support of Robert Dick, who he claimed had helped implement the New York School Law and hence was eminently qualified.[4]

This provoked a riposte from 'Ex Domini,' who argued that all the candidates were undoubtedly motivated by a desire for high pay and who defended Captain Douglass as one whose 'conduct and character ... are above a newspaper eulogy.'[5] The council minutes for the following session have been lost, but at it Rev. Alexander Mann (1800–84) of Pakenham was appointed Bathurst District superintendent of schools, an office he held until April 1847.

Mann was born in Tarland, Aberdeenshire, and educated at King's College, Aberdeen. He worked for a time as a tutor to Lord Aberdeen's family, was ordained in 1840 and appointed by the Colonial Committee as a missionary in the Bathurst District. He was located in the village of Pakenham, which had been established and was dominated economically and politically by Andrew Dickson.[6] Both Mann's church and presbytery were built at Dickson's expense. From Pakenham, Mann ministered to the townships of Fitzroy, Torbolton, Pakenham, McNab, and Horton. He was married to a woman fifteen years his junior and supporting a young family of four.

Mann was a Pakenham common-school commissioner in 1842–3, chairing the commission when attempts were made to secure a grammar school for the village. He agitated for the compulsory use of the Scriptures as a school class book.[7] Active also in the temperance movement, Mann was supported financially by the Clergy Reserves fund and by his parishoners. He was granted an honorary DD from Queen's University in 1876.[8]

According to his own account, Mann was appointed inspector without applying. Council offered him £50 a year and demanded £4,000 in sureties. Mann took the appointment, likely in response to urging from his patron, Andrew Dickson, but couldn't be confirmed until the council meeting in September. Thus he was to get only £12.10 for 1844, which tempted him to resign. Assistant Superintendent Murray pleaded with him to remain, for his resignation 'would be attended with very serious consequences to the poor teachers.' Murray wrote to the district council, urging the payment of Mann's salary in full.[9]

In 1844–5, Mann attempted to use the monies set aside for schools in new townships to subsidize a teacher-training project. 'Finding comparatively few Teachers in this District possessed of knowledge commensurate with the requirements of the School Act,' he wrote to McNab, 'desiring to advance by every means in my power the interests of education in this section of the Province, and seeing no immediate prospect of the organization of a Training School, I have, on my own responsibility, employed a gentleman of distinguished ability, to instruct those Schoolmasters who may be solicitous of improvement.' But because the fees charged were high, the enterprise was faltering, so Mann sought to fund it out of the school monies. Assistant Superintendent McNab refused to allow this.[10]

In his report for 1845, Mann announced the failure of his scheme from the fact that his salary was too low to do it without aid. Normal schools were desperately needed, Mann insisted, and he revealed that he had given 'no regular certificate' to any teacher in the district. This is hardly likely to have endeared him to the teachers, some of whom were very well educated, but Mann insisted that education was neglected and 'the people ... require to have their attention specially directed to its paramount consequence.'[11]

Mann's educational activities were clearly oriented towards the central Education Office. As far was one can see, he made no effort to interest Council in his plans for a training school, despite the presence on Council and in Perth village of several important educational activists. His relations with Bathurst Council became exceptionally bitter. Opposition to central control of education was at least as strong in the Bathurst District as anywhere else in the colony. An editorial greeted the publication of the School Act of 1846 with a denunciation of Ryerson's powers 'to practice the Prussian system of "paternal" despotism' and the *Bathurst Courier* reprinted the critical opinions of the Toronto press as well.[12] In a debate between the central and local authorities, Mann was seen to side with the former and was pressured to resign.

The provincial government redrew the boundaries of the Bathurst District in 1846 in a gerrymander. In consequence, Council could not achieve a quorum until new township elections were held, and hence the school tax for 1845 could not be levied. The schools had been open, none the less, and trustees had engaged teachers in the expectation of the school grant. When this was not forthcoming, many trustees advanced teachers' salaries out of their own pockets.

Under the School Act of 1843, the provincial grant could not be paid to districts that had not matched it by taxation and could be paid, in any case, only to legally qualified teachers. Technically, even trustees who had paid teachers themselves could not be reimbursed directly out of the school fund, even though, in many school sections, local voluntary contributions equalled or surpassed a school tax.

Council attempted to remedy this situation by passing a by-law to enable the district to receive the provincial school monies before or without levying a school tax. The district superintendent was instructed to apply for the provincial school monies and to pay these in the manner and to the persons Council would direct.

One councillor warned that, if Council did not levy a tax at once for 1845, it would face the prospect of a double tax in 1846 or the forfeiture of the school grant. But because voluntary contributions had supported the schools for 1845, Council's education committee opposed a tax. Alexander Mann was ordered to pay the school monies to township superintendents and was offered Council's protection for so doing.

Although it was claimed that Mann had agreed to this, he refused to pay the school monies without consulting Ryerson. Ryerson declared any such proceeding illegal and threatened the district with the loss of all future school money. Vicious denunciations of Ryerson followed in the press.[13]

Council petitioned Parliament for the payment of the school monies without the levying of a rate, but without success. Malcolm Cameron then secured an act of Parliament allowing payment of the 1845 monies under the direction of Council, provided that a rate in 1846 be levied to raise an amount equivalent to that held by Mann. But this act lapsed before the rate was collected, and a second act was required before the monies were finally paid. Ryerson, Mann, and the School Act of 1846 were seen to have disrupted common schooling in the Bathurst District.[14]

Mann was pressured to resign, and his performance was attacked even as he was replaced. Mann claimed he could not have broken the law simply on the order of Council and maintained that he had always said he would consult Ryerson before acting. This led to a particularly angry reply from Murdoch McDonnell who revealed that Mann had never even inspected the schools. 'It seems,' wrote McDonnell,

that no clergyman deriving an income from the Clergy Reserve[s] Fund, can derive any portion of his living for services not performed by him in the clerical capacity; and that the late superintendent was advised, that he must either relinquish his salary for being superintendent, or his right to receive a share of the Reserve[s] Fund. It further appears that the Rev. gentleman did not lay before the District Council, when in sessions, the instructions prohibitory of his continuing to be superintendent; and that in consequence of the ignorance of that body relative to the existence of clergymen's acting in any other than a clerical capacity, it appointed Mr. Padfield, Episcopal minister of Beck-with, to the office of superintendent.

McDonnell hoped that Padfield would act, at least for the time being, and urged trustees to send their reports for 1846, which Mann refused to receive, to the district clerk.

In fact, the prohibition of which McDonnell wrote applied only to Presbyterians, not to Episcopalians like Padfield. For Mann, a share in the Reserves fund was far more lucrative than the school superintendency. The fund paid him more than £153 in 1846 and more than £173 in 1847, both sums in addition to support from his congregation.[15]

Council's education committee expressed its 'unqualified disapprobation' of Mann's conduct in this matter, especially in not paying monies after he had 'pledged himself' to do so. The committee noted with chagrin that the school monies had been paid for both 1845 and 1846 in the neighbouring Dalhousie District without the levying of any tax.[16]

Mann defended himself. 'At the former meeting of the Council,' he wrote, 'I gave intimation by letter, that I ought not to be put in nomination for the office of District Superintendent, as I could not accept of the appointment.' He had 'never concealed' the reason for this, and 'only agreed to officiate until the termination of 1846,' that is, before the school reports were due. Still, he insisted, 'I in no case refused to receive reports which were prepared and transmitted according to proper form.' Accusations of duplicity against him were entirely false, Mann said. He had never received an order from Council to pay monies while Council was in session, and if he had seen the order he would have refused to agree to it. Council had consistently refused his advice in the matter. Later, Mann again insisted he had only ever agreed to obey Council after consulting

Ryerson, and the only trustee reports he had refused to accept were those improperly submitted.

Judge Murdoch joined in the attacks on Mann in April 1847. Murdoch explained that, because the township superintendents created by the act of 1843 ceased to exist on 1 January 1847, Ryerson had sent a circular to Mann telling him to collect township school reports in December 1846. But Mann neglected to do so, and now the township superintendents were threatened by Ryerson with legal penalty. Mann replied that the circular sent to him by Ryerson was private and there had been no need to publish its contents for the information of township superintendents. However, he had published Ryerson's letter praising his school report for 1846.[17]

The matter of the 1845 school monies was not resolved until October 1847, when Council finally passed a by-law to raise a school tax for 1845 and arranged with Mann and James Padfield for the payment of the money to teachers.[18] But ill-feeling continued to run high. The whole affair was rehashed by the education committee in October 1847, Mann was again denounced for having consulted Ryerson, and a committee was struck to draw up suggestions for the revision of the School Act to be presented to Ryerson at his impending visit to Perth.[19]

Mann's successor was James Padfield (1802–79), a man whose early antecedents are unclear. An Englishman who was appointed master of the Johnstown District Grammar School in 1827, Padfield moved to Upper Canada College in 1829, working until 1833 as master of the preparatory school. He earned more than £150 at the college, which was 'considerably below his colleagues in the senior forms.' However, Padfield's qualifications were said to be 'not on a par with those of his senior-form counterparts.' Class sizes in the lower school were quite large, and Padfield taught English reading, writing and spelling, arithmetic, and the first elements of Latin.[20] Padfield joined the Church of England in 1831 and, under Archdeacon John Strachan's direction, worked as a lay reader and catechist. With some other masters of the college and some of Strachan's students, he manned the mission stations Strachan established in the Home District.[21] He was ordained a deacon by Bishop Stewart in April 1833 at York and then assigned to March and Huntley townships in the Dalhousie District.[22] Ordained a priest in March Township in August 1834, Padfield travelled an irregular circuit in this and neighbouring townships for the next several years. His church in Horaceville was built at the expense of Hamnett Pinhey, later inspector of the neighbouring Dalhousie District.[23]

In 1839, Padfield was assigned to Beckwith Township in the Bathurst District, and in March of that year he preached before the members of the Eastern District Clerical Association in Williamsburgh.[24] He served as Beckwith Township superintendent from 1844 to 1846 and lived in the flourishing village of

Franktown until 1852, when he was assigned to Carrying Place, 1853–4, and finally to Burford, where he remained from 1855 until his death in 1879. He was married and supporting a household, including eleven children, in 1852. His eldest daughter married Joshua Adams in August 1849.[25]

Padfield was appointed at a district council meeting in February 1847. The education committee of Council said there were four candidates, all equally qualified, more or less, for the job: Padfield, J.A. Murdoch (the district judge), William Sommerville (a schoolmaster in Perth), and James Allan (the postmaster, a book dealer, and son of the first Bathurst superintendent). The committee urged the council simply to vote. Padfield won, and posted his sureties in the amount of £4,000 from Alexander McMillan, James Shaw, Rev. M. Harris, and Thomas McCrae. The salary for district superintendent was raised to £100 per annum.[26]

As we have seen, the appointment was the cause of some unease in the district, but Padfield functioned to the general satisfaction of Council. True, his confession in his first report for 1847 that sickness and the necessity of remaining at home to pay the school monies of 1845 had prevented 'so full a visitation of the schools' as he wished led Council to pass a by-law specifying his duties.[27] But, after this, Padfield managed to avoid the contentious relations with Council that Alexander Mann had entertained, despite the fact that some of the councillors were among the sharpest critics of the Ryersonian administration.

Relations between the Education Office and the district council, sore already after conflicts over the school monies, were markedly worsened by the memorial on the School Law passed by Council at its February 1848 session. This document attacked the prevailing organization of common schooling. Two other disputes raged between Ryerson and the council in 1848. One of these concerned the location of the legal schoolhouse in section 6 of Ramsay Township and the other the legality of a trustee election in section 4 of Pakenham Township. Both provoked a number of angry exchanges between Council and the chief superintendent of education. There was a strong element of bear-baiting in these matters, as the Reform-dominated council anticipated Ryerson's overthrow and as Ryerson responded angrily to what must have seemed to him intentionally obstructionist activity.

The issue in section 6, Ramsay, was the legitimacy of the old section school or of a new school built by a new set of trustees as the official school. Ryerson claimed the district council should decide; the council claimed this was Ryerson's duty under the act.[28]

In section 4, Pakenham, the issue was the legality of the trustees' election, and Council argued that all elections under the act of 1846 might be illegal. Briefly, the act had stated that notice of the January 1847 trustee elections was to be given by the sitting trustees under the act of 1843, except in newly formed sections, where it was to be given by the district council. The boundaries of section 4 had been altered by Council, which claimed this made it a new section. And, in any case, Council argued, since the act of 1846 repealed that of 1843, all sections were now new sections, all elections for 1847 should have been announced by the councils, and hence all trustees sitting were doing so illegally throughout the colony. Ryerson claimed that a school section with an established school, and sitting trustees did not cease to be a continuously existing section simply because the council altered its boundaries. This section was not new, and the more general point was ridiculous. Ryerson also claimed that 'three fourths of the complaints' to the education office until the end of 1846 surrounded the annual election of trustees and the performance of township superintendents.[29]

Padfield managed to remain aloof from these conflicts. His annual report of 1848 so impressed the councillors that they ordered it printed and distributed to the teachers in the district as a means of encouraging improvement. In this document Padfield noted, 'there are 120 schools in operation at present ... I have visited each of these Schools once, with a few exceptions for the most part of such as were not in operation when I was in their respective neigbourhoods; – some of them twice; and a few oftener.'

The text was an echo of the views of the common schools shared by most men of his class: he deplored irregular attendance, small schoolhouses, and the use of disparate texts; better audiences for the quarterly examinations and better school accommodation were necessary, but, on the whole, things were improving. Padfield named the best schoolmasters in the district as a spur to emulation. It is clear from this report that his school visits were unexpected.[30] His other surviving report, from 1849, mainly stated that the schools were getting on well, but the district education committee was sufficiently content with his work to suggest that Council pay all of his contingencies.[31]

Both Alexander Mann and James Padfield were particularly well-placed to serve as school inspectors. As itinerant clerics, they had a detailed knowledge of the district, especially given that schoolhouses typically did double duty as churches. Mann, however, produced no effective superintendence, allied himself with the chief superintendent, and was forced to resign.

Padfield's congenial relations with Council may well have been attributable to the relative coldness of his relations with Ryerson, for whom Padfield had undoubtedly appeared as a despoiler of the public bounty, both as a teacher at Upper Canada College and as a member of the Church of England. While other superintendents kept the Education Office abreast of local educational politics, as far as one can see, Ryerson heard nothing about the tempestuous agitations against the school acts in Bathurst from Padfield. It was local teachers, including the sycophantic Johnston Neilson, who warned Ryerson of the 'Scotch Radicals' at work against him in the district, rather than Padfield, who was certainly in a position to know what was taking place.[32] Indeed, in his final report as district superintendent, Padfield expressed his opposition to the School Act of 1850, which he found cumbersome and inefficient. He opposed the elimination of the office of district superintendent, in sharp contrast to almost all the other superintendents who, in response to prodding from Ryerson and Hincks, had publicly supported its abolition.

The dominance of propertied men and their clerical allies in educational matters in the Bathurst District is clear, but there were divisions among them. The 'Scotch Radical' tradition in this district settled initially by the Paisley weavers favoured education as a means to moral and political discipline in society, yet stressed the local self-management of this discipline. The experience of the Bathurst District superintendents was shaped by their positions on the main axis of central versus local control, as it was by their positions in the religious establishment. Their activities (and non-activities) as school inspectors influenced colonial educational politics as a whole.

The Brock District

The three men who occupied the position of Brock District superintendent of Education were closely connected in a range of moral and cultural activities aimed at social improvement. Newton Bosworth (1778–1848) and W.H. Landon (1805–86) were both Baptist ministers, and George Hendry (c. 1810–47) was a small master cabinetmaker. Landon arrived in the Woodstock area in 1822, Hendry likely in the 1830s, and Bosworth in 1842.

Their relations with one another were many and varied. Bosworth's appointment to the Woodstock pastorate was witnessed by Landon. Landon was vice-president of the Reading Society in 1837, when Hendry was on the management committee, and presided over the meeting on 18 June 1838 at which Hendry read an essay titled 'Is the Stage Conducive to Morality.' Hendry's partner, John Bain, was president of what became the Woodstock Subscription Library in 1840, and he and Hendry alternated in the positions of president and vice-president for several years. Landon was a member throughout the period. All three men were active members of the Woodstock Temperance Society. Hendry and Landon were founding members of the Brock District Building Society. All three were active in the Woodstock Mechanics' Institute, with Hendry as its secretary from its formation in 1844 until his death in 1847. Landon chaired the first meeting of the Woodstock Irish and Scottish relief fund, to which Hendry's partner was a large contributor, and many other such connections existed.[33] These men were committed to rational religion, social improvement through intellectual development, and self-help. Hendry was by far the most politically active, in the Reform party, but the others shared many of his social views. For their time and circumstances, they held progressive views on many social questions.

Newton Bosworth was the first of this triumvirate to hold the office of district superintendent. At sixty-six, the second-oldest member of the inspectoral corps, he worked from 1844 until 1846. Bosworth was the son of a schoolmaster and received his early education in Peterborough, England. He became an assistant teacher in the same town in 1795 and went to Cambridge University in 1800. He was an early and active member of the movement for the 'diffusion of useful knowledge.' His *Accidents of Human Life; with hints for their prevention or removal of their consequences* appeared in London in 1813 (reprinted in New York 1814; second edition London 1834), and his support for the British and Foreign School Society suggests a close connection with rational dissent.

Bosworth emigrated to Canada in 1834 and around this time converted to the Baptist religion. From 1835 to 1839, he was minister of St Helen's in Montreal, where he published two works of social commentary. The first, *The Aspect and Influence of Christianity Upon the Commercial Character* (Montreal: Wm. Greig 1837), was published on the eve of the Rebellion with the hope that it 'might prove useful at the present crisis,' influencing Lower Canada. Here Bosworth stressed the 'manifold and obvious' advantages of the growth of international commerce: 'It promotes the intercourse of nations – enlarges the boundaries of knowledge, – contributes to the welfare of mankind by the interchange of commodities, supplying the wants of one country by the excess of another,' and, last, but certainly not least, 'it opens facilities for the introduction of the Gospel into all lands and nations.'[34]

But the growth of commerce also had its moral and social dangers, especially the growth of a 'rapacious spirit,' which was visible even in 'our own traders.' Bosworth urged his readers to direct their attention not to the dangers of eternal damnation in the future, but to the moral danger that threatened their lives from inattention to the virtues of integrity, honesty, diligence, and moderation in commercial relations.[35] Like many members of the religious intelligentsia, Bosworth believed capitalist development was a force of social well-being if guided by sound moral discipline.

Bosworth's *Hochelaga Depicta; The Early History and the Present State of the City and Island of Montreal* (Montreal: Greig 1839; second edition, 1846) was very influential and spawned a number of imitations. The work contained a general overview of the origins and development of Montreal, with a detailed description of its topography, facilities, and institutions. Bosworth provided an account of the Canadian Baptist Missionary Society, in which he was himself involved. In Ireland, he claimed, the Baptists had been very 'effective' in their educational efforts, and Bosworth clearly thought similar efforts were needed among the French Catholics. He emphasized his belief that 'education is essential to the perfection and the stability of the social state.' While in Montreal, Bosworth was active in founding the Canada Baptist College.[36]

From 1839 to 1843, Bosworth made evangelical tours in Upper Canada. He was pastor of the Woodstock Baptist Church in 1843, but resigned over his refusal to allow women to speak in church. From late 1845 until his death in 1848 he was pastor of the Baptist Church in Paris, Canada West.[37]

From his earliest appearance in the Brock District, Bosworth involved himself in efforts at moral and intellectual improvement. For instance, he gave lectures titled 'The Nature and Property of Matter' to the Paris Mutual Society and Circulating Library and later, to the Paris Mechanics' Institute, 'The Progress of Discovery in the Sciences and Arts, and their Influence Upon the Mental and Moral Condition of Society.'[38] He was appointed Brock District superintendent of education at the February 1844 sessions of the district council.

There were five applicants for the position: Bosworth; two teachers; W. Bettridge, the Rector of Woodstock; and George Murray of the Scotch Secession Church in Blenheim. The rector was initially preferred, until the councillors discovered the position was meant to be salaried, whereupon he withdrew. Bosworth was appointed and the Tory editor of the Woodstock *Herald* remarked 'the choice is a very good one; but the salary is absurdly inadequate. It will not do much more than pay his postage and stationery bill.' Council initially voted £30, although this sum was raised to £50 in November.[39]

Bosworth was obliged to post a performance bond of £1,500 and two bonds of £750 to assume office. In mid-1844 he claimed that he had received no pay whatsoever for his duties under the act of 1843 and asked Assistant Superintendent Murray if he could deduct a percentage of the monies passing through his hands. Murray told him to see if the inspector general would accept his accounts. In reply to McNab's circular on pay, Bosworth said 'neither the County Sup't. nor any of the Township Supts has yet been paid his salary for the past year; but we are expecting to receive what is due to us from the funds of the District.' Bosworth was subsidizing the superintendency, although inspecting schools did overlap with the practical work of his mission.[40]

The School Act of 1841 undermined common-school organization in the Brock District. At the end of 1842, only twenty-five schools were reported under the act and, in Norwich Township, which had been divided into fifteen school districts, there was 'no school reported to have been in operation for the last year.'[41] Bosworth began by attempting to find out from Robert Murray what form of examination he should use for teachers. Murray, who had recently lost his office clerk, responded that there was too much work at the central office for the preparation of forms. Bosworth was left to decide himself on the qualifications of teachers.

He conducted an active school inspection in 1844 and corresponded with local teachers and with the Education Office about what he saw as needed reforms. He told the teachers 'after a careful inspection of all the Schools in the District that were in operation when I visited the respective Townships,' he was impressed with their quality. There were many good teachers in the district, but Bosworth encouraged teachers to unite for mutual improvement, something those in Burford were already doing.[42]

In correspondence to the Education Office, Bosworth's main interest was with school books. He urged the creation of a government-appointed committee 'to select or prepare a series of books to be used in the Common Schools' that should be printed on the government press and sold at subsidized rates by the teachers. The most serious obstacle to 'improvement' in Bosworth's view was diversity in school books. 'In some cases I found 3, and in others 4 spelling books of different kinds in the same school,' he wrote. Bosworth himself secured a supply of books from the British and Foreign School Society and distributed them in the district.[43]

In his report to the Education Office for 1845, Bosworth again stressed this point, saying that the Irish National school books would be well suited for Canada, but that he personally preferred those produced by the British and Foreign School Society. On the whole he thought the act of 1843 worked well, although he believed inspectors should be empowered to levy a tax for the construction of schoolhouses and that some way of solving disputes about schoolhouse locations was needed. In the district there were four schools Bosworth considered to be 'in a high state of excellence and prosperity,' but he was generally dissatisfied with the teaching of writing, which seemed to be 'without any regard to rule or system.'[44]

In the following year, Bosworth reported that the number and condition of the schools were generally improving. He named the best schools and teachers he had found in each township, noting that, while some teachers were underqualified, many were performing very well and some were qualified to give more advanced instruction. He did maintain that parents in several areas 'continued to feel little interest in a subject so closely connected with the welfare of their offspring,' but suggested the creation of a prize fund for students and teachers might help overcome this lack.[45]

On the verge of his retirement in 1846, Bosworth wrote at length to the provincial secretary with suggestions for improvements to the School Act. The main problem as he saw it had to do with the impotence of the district council to decide where schoolhouses should be located and limitations on its powers of educational taxation. Disputes among trustees and section residents about the location of schoolhouses so delayed the construction of schools as to cost many sections their shares of the government grant. Bosworth suggested that township or county superintendents be empowered to decide these questions on appeal. He also claimed that trustees were incompetent in such matters as the selection of school texts. Some trustees had told him that, even if they were competent, the diversity of opinion about texts would be greater still. As a remedy, Bosworth suggested that county superintendents be allowed to specify the texts to be used, or that the government appropriation be withheld from schools not using satisfactory texts.

Finally, Bosworth urged the establishment of a normal school and the hiring of a qualified professor from the British and Foreign School Society in London or the Irish National Board of Education. Graduates of the normal school could be sent to teach in local model schools, with the beneficial effect that 'a degree of uniform and efficient teaching would soon become general throughout the land, to the great advantage of the rising generation and the advancement of our population in intelligence and moral character.'[46] These remarks suggested many of the things soon contained in the School Act of 1846, although Bosworth himself never commented on it and although the Baptist *Register* opposed both it and the act of 1847.[47] Bosworth chaffed under the lack of power he possessed as district superintendent, but he does not seem to have supported a radical educational centralization. As he put it on the verge of his retirement, 'though I have had much pleasure, and I hope done some little good, in these two years visitations, they have taken me so much from my duties at home that I am glad to retire from the office, especially as my power of effecting reforms is so restricted by the want of authority in the school act for introducing them as to render any attempt of this kind all but useless.'[48] Bosworth had worked 'with a sincere desire to improve the state of Education in the District of Brock,' but had done so 'all along under the impression that if I had been invested by the School Act with powers superior to those of a mere inspector and adviser the results of my efforts would ... have been more beneficial.'[49]

Bosworth offered a tentative resignation to Council in February 1846, stating that he had moved out of the county and that one of his sureties had left the country. He offered to serve again if Council thought the 'interests of Education should suffer' from his departure, but, when Council did move to re-elect him, he resigned unconditionally. Council appointed George Hendry, after an interesting debate about his class position and education.

Of the three Brock District superintendents, Hendry was the most active in party politics. How he would have reacted to the crucial political events of 1849 is a moot question, given his premature death, but he was an energetic and active Reformer when it was still a mark of pride for a member of that party to declare himself an artisanal worker.

Hendry was born in Banffshire, Scotland, and beyond this no information about his origins has been uncovered. The earliest record of him in the district is as a member of the Reading Society in 1835. With his partner John Bain, he was one of the subscribers to Goodwin's School House in 1839.[50] In 1840, 'Hendry & Bain, Upholsterers & Cabinet Makers' were advertising in the Woodstock newspaper their large stock of furniture, their premier position in the trade, their ability to produce furniture to order, and that 'Lumber, Grain, Feathers, &c' were 'taken in exchange for Furniture.' Bain kept the business after Hendry's death, adding undertaking as a sideline. His two sons, John, Jr, and George, developed what became the largest wagon factory in the country, with about 200 employees in 1900.[51]

Hendry's business enabled him to support a family and to devote a considerable amount of time to cultural, political, and administrative activities.[52] He served as a school trustee under the Upper Canada School Act, chaired the Board of Common School Commissioners for East Oxford under the act of 1841, and was appointed superintendent for that township in 1844. He was East Oxford's returning officer and, during 1844–7, a district auditor. In a period where even urban businesses were involved in exchange in kind, some of these offices would have provided Hendry with welcome sources of cash: the inspector's office was worth £100 a year. Had Hendry lived, his close connection to Francis Hincks would likely have propelled him to financial success, as such a connection did William Hutton. Already in 1847, Hendry was acting as Hincks's assignee in Lake Huron mining schemes.[53]

From the outset, Tory members of Council questioned Hendry's election. Although Bosworth suggested Hendry as his successor, Councillor Ward expressed 'some doubts as to the qualifications of the candidate.' This wasn't because Hendry was 'only a mechanic,' but because the office demanded 'a person of classical attainments, which, judging from the reports given in by Mr. Hendry as Auditor,' Ward 'did not conceive him to be.' However, Hendry's Reform ally T.S. Shenston came to his defence, arguing that 'he did not see the necessity for classical attainments in a Superintendent of common schools' and that, since Hendry was 'well acquainted with the School Act, he was likely to be able to carry its provisions into effect.'[54] Hendry was appointed, but the matter was later raised in Parliament. Riddell, the Tory member for Oxford, argued against allowing district councils to appoint school inspectors in the debates over the School Act 'on the ground of their incompetency to select, and instanced the appointment in [the Brock] District of a Mechanic.' Hendry was described as 'a most unfit person.'[55]

From his practical experience, Hendry was critical of the office of township superintendent. He visited all 108 schools in the district in 1845–6, but, with one exception, the teachers were certified by the township superintendents. These officers produced what Hendy saw as poor reports, and retarded the delivery of his own report. 'Each one seems to have a financial year of his own,' Hendry complained, 'a course which has led to a great deal of confusion.'[56] Rev. George Murray, the superintendent for Blenheim, produced a report which was 'not only informal' but 'also almost unintelligible.' When Hendry asked for clarification, Murray 'positively declined making any alteration in it further than to mention the amount of the balance in his possession.'[57]

But Hendry did not regard the act of 1846 as much superior because school visitors were allowed to grant certificates. He gave public warning that he intended to 'be most rigid in granting certificates to those alone who were thoroughly qualified.'[58]

With one interesting exception, and despite his party politics, Hendry's relations with Ryerson, whom he seems to have distinguished from the minis-try, were quite cordial. Hendry defended Ryerson against the angry complaints of teachers who had not been paid the government money in September 1846, and Ryerson promised Hendry his 'aid in all cases where I see ... an earnest and disinterested desire to accomplish to the greatest extent the patriotic objects of the School Act.'[59] Together they considered measures for the encouragement of district taxation for schoolhouse construction and repair and Ryerson explained his textbook policy at length to Hendry.[60] Ryerson allowed Hendry some of his costs out of residual school monies for 1846, encouraged him to distribute some of these monies to needy schools at his own discretion and proposed to consult with him about the remainder.[61]

Their dispute was over the nature of educational intelligence. Ryerson had published an educational table in the *Christian Guardian* in October 1846 that purported to show that, on average, teachers had earned only £29 in the preceding year. Hendry sent to Ryerson for his comments a corrective he proposed to submit to the *Guardian*. In it, Hendry suggested that Ryerson's calculation of salaries was low because he had not counted the pay teachers received in the form of room and board. Many teachers continued to 'board round,' but trustees did not usually report this as part of the teachers' income. In the Brock District, it seemed, by Ryerson's calculation, that teachers on average earned £38 in 1845, but Hendry argued that the true figure was closer to £42. In addition, he argued that, in Brock, salaries had increased under the act of 1843. Men, on average, earned about £50, although several had more than £70 and at least one male teacher earned £87.10.[62]

But Ryerson had not claimed teachers made £29 out of a simple love of veracity. This piece of political intelligence, published during the continuing debate over the School Act of 1846, was designed to bolster his contention that the act of 1843 was incapable of producing improvement. Ryerson replied with heat that Hendry's calculations were erroneous because to calculate room and board as a part of teachers' salaries was improper: no one who boarded a teacher could have any idea of sound teaching. For Ryerson, the moral and political question of control over teachers and of teachers' integration into the community predominated.[63]

In response, Hendry wrote 'no one can have greater objections to the practise of "boarding round" than I have, but it being an incontrovertible fact that such is practised, to a considerable extent, we must not shut our eyes to it. The ulcer and the gangrene are unsightly appearances, but he would be an unwise physician who would, on that account neglect to attend to them.' However, not wishing to cause controversy or have his motives misunderstood, Hendry did not submit his remarks to the *Guardian*.[64] Hendry deferred to Ryerson in this matter, despite his Reform affiliations. One suspects his hesitation might have to do with his own perception of his social position and background.

Hendry died on 4 October 1847, while the Brock District Council was in session and while it had the memorial of the Newcastle District Council on the School Act under consideration. How Hendry would have reacted must remain a matter of speculation, but Ryerson acquired a strong ally in his successor, Rev. W.H. Landon.

Landon, the first ordained pastor of the 'open communion' Baptist chapel, arrived in the Woodstock area in 1822 from Batavia, New York. By the early 1840s, he was solidly established in the community and involved in a large number of projects for cultural and social improvement. As a member of the 'open communion,' Landon, like Bosworth before him, had a practical experience at shaping and guiding the developing powers of self-expression of members of the community and of securing popular consent to a structure of dominance. One of Landon's descendants has remarked, 'In some of the Baptist churches in the western part of the province one week day in each month was set aside as an occasion for confessing orally to the Articles of Faith which were read aloud by the church clerk. After a sermon the individual members were expected to "improve their gifts" by addressing the meeting. Elder W.H. Landon, of Oxford, has left the comment that the people had to be taught cautiously that the Holy Spirit had not conferred the same gifts upon all men and women. It took many years to have this comprehended.' This depiction captures well the 'improving' project of these reformers: a limited democratization in the realm of self-expression (outside of church for male proprietors only), but one contained within clearly specified forms, either of religious or of political faith, and guided by those with superior social or spiritual gifts.[65]

Landon was also directly involved in local schooling. He was a district grammar-school trustee and, with his sister, ran a school for young ladies in his house.[66] He described his occupation as 'Editor' in his work as Woodstock census enumerator in 1852, by which date he was also married.[67] As a trustee with T.S. Shenston, the district clerk of school section 2 in Woodstock, Landon achieved an important victory for the 'friends of improvement' over the council's view of populist democracy. In February 1847, Council had refused school trustees' petitions to tax for school improvements in the Woodstock school districts, because the majority of the property holders in the districts had not signed. Landon, Shenston, and Amos Goodwin, trustees in section 2, argued that, as trustees, they could not possibly reconcile the conflicting views in their section, given the rich who refused any tax for the education of the poor and the poor who could not appreciate the merits of education. After a correspondence with the chief superintendent, Council agreed to tax in response to trustees' petitions. Ryerson argued, and Council eventually accepted that trustees expressed the educational will of the school section, whatever its ratepayers might say.[68]

Landon was appointed district superintendent at the October 1847 sessions of Council. At the same session, by a large majority, Council endorsed the Newcastle council's description of the School Act of 1846 as 'a compilation of unnecessary machinery, whose provisions are almost impracticable ... the only satisfactory amendment will be its total repeal, and the substitution of a far more simple system, and one that will be more under the controal of the local authorities.'[69] Landon was not yet able to pronounce on such questions as district superintendent.

From the outset, Landon and Ryerson saw themselves to be involved in a common project about which they had no fundamental disagreements.[70] Ryerson supported Landon's distribution of unexpended school balances for 1847.[71] Together they planned ways to overcome the actions of 'ignorant' school trustees, and Ryerson encouraged Landon to disqualify any teacher he felt did not perform adequately: 'This is the only way we can protect the children of the country in particular cases from the conduct of ignorant and pernicious trustees and their supporters. I think that greater evil than good would arise from doing away or interfering with the popular elective system of trustees; but the evils incident to it among the little informed sections of the community, must in the mean time, be checked and counteracted in every possible way until the people at large become more intelligent.'[72] Both gave the interests of 'improvement' precedence over forms of representative government when it suited them and both saw local government as an education for 'the people.'

In February 1848, Landon prevented the Brock councillors from endorsing

Gore Council's memorial on the School Act, which called for its repeal and for the vesting of all educational powers in district councils. Landon opposed the repeal of the act and made a strong argument in favour of public education. New countries like Canada, he maintained, had to learn from the experience of others, and the School Law was a copy of that in force in New York State. It could stand improvement, but its continuation was the key to social progress. Landon argued that public education would open all occupations and political offices in the country and would give power to the people as a whole. 'This is an age of improvement. Society is in a state of transition and progress. The desire of the people for education is a consequence of that progress and a part of it.' The councillors were convinced, and Landon's address to them was published.[73] Ryerson himself took the occasion of a dispute over the outstanding debts of a school district Brock Council had divided to remark, 'It is strange that in those very places where a more exclusive local control of School affairs is demanded, all the difficulties connected with such School affairs arise from the imperfect manner in which the local control already provided for by law is exercised.'[74]

Landon certainly agreed. In response to a request from the *Journal of Education*, he published a lengthy analysis of the necessary reforms in educational organization, which included removing the appointment of educational inspectors from the district councils. Canada West needed not more schools, but free schools supported by taxation. This change demanded a campaign to convince people of the benefits of such institutions. There were three pressing reforms, according to Landon: '1st a system of thorough inspection, connected with measures to improve the state of public knowledge & feeling on the subject, by lectures and the circulation, among the people, of suitable publications, &c. 2nd Encouragement & aid to secure suitable premises; and 3rd The supply of Books of reference and illustrative apparatus.' He paid particular attention to the qualities of inspectors.

The Inspectors or Superintendents should be practical & experienced Educators. To be Educated men is not enough. They should understand, in detail, the process by which knowledge, of the most elementary kinds, is most readily imparted. They should have an exact knowledge of the rural and labouring population of our Country; and be able to enter into the feelings & wishes, and even to understand the prejudices & dislikes of those classes of our fellow countrymen. They should be men who by kindness, urbanity and untiring industry, might acquire an influence, and diffuse a portion of their own elevated spirit & generous sentiments among the people at large.

This was precisely the model of administrative paternalism shared by liberal reformers, but Landon believed 'so long as the local Municipal Councils have the appointment of the only inspectors known to our schools, not many such men will be employed.'[75]

These were not the views of a minor local official, but of someone at the centre of a diverse movement for social improvement whose members were recruited from urban clerks, artisanal workers, small masters, clergymen, and some members of the rising capitalist class. Landon's own social standing was high, and was undoubtedly enhanced by his having Lord Elgin as a house guest in 1849.[76]

At the end of his superintendence, Landon made a final intervention which supported the settlement of 1850. In answer to Hincks's circular, Landon secured the approval of the new county council for most of Ryerson's revisions. Here the key compromises Ryerson introduced were supported: rate-bills were allowed, but could be abolished at local option; trustees were to be individually liable for misdeeds; county boards could examine teachers, but there would be central control over books; the distribution of the grant would be according to average attendance; and Landon urged the appointment of county, rather than township superintendents. He served himself as superintendent for about half the county for much of the 1850s.[77]

Collectively, the Brock District superintendents did much to further the educational project locally. This activity undoubtedly sustained the extension of the powers of the Education Office and solidified the developing forms of educational governance emanating from the centre. However, it is important to notice that these men were themselves divided, within a broad political consensus, over the organization of 'improvement,' particularly with regard to the powers that should attach to local governmental bodies. Both Bosworth and Hendry tended to support local efforts at self-improvement and the efforts at mutual improvement by teachers, while Landon was more clearly oriented towards the construction of a central authority. These differences were real and important, although they may well have been overshadowed by the political crisis of 1849, had Hendry and Bosworth lived.

How well Landon himself acted to 'enter into the feelings and wishes' of the people in order to improve them remains obscure, but it is at least clear that he saw this approach as an explicit objective of educational inspection. The role of the 'better informed' sections of society, the rising middle class, was to shape and guide popular consciousness in support of social improvement. Landon pursued this objective as a minister of religion, an educational reformer, a newspaper editor, and a railway-company promoter.

In the Brock District, school inspectors worked to temper the opposition of local government to public education and to extend the public educational project. Educational superintendence in the Dalhousie District was markedly different.

The Dalhousie District

In the Dalhousie District, attempts to construct a bureaucratic educational administration were opposed by members of a self-constituted gentry. The Dalhousie District was largely settled by English army and naval officers on half-pay who were provided with substantial government land grants. These settlers attempted to re-create their vision of an English landed gentry in Upper Canada and transformed military rank and social bearing into a rigid local hierarchy. They defined and sustained rigid class distinctions and arrogated to themselves the privileges of administering justice, religion, and education. To these people, the limited democratization of civil administration implicit in the District Councils Act of 1841 and in the successive school acts was repugnant, and they worked to subvert it. The political complexion of this local ruling class is perfectly visible in the countenance of the first Dalhousie superintendent of education, Hamnett Kirkes Pinhey (1784–1857).

Pinhey was born in Plymouth, England, and raised in London. He attended Christ's Hospital from 1792 to 1799, and then went into the mercantile trade. He enjoyed considerable initial success in this war period and was voted a sum of money by Parliament for running the Napoleonic blockade. In 1812 he married Mary Tasker, the daughter of a London merchant exporter.

Pinhey was engaged in a marine insurance partnership, the failure of which, in 1814, was followed by three years of litigation and led him to retire from trade in 1819. Now a governor of Christ's Hospital and a citizen and liveryman of the Company of Grocers, he petitioned the colonial secretary for a Canadian land grant. The petition was successful, and, in April 1820, Pinhey sailed to Canada with £300 in gold and silver. He settled in March Township on the Ottawa River, and the following summer his wife and children joined him, with another £800 worth of possessions.[78] By English standards, this was a rather modest fortune, but quite enough for someone with Pinhey's pretensions in Upper Canada.

Pinhey mapped his own land grant, employing, as he put it, twenty-five to thirty 'of my own countrymen' to do it. Governor Dalhousie spent the night on the property in the 1820s and was so impressed that he granted Pinhey another 600 acres. Pinhey eventually held 2,000 acres. On the banks of the Ottawa, he constructed an imitation English manor, with a stone house, saw and grist mills, and a stone church, which was consecrated in 1834. Pinhey named his settlement 'Horaceville' after his eldest son and was township warden in the 1820s for March.[79]

Throughout the 1830s, Pinhey was 'at the core of a local compact.'[80] He was an agent for the Canada Company and involved himself, in this decade and later, in a variety of schemes for local improvement, including agricultural societies, road companies, and the Ottawa Emigration Society. He acted as a private banker before the organization of banks in the district.

Pinhey bribed his way into the colonial Parliament in 1832 but lost his seat when it was shown that most of those who voted for him held only tickets of location. He was a Tory and a staunch opponent of political reform, supporting William Lyon Mackenzie's expulsion from the Assembly in 1832 on the grounds that Mackenzie was 'a man unworthy to sit in the same room' with gentlemen, and writing anti-reform letters under the pseudonyms 'Vesper' and 'Poor Correspondent' in the Bytown *Gazette*.[81]

Pinhey was the councillor for March in the first Dalhousie District Council and sat on the education committee as well. He was appointed district superintendent of schools in 1844 and elected warden in 1846. In 1847 he was named to the Legislative Council.

Pinhey's view of the act of 1843 was succinctly expressed in his pseudonymous reaction to a pamphlet containing its provisions: 'The nauseating nonsense!' At the May 1844 sessions of Dalhousie Council, which Pinhey chaired, it was discovered (or claimed) that all of the township superintendents had refused to serve. They attributed this to the lowness of the pay offered, to their own incapacity, or to the unpopularity and unintelligibility of the School Act of 1843. A by-law named Pinhey *both* township and district superintendent. This council meeting also refused to levy a district school tax, on the grounds that taxation would reduce voluntary subscriptions for the schools. Pinhey claimed that for March, subscriptions generated £50, but a tax would only produce £40. Council did vote to levy a rate for the establishment of a district model school to be under Pinhey's supervision. £110 was raised for the school in 1844.[82]

Pinhey's views about Canadian educational organization were expressed in a lengthy communication to acting Assistant Superintendent of Education McNab in September 1845, part of which dealt with the district model school. According to Pinhey,

in each district such a school, should be the governing Model of all the Common Schools and that put in practice could be a near approximation to one uniform system throughout West Canada – hitherto scarcely two common Schools have any similitude in form and matter, and indeed in some of them, they can hardly be said to have any system at all ... I need not tell you that the parents generally are very incompetent judges of the Scholastic acquirements of a Teacher, and that among them a man too lazy or too feeble to gain a livelihood by manual labour finds no great difficulty in passing himself off as a 'Scholar' altho' he shall not be able to spell the word itself; this is a lamentable fact that my short experience and acquaintance with the 'Teachers' has disclosed to me.

Needless to say the parents here spoken of were not also retired English grocers, magistrates, or councillors. In any case, Pinhey warned, it was 'very premature,' even in this condition, for 'the District Superintendent formally and *ex officio* by examination and rejection to disqualify the non-educated Teachers.' To do so would only mean that 'parents of the children would be vociferous in their demands to be supplied officially with a successor ... a demand that could not be complied with.' But while the 'Evil' thus described could not be 'overcome peremptorily and harshly,' it might none the less 'be ingeniously and gradually subdued.' How? Well, Pinhey himself had largely done so in Dalhousie. Here the School Act was 'deemed to be too complex and too prolix'; the township superintendents had all refused to serve, and so the district council had had to do all the work. Pinhey had required all the teachers in the district to assemble at the Model School with a list of attendance at their schools signed by the trustees, sworn before a magistrate, and agreed to by a district councillor, before he would pay them. In this way he claimed, educational harmony was produced. Pinhey concluded that the School Act should be revised to allow district councils to manage all educational matters, and McNab replied that some amendments to the act might well be needed.[83] Pinhey arrogated to himself the power of certifying teachers – as did several other district superintendents. Yet, in his case, this move was clearly meant to strengthen the personal control exerted over local education by the aspiring gentry of the Dalhousie District.

In 1846, Pinhey again announced that 'it was deemed by the Council unnecessary & impolitic to hazard the suppression of the voluntary by an arbitrary assessment': no educational tax was levied for 1845, beyond the £130 raised for Pinhey's model school. Voluntary contributions were said to be three times the parliamentary school grant. In each of the first three years, Pinhey was in office, the district received the legislative school grant without raising the matching grants by taxation as required by law, despite the refusal of the Education Office to do this in the adjoining Bathurst District.[84]

'The Common Schools are very indifferently conducted,' Pinhey wrote in his annual report for 1845, 'and the masters in general very inadequate to perform the duties required of them.' He also claimed that 'the present Common School act has been very unpopular in this District and the New Act now in progress through the legislature is looked forward to, with much more interest.'[85]

Yet, Council again refused to levy a general school tax for 1846. A by-law in February 1847 provided for the taxing of those townships that petitioned Council to do so, but no township did. Pinhey claimed that he had gone to the meeting in March Township 'to feel my way for a general School Tax –; the Tax was almost universally deprecated.' What people wanted was a subscription list, and so Pinhey started one, 'laid it on the Town clerk's table for every man to come up and sign his name and state the sum he would covenant to contribute. The contribution was ample – generous – but I found, as other Councillors had found, that the sum subscribed was chiefly from those who had no further interest in the question than that of *educating* other people's children.' In other words, the self-constituted gentry of March was prepared to provide only a charity education for the children of the poor.[86]

Pinhey involved himself heavily in educational matters. He wrote at length to Ryerson in February 1847 about his examination of teachers:

I have felt it my duty with a *necessary* liberality to qualify 56 only out of near 100 applicants: many rejected by me will be more successful under Cl. XVI of the Act [which allowed visitors to grant certificates]. I believe the mass of the people ... of this district less intelligent than in others, and in truth *I hope* this is the fact – I fear there will be both perplexity and perversity to contend with in the 'working' of the act for some time, but still tho' we may not reach perfection, if we get half way towards it, we shall have done something worth doing.

Pinhey's own sense of his world-historic social mission appeared again in his concluding remarks: 'I have been four years in the service and contemplate retiring at the close of the fifth – when it is *possible* I may be enabled to say "I have done the state some service." '[87] He mentioned that the Dalhousie District model school was not then in operation, but would recommence in October. He proposed to support it out of the school fund, something illegal, but against which Ryerson did not protest.[88]

In 1847, Ryerson was inclined to agree with Pinhey's assessment of Pinhey's own service to education and the state. He expressed his hope that Pinhey would not resign when 'you are just beginning to realize the presages of those improvements for which you have so vigorously laboured. You have gained an important step in at length getting a School Assessment for the District.'[89] But his attitude changed somewhat after the elections of 1848, when the Dalhousie District Council added its voice to the opposition to the School Act and when the district school tax did not materialize. Ryerson wrote to Pinhey that the School Act had produced great educational progress in some districts, and if this wasn't the case in Dalhousie, the fault lay with the local gentry: 'If the law has operated to the improvement of the Schools and convenience of the people in some Districts; and if it is otherwise in other Districts, it is plain that there must be something wrong in the state of Society or in the administrations of the law, or both, in such Districts.' Ryerson claimed the district council had performed poorly at administering the law and at informing people of its provisions. He hoped this fault would be corrected in the future through the publication of the

Journal of Education. Now Pinhey himself contemplated retirement, but he opposed the appointment of John Flood. Ryerson continued, 'you intimate that there is reluctance in your Council to appoint a clergyman as District Superintendent of Common Schools. There are several clergymen of different religious persuasions filling that office in different Districts, and I think they are, on an average, the most efficient District Superintendents in Upper Canada.'[90] Pinhey blocked any new appointment until the autumn of 1848.

In February 1849, Pinhey invited Ryerson to 'felicitate' him 'on being at last relieved from the performance of the duties of an office, which duties by statute have been so antagonistic to the feelings of a large majority of the people.' Pinhey announced again that the council had refused any general school tax, agreeing only to pass by-laws for sections where trustees petitioned for a tax. Ryerson replied rather coldly that no government grant would be given, except to match money raised by local assessment. The new Reform ministry was much less sympathetic to Ryerson's arbitrary interpretations of the provisions of the law than Pinhey's friends in the prior Tory administration had been.[91]

While Pinhey was replaced as district superintendent by John Flood late in 1848 or early in 1849, the legacy of his paternal administration of the educational funds of the district remained, and Ryerson continued to lend official support to Pinhey's activities. In June 1849, for instance, a teacher named M'Gillicuddy complained that Pinhey had distributed unfairly the Huntly Township school fund for 1848. Pinhey explained: 'In the Township of Huntly the School sections had been so ... entangled I could not unravel them, not even with the assistance of their two Councillors and the Teachers and Trustees themselves; so I proposed to ... the Councillors, that they should call a meeting of all the Teachers and Trustees within their Township and whatever might be then and there agreed as to the appropriation of the sum in my hands due the Township provided there were no dissentients I would ratify.' Yet Pinhey did not dispose as he did propose. Everyone at the meeting agreed to share and share alike in the school fund, but a teacher named Scully complained that his school had been open longer than M'Gillicuddy's and was a better school, so Pinhey withheld some of M'Gillicuddy's share and gave it to Scully. Ryerson concurred, although in similar instances involving other superintendents precisely this kind of behaviour was opposed as arbitrariness.[92]

Throughout the period 1841–50, the Dalhousie District Council refused to levy a general school tax. Indeed, the village of Richmond may well have been the last established village in the colony to organize a school under the provisions of the act of 1850 (in 1857). The suggestion is strong in the archival evidence that Pinhey himself was as much opposed as anyone else in the council to educational taxation, yet Ryerson's relations with Pinhey were more than cordial throughout this period. Pinhey was one of the three superintendents Ryerson formally consulted about his draft School Act of 1846. Ryerson subsidized Pinhey's local educational efforts out of the school fund, although these reeked of patronage, and defended Pinhey against the claims of teachers that he defrauded them of their salaries.[93] He repeatedly praised Pinhey's educational efforts, and it was only after the election of the Reform ministry in 1848 and the publication of the Dalhousie District Council's memorial on the School Act that a note of criticism appeared in Ryerson's communications. Pinhey's successor, John Flood, whose appointment Pinhey opposed, received no school census from him, and declared in 1849 that 'Mr. Pinhey paid the money here contrary to the law & exerted himself to strengthen every prejudice against the School Act.'[94] Either Ryerson was naïve or Pinhey was too powerful, before 1848, for criticism.

Pinhey was replaced as district superintendent in October 1848 by the Rev. John Flood (1811–post 1871), who held the office until its abolition in 1850. Flood had been raised a Roman Catholic, but converted to the Episcopal church and was appointed the first minister of Huntly Township church. He was active on the Township School Commission for Goulbourn, and in 1843 defended the claims of women teachers to a share in the government school monies.[95] He was known locally for his taste for literature and for the fact that he 'pursued his reading by firelight and fat pine chips instead of the dip of those times.' After the abolition of the district superintendents in 1850, Flood was appointed township superintendent for North Gower, at £31 per annum.[96]

Flood was married in 1842 and appointed one of the trustees of the Richmond Grammar School in 1845.[97] The school was barely viable and the difficulty of retaining a qualified master plagued the trustees. On at least two occasions, they attempted to appoint Flood himself master of the school.

The trustees urged their MPP, William Morris, to support Flood's application, noting that he would teach in the Latin department, and that 'Mr. Flood (a very worthy man) gets no support from his Parishioners and is straitened in his circumstances.' Morris passed this letter on to the ministry, with the marginal note 'I do not approve the appointment of clergymen as schoolmasters.' To this first application of the trustees, Secretary Daly announced the government's belief in 'the inexpediency of appointing Clergymen teachers of Grammar Schools where it can possibly be avoided.' The trustees were advised 'should Mr. Flood be indisposed to relinquish his clerical charge, to make another recommendation.' After the trustees had been obliged to remove Mr Cruickshanks early in 1846 'on account of his having fallen into a habit of intoxication and neglecting his duties,' Flood again applied for the position. He maintained, in April 1846, that his salary 'as clergyman is so inadequate that if the school be still refused, I must engage in some other secular employment.' Taking the school would thus not interfere with his clerical duties, and Flood added that, if he weren't appointed, he would probably open a competing school in Richmond. This application was also refused.[98] Flood was none the less earning £100 a year from the Reserves fund.

The office of district superintendent did little to alleviate Flood's financial problems. He seems to have received only £15 for his labours in 1849, and Ryerson offered only a vague promise of help from the discretionary school monies.[99]

Flood's relations with the Education Office were markedly different from Pinhey's, in part because of the changed political climate under the Reform administration, despite his eagerness to promote a large part of the office's view of educational 'improvement.' Where Pinhey was allowed a large discretion, which enabled him to work against the School Act, Flood was held narrowly to the letter of the law. Ryerson's own political position was weakened by Reform attacks, which led him to refer matters of financial discretion more closely to the ministry than he had done in the past. Especially in the face of cries for retrenchment and 'responsibility' from the left of his party, Baldwin urged a more universalistic educational financial management. While Ryerson was prepared to defer to Pinhey, even after Pinhey's agitations against the School Act should have been amply clear to him, he was not prepared or not able to defer to Flood, this clergyman in 'straitened circumstances.'

I do not wish to overstate the case. Ryerson did not insist that the Dalhousie Council levy a general school tax. He confided the entire appropriation for the district to Flood and allowed him to distribute it in 1849 to townships and even individual school sections where a property tax for the schools was levied.[100] Yet he insisted that no money be granted until a tax was levied, and voluntary subscriptions were not to take the place of a tax, as they had under Pinhey. In many parts of the district, the teachers were paid only in kind in 1849, and Flood suggested to Ryerson, 'if you will wink at the matter, I will pay the poor men.' Ryerson consulted Baldwin, who refused to allow such payment.[101] In 1850, Ryerson insisted that the townships, which now had powers of taxation under the Municipal Councils Act, must levy a school tax to receive the government grant.[102]

Still, Flood exerted a energetic superintendence in the district, and attempted actively to counter the paternalistic influence of his predecessor. Early in 1849, he toured the district 'to deliver lectures in several parts of each Township in support of taxing for common schools' and visited even the schools not subsidized by the school grant.[103] He declined to accept any of the grant money for 1849 until he had attempted to persuade the council to levy a rate, but this attempt foundered on the absence of an educational census, something Pinhey was supposed to have made. After his lectures, Flood claimed that 'many who had been taught to consider the School Act, "A Damnable Bill" I have led to see it in a different light,' and Council was ready to tax for the schools in August, but the absence of a census made this impossible. Only four sections in Fitzroy levied a school tax in this year.[104]

In delivering his annual report for 1849, Flood again complained of Pinhey. 'I have been surprised to see that Mr. Pinhey has reported that he visited all the schools of the Dalhousie District in the year 1848,' Flood wrote, 'when I know well that he did not visit any of them.' In Gloucester Township, Flood complained that people paid no attention to the School Act. When he told them the conditions under which he could pay them, the township council passed a by-law telling Flood to pay them the money anyway, 'and Mr. Pinhey came in supporting them and trying to overwhelm me.'[105]

The School Act of 1850 eventually came into effect in this part of the colony, although the prejudices of the 'gentry' retarded its operation. Flood was active throughout the 1850s as a township school superintendent, and as one of the more perceptive commentators on the operation of the act.[106]

Conclusion

Regional variations in the colonial class structure and variations in the political complexion of colonial districts shaped the practical operation of educational inspection and influenced the experience of inspectors. These regional events point to the creation of a novel dynamic of political rule involving central and local states. The realization of central political objectives came increasingly to depend on the existence of alliances between central projects and local political activists, although, with its controls over finance, the centre was in a strong position. Superintendents could do much to further or to block central policy in their districts.

These three cases also point to a larger political process under way in the 1840s, that of freeing 'the interests of education' both from the control of entrenched élites and from populist democracy. Representatives elected by men of property were empowered to decide a range of educational questions, even where their decisions were opposed by a majority of those subjected to them. At the same time, principles of bureaucratic administration increasingly limited the idiosyncratic impulses of a would-be gentry and the autonomy of local government bodies. Thus the domain of education was placed firmly in the developing capitalist state system, and key state servants were allowed to administer and define 'the interests of education.'

The central authority pushed successfully for a heightened control over local state servants. Under the act of 1850, superintendents were far more closely regulated than under the acts of 1843, 1846, and 1847. Yet, before 1850, superintendents had a wide latitude for activity. Chapter 8 points both to the power of inspection and to the development of pressure for administrative standardization.

8 From Class Culture
to Bureaucratic Procedure

The question of the origins of bureaucratic management in public education has occupied an important place in recent educational historiography. Several accounts have argued that the common-school reform movement of the mid-nineteenth century created institutions that, from their sheer size, could be managed only bureaucratically. Some writers have maintained that increases in scale were accompanied by popular demands for bureaucratic organization, while others have seen bureaucratic procedure as a mechanism of class domination.[1] Yet there has been a tendency, especially in more conservative accounts, to regard elements of bureaucratic management as 'efficient': as rapid, economic, and effective means to desired ends, and, it is sometimes argued, for that reason bureaucratic management was historically necessary.

Such accounts tend to distance elements of bureaucratic organization both from their political roots and from their implicit political character. Seeking the origins of hierarchical organizations in technical necessity obscures the political interests of bureaucratic cadres and state servants, while it ignores or overshadows the specifically educational elements of bureaucratic arrangements themselves. For no bureaucracy can function unless those subject to it adopt specific attitudes, habits, beliefs, and orientations; attitudes to authority, habits of punctuality, regularity, and consistency, beliefs about the abstract nature and legitimacy of authority and expertise: orientations to rules and procedures. These attitudes, habits, beliefs, and orientations do not themselves spring into existence out of technical necessity; they are the products of complex and protracted social conflicts. Such character traits (or forms of subjectivity) were the conscious objectives of those interested in 'training the people for representative government.'[2] The role of bureaucratic institutions as what J.S. Mill called the great 'Normal School' for the people has been neglected in the literature, despite the insistence of 'revisionist' writers that 'education' is not simply about schools.

Bureaucratic administrative systems have substance. 'Efficiency,' as Emile Durkheim pointed out a century ago, is an ethical construct, one whose adoption involves a moral and political choice. Its institutionalization should be taken as an instance of cultural power relations. Where the origin of social arrangements in political, cultural, and moral choices has disappeared or has come to appear as a neutral technical matter, where bureaucracy has become 'efficiency,' one faces a situation of cultural and political hegemony.[3]

I argue in this chapter that the substance of bureaucratic administration in schooling in Canada West was largely constituted by the moral, cultural, and political interests of the rising middle classes. I do not argue that such administration took place in a social vacuum, that capitalists, clergymen, merchants, and professionals had a free hand, or that popular action and reaction were unimportant in bureaucratic development. I do not argue that the rising middle classes were unanimous in their educational politics, nor do I argue that their politics were wholly enlightened or wholly reactionary. I do argue that these people's interests defined the 'interests of education,' and that their experience in attempting to further these interests led and constrained them to adopt bureaucratic methods of organization. The creation of the relatively autonomous 'interests of education' was an essential moment in state formation. But there were always other possible methods of organizing social institutions: the Clear Grit platform of 1850, with its planks drawn from the English Chartists, is a case in point, and many local, communitarian movements existed in Canada West in this period. Centralized, bureaucratic management triumphed only by eliminating or marginalizing such alternatives.

While the central educational authority came to see that the efficacy of its policy lay ordinarily in a regular, uniform, and consistent application of general principles to specific cases, the principles in question sustained a web of authority relations. Bureaucratic procedure was, at times, urged upon field officers as a means to defend particular substantive policies, to eliminate 'grounds for complaint.' It affected the form of judgments without changing their substance.[4]

'Rationalized' and 'Non-Rationalized' Rule

It is useful to bear in mind in what follows a distinction between 'rationalized' (legal) and 'non-rationalized' (moral/ideological) elements of governance. The former term refers to elements that were bureaucratic, at least in tendency, practices and procedures relatively indifferent to the personae of practitioners. The latter term refers to elements whose thrust is particularly moral-regulatory; elements whose efficacy lies in whole or in part in the power of social classes and groups to define the moral, the culturally worthy, the proper, and the appropriate in the realms of behaviour and consciousness, and to endow these partial definitions with a general prestige.[5]

This distinction evokes that drawn by Gramsci between 'two major superstructural "levels": the one that can be called "civil society," that is the ensemble of organisms commonly called "private," and that of "political society" or "the State." These two levels correspond on the one hand to the function of "hegemony" which the dominant group exercises throughout society and on the other hand to that of "direct domination" or command exercised through the State and "juridical government". The functions in question are precisely organisational and connective.' Gramsci continues this passage, which stresses the importance of 'intellectuals' in processes of rule, with a further elaboration of the distinction between 'social hegemony and political government.' 'Social hegemony' means 'the "spontaneous" consent given by the great masses of the population to the general direction imposed on social life by the dominant fundamental group; this consent is "historically" caused by the prestige (and consequent confidence) which the dominant group enjoys because of its position and function in the world of production.' 'Political government' refers to 'the apparatus of state coercive power which "legally" enforces discipline on those groups who do not "consent" either actively or passively. This apparatus is, however, constituted for the whole of society in anticipation of moments of crisis of command and direction when spontaneous consent has failed.'[6]

Mid-nineteenth-century governance in the Canadas involved an extension and intensification of rationalized state forms. The 1840s, especially, were a transitional decade in which non-rationalized forms of rule were in decline. But the development of rationalized political administration owed a considerable amount to the institutionalization of specific non-rationalized ways of ruling. And rationalized state forms continued to coexist with and depend upon non-rationalized forms of rule.[7]

Inspectors, for instance, gathered specific items of information in an increasingly standardized manner for a central authority. But standardization was a process that affected the form and not primarily the substance of their judgments. Again, access to local schools by inspectors was at least facilitated by their manner of dress, self-presentation, and other things marking them as a particular 'kind of person.' The transition in Canada West from rule by individual male proprietors to rule by the elected representatives of all male proprietors, and ultimately of all 'citizens,' was facilitated by continuity in the class and moral character of the first public officials and members of earlier 'compacts.'

Authority has a cultural basis, and, for at least the first half of the nineteenth century, one of the cultural prerogatives of men in the dominant classes was that of entering into the lives of and informing themselves about those beneath them. One of the cultural consequences of bureaucratic state administration and bourgeois class structure has been the erosion of this paternalistic right of men in the dominant classes as individuals to know the lives of others. The decline of the power of individual rulers to know the ruled personally has been paralleled by a proliferation of impersonal forms of state knowledge. Yet this established right and privilege were essential for the operation of the educational inspectorate in its earliest period. Bureaucratic administration developed out of, and was for a time continuous with, the methods of governance that preceded it.

Finance

'All states,' Weber reminds us, 'may be classified according to whether they rest on the principle that the staff of men themselves *own* the administrative means, or whether the staff is "separated" from these means of administration.'[8] One dimension of educational administration in the 1840s in Canada West was the development of pressure for rationalized management.

There were a variety of efforts to standardize procedures and to make them relatively indifferent to the personae of office holders, ranging from the organization of an education office with its own architectural identity, in place of Egerton Ryerson's house where the General Board of Education met during much of 1847, to matters of correspondence. Alexander McNab was chastised for including several requests of the government in the same communication. The documents generated by inspection were not to be the personal property of inspectors.[9]

The school acts created a financial framework for educational 'improvement.' The acts allowed for initiatives by a particular class of men, and provided central and district state servants with leverage over educational practice. The administration of the school grant was of central importance.

Nowhere in Canadian financial administration did agencies tax narrowly to spending estimates. Monies were expended or services performed, and tax revenues raised only after the fact. The same approach was taken to all educational offices as well. Teachers were paid yearly, in August at the earliest, after their year's labour. The school grant was placed at the disposal of the district superintendents, usually after the school taxes were placed on the collector's roll, but often before the tax was collected.

Two 'irrational' consequences ensued. First, only licensed teachers could draw the school grant, but, throughout the 1840s, and despite the agitations of the Education Office, teachers continued to present themselves for certification only when they came to collect their pay. Inspectors found themselves engaged in bitter disputes when they refused to pay unqualified teachers who had kept schools.[10]

Second, superintendents held the entire school monies until these were paid to teachers. There is no evidence to suggest separate accounts for school monies were kept; the opposite seems to have been the general practice. And although the Education Office expected district councils to pay the salaries of district and township superintendents out of general funds, superintendents were commonly paid a percentage of the monies passing through their hands. Such was also true of township collectors and district clerks. The fund actually reaching teachers or devoted to educational 'improvement' was substantially diminished for this reason.[11]

The Education Office attempted to end this practice, writing to district councils that superintendents' salaries were to be paid out of district funds and that school monies were intended solely for the payment of teachers. One of the contentious educational issues between radical and moderate Reformers in 1849 was the attempt by Malcolm Cameron to reduce educational taxation by paying educational administrators out of the school fund in poor townships. Despite the opposition of the Education Office, some superintendents continued to draw their own salaries from the school monies in their possession until the educational reforms of 1850.[12]

The Education Office was initially constrained to deliver school monies into the care of the respectable men chosen as district superintendents, but, by mid-1845, the office already had reason for unease. As we have seen, acting Assistant Superintendent McNab received an anonymous letter accusing Elias Burnham, Colborne District superintendent, of misusing the school monies and called him to account. Complaints that Dr McLean, the Kingston superintendent, had not divided money fairly led to a similar demand for an accounting in 1847. The vulnerability of the superintendents to such demands was impressed upon them.[13]

Late in 1845 John Steele, the warden and district superintendent for the Newcastle District, a trustee of Queen's College and a man extremely active in support of public improvement, was removed by order-in-council from the wardenship, which he had held for only a few months. In a letter to the press, Steele denied the provincial secretary's claim that he was in 'difficulties ... in matters connected with public moneys,' but sometime within the next six months he had ceased to be district superintendent of schools. Steele's financial problems likely concerned the school monies.[14]

'Mr Bignall's Villainy'

The limitations of allowing 'choice men' to hold the school monies was forcefully demonstrated by the activities of John Bignall, Huron District superintendent. Bignall was extremely lax in his accounting and reporting procedures from his first appointment. It is not clear he presented any systematic report in 1844 or 1845. He responded to Assistant Superintendent Murray's demands for a report in the earlier year with the statement that he hadn't completed it, as he was 'living eight miles from the village, and [was] busily employed just now in getting in [his] crops.'[15] His report for 1847 was lacking in detail, but he did assure the Education Office that he had managed to make Council appropriate £100 for the purchase of Irish school books.[16] However, little if any school money was actually reaching teachers. Public attacks on Bignall's non-performance by Thomas Macqueen, the Reform editor of the *Huron Signal*, were sharp. Macqueen wrote of the district superintendents: 'We cannot see the necessity or the justifiable policy of squandering the educational funds upon such office holders ... to give away a large sum of money to a man for doing nothing but writing a few pages annually, and dividing a few hundred pounds among the half-paid teachers of his limits, and perhaps making a race once, or at most twice a year, merely popping his head, like Peter Pry, into the door of each school house he passes, is rather too much.' Bignall was an unusually large and fat man for his time, and Macqueen claimed that many of the superintendents 'have apparently been intended by nature as draymen for some respectable brewery, and their sottish stupidity, associated with the cause of education, exhibits a specimen of the truly ridiculous.' The remark earned him a visit from Bignall, who offered to alter Macqueen's phrenological chart.[17]

Public meetings of school trustees followed in Goderich in March 1848 'for the purpose of taking into consideration the reason of the District moneys not having been paid to the school teachers for the last year.' A resolution of a meeting at which Bignall's non-performance was complained of loudly led to memoranda addressed to both the district council and the district superintendent himself, as well as to a letter to the Education Office.

Bignall responded that he was 'prepared and anxious to answer any attack that has been made upon me, as a public servant,' and Ryerson himself intervened to chastise Bignall's critics and to express his entire confidence in Bignall's financial management. 'I am sure Mr. Bignall's explanation must have satisfied you, as it has me, that no blame whatever was attributable to him for the delay in the payment of the moneys in question, and that you did him great injustice in complaining of his conduct to this office, before you received his explanation.'[18]

But, at the May meetings of Huron Council, questions were again raised about Bignall's activities. One councillor wondered if Bignall had, in fact, reported to the Education Office in 1844 and 1845, if not, why he had not been fined by the chief superintendent, if so, why the district had received so little school money. When Bignall did not respond, Council moved at its October sessions in 1848 to require him to appear, with all of his correspondence with Egerton

Ryerson between 1846 and 1848. Ryerson himself noted that Bignall had not included his audited accounts with his school report for 1847 and urged him to send these to the Education Office.[19]

Bignall ignored Council's summons, and a motion passed on 7 October 1848, declaring the position of district superintendent vacant if Bignall did not appear with all his papers at the February sessions. Then an information was laid against Bignall on 9 October for embezzlement after it was discovered he had fled with the school monies. Council had failed to receive adequate sureties, and the taxpayers were constrained to make good the loss.[20]

To add to his own embarrassment, Ryerson had corresponded with Bignall shortly before his disappearance about ways in which Bignall could convert the school monies into cash. The grant was typically paid in the form of government debentures convertible only at a discount. Some superintendents attempted to reduce the loss occasioned to teachers from this cause by travelling themselves to Montreal, where discounts were lower, and carrying the school monies back with them. There were various schemes afoot for making up the discounted sum.[21]

At the other end of the colony the following summer, the Eastern District superintendent absconded with £500 and, in July 1849, Ryerson watched as the Colborne District Council fired Benjamin Hayter after he refused to pay surplus school monies into the district treasury, something which would have violated the School Act.[22]

These instances of peculation led to the management of school monies by county treasurers under the School Act of 1850 and to the introduction of annual audits. 'Under this system,' Ryerson noted, 'local Superintendents will be under no temptation, at any time, from considerations of personal convenience, to withhold or delay the payment of school moneys.'[23] The experience of educational administration demonstrated that personal management of public finance threatened the educational project.

Superintendence as a Vocation

At the other end of the spectrum, many of the educational inspectors subsidized the office out of their own pockets. Samuel Ardagh spent £44 on postage, stationery, and travel in 1844, but received only £25 from Simcoe District Council. Newton Bosworth was eventually awarded £50 from Brock Council for his efforts in 1844 and 1846, an amount regarded as insufficient to cover his correspondence costs. William Fraser complained that the superintendency of the Eastern District cost him £7 of his own money in 1849, a sum he could ill afford. John Flood, William Clarke, and others served gratuitously for longer or shorter periods.[24]

That is not to say that inspectors were all men of 'public spirit,' for many of them served without pay as a speculation, or quit when they realized that no pay was forthcoming. Some superintendents responded to the low pay offered them by district councils by performing only clerical functions, but others were particularly active in educational inspection and propaganda – 'the good cause,' William Hutton called it. Moral leadership and commitment were central to the operation of the inspectorate.

Superintendents were salaried public officials, but many of them lived 'for' rather than 'off' public administration. Their personal commitment was an important element in their inspectoral activities.[25]

Inspectors were placed to make and enforce *determinations* about the quality of teaching and learning, about the condition of education, and about what 'needed to be done,' although not without opposition. Financially, their room to manoeuvre was sustained by clauses allowing for the discretionary expenditure of surplus school monies. Initially, superintendents were granted wide latitude; especially true in the Dalhousie District, where, for five years, Hamnett Pinhey was allowed to distribute the state school grant in ways that seemed to him *personally* to be appropriate. But other superintendents also enjoyed discretionary power.[26]

Despite the fact that the School Act of 1843 recognized only *one* state school in any school section, John Strachan of the Midland District was allowed to subsidize two to promote 'harmony' in one section. Ryerson wrote, 'in cases in which we have any discretion we should administer and apply the law ... in such a way as will contribute most to the harmony & wishes of the community.'[27] McNab permitted Ardagh to distribute surplus monies in 1845 in any way upon which he and the local superintendents could agree.[28] The practice continued under the act of 1846. Ryerson encouraged George Hendry to distribute surplus monies to needy schools and commented on the discretionary monies clause to Charles Fletcher: 'I have found this clause of the Act extremely useful in many instances – enabling District Superintendents to maintain the law on the one hand, and yet on the other meet various special cases which clearly form exceptions to the general rule.'[29] ·

The Terrain of Inspection

While they were employed by district councils and, after 1846, legally bound to follow the instructions of the chief superintendent, district inspectors exerted a considerable influence over the conduct of local educational development. The powers they exerted went far beyond those specified by statute. Many of the things they did were not demanded of them by the School Act, and they were able to do many things by virtue of the prestige that their social positions conferred upon them.

Gramsci reminds us that the dominant class in any society must not only dominate but also lead if it is to remain in power. The district school inspectors occupied a terrain that allowed them to define 'the road to progress.' And, while their definitions were not always or automatically accepted, they were significant in establishing particular conceptions of 'what needed to be done' in education.

The superintendents agitated for educational improvement and exerted a degree of discretion explicitly encouraged by the Education Office.[30] Many of them urged the adoption of the Irish National school books before these were made the official texts in 1847. They proposed revisions to the curriculum in areas in which they found it weak, Canadian history and geography, for instance. They pushed for 'improved' schoolhouses, by which they understood buildings with cross-ventilation, privies, wells, and woodsheds, and, in some cases, separate entrances and separate seating arrangements for boys and girls. They tried to establish new schools and sometimes offered to subsidize them out of their own monies.[31] They counselled teachers to use gentle methods and to dispense with corporal punishment. While I do not think the only measure of political practice is the *intentions* of activists, many of these men were motivated by a sincere desire to make what they considered a better world, and, in contemporary terms, several of them were politically progressive.

While the superintendents sometimes opposed their own conceptions of educational improvement to those of the Education Office, this opposition did not call into question the more general educational project: that respectable men of property should regulate the educational development of society and that the principles of social order should be implanted in the young through training.

Intelligence

English debate over the nineteenth-century 'revolution in government' has stressed the centrality of the generation of public perceptions of social 'problems' by strategically situated intellectuals in processes of state formation.[32] 'Scientific' views of social problems were a product of information-gathering by inspectors; this was certainly the case in Canada West. On the basis of their access to and intelligence-gathering in what had formerly been community institutions, district superintendents of education developed particular views of educational conditions and of what needed to be done to improve them. These views were important resources in educational politics.

As superintendent of education for Canada West, Egerton Ryerson was aware from the outset that official educational statistics could play an important role in sustaining the educational project. From his first annual reports, he published comparative statistical tables intended to demonstrate the 'advance' and 'improvement' of the school system, in comparison both with preceding years and with educational development in parts of the United States. He complained bitterly when the confusion provoked by the School Act of 1846 led to less detailed reporting from inspectors.[33] 'Believing that one of the most serious obstacles to the progress of Common School instruction in the country was the ignorance and consequently indifference, which exists as to its real state,' Ryerson had 'prepared and got printed a Table of Statistics of Common Schools in Upper Canada.' He sent a copy of this to every district council and newspaper editor, 'besides many others' in the colony.[34]

As the Reform ministry prepared to consider a new school bill early in 1849, Ryerson wrote to his parliamentary ally J.C. Morrison, asking him to secure a large printing of the school report for 1848. 'As you have seen some of the statistical tables which it contains,' Ryerson commented, 'you know their relative importance ... The wide diffusion of such information among a people is important to the advancement of popular education at any time, but it is essential in the commencement of a system.' To his dismay, Parliament refused a large printing.[35] In his defence of the acts of 1846 and 1847 to the ministry after the passage of the Cameron act, Ryerson drew heavily upon statistics generated by district superintendents to claim that the acts had increased the interest of the respectable classes in the schools, despite his earlier hesitations about the reliability of such statistics.[36] 'Does Public Sentiment in Favour of Popular Education Increase in Upper Canada?' asked Hodgins in the *Journal of Education* in the middle of the educational crisis. The growing numbers of children in the schools and of visits to schools by members of the respectable classes and the success of the free school system in those districts where it was in place provided a strong answer in the affirmative![37] And Ryerson concluded his annual report for 1848, reprinted in large part in the *Journal of Education* in September 1849, with the observation that '*these statistics evince that practical and general exertion, rather than theoretical and up-rooting legislation*, is required to place the Common School system of Upper Canada upon a level with those of the oldest States of America.'[38] The defence of the educational interest involved ideological work aimed at establishing a view of existing social conditions, at defining needed improvements, and at limiting parliamentary 'interference.'

The educational superintendents were involved in the production of the intelligence on which such 'scientific' views of educational progress were formulated. Their views provided the basis for informed debate about educational organization and development. Information-gathering by superintendents was absolutely indispensable to the operation of the acts. There was even no reliable census in the colony before 1848, and the state grant was distributed according to population. Superintendents drew up censuses of school districts.[39]

From the outset, however, inspectors were left largely to devise their own standards for evaluating educational questions. Many of them sought standardized report forms when they took office, but until 1847 such forms were not generally available.[40] The criteria by which teachers and schools were evaluated and the organization of information reported were left largely to the superintendents themselves until 1847, and only general guidelines were specified thereafter. Thus, the observable regularities in inspectoral reporting stemmed initially from the common perceptions of inspectors, from their participation in a common class culture.

The Organization of Educational Intelligence

The central authority worked to standardize intelligence-gathering and reporting by inspectors. In contrast to the situation in many European countries, regular and formal contact between the Education Office and district superintendents was limited in Canada West. There was no central superintendents' headquarters in the colony, and superintendents had not taken any serious steps towards professional organization by 1850. Under the tenure of Murray and McNab, individual correspondence and personal visits to the Education Office exhausted the contact inspectors had with the central office, although there were instances of the central authority encouraging field officers to organize local intelligence in congenial ways. Despite evidence of their receptivity to direction from the centre, inspectors were initially left more or less to their own devices.[41] Ryerson's attempts to secure a stronger central control over superintendents in the acts of 1846 and 1847 were only moderately successful. He was empowered to instruct these officials, but not to appoint or dismiss them, nor to summon them to Toronto for a collective information session. Thus he was left to undertake other propaganda efforts and to exercise his authority to specify rules and regulations. Successive circulars from the central office encouraged and cajoled inspectors to approximate the office's model of sound practice. Books of forms and instructions were distributed after 1847, seeking to standardize the kinds of information collected and the kinds of agreements struck between educational agents. Ryerson undertook a province-wide tour in the autumn of 1847, spreading the common-school gospel in lectures to the 'respectable' residents of most district towns, and meeting, often for the first time, with his field officers. Most of these public meetings produced resolutions in favour of aspects of educational reform sought by Ryerson: free schooling, compulsory attendance, normal training, and so on.[42]

In addition to these initiatives, John George Hodgins, under Ryerson's tutelage, undertook to edit a *Journal of Education for Upper Canada* to provide a public forum for the educational interest. The journal first appeared in 1848, funded by Ryerson and Hodgins themselves. A key victory for Ryerson in the subsequent educational crisis was the securing of official funding for this enterprise and its recognition as the legitimate source of official communications from the Education Office.

Initially, however, the journal was dependent upon private subscriptions, and superintendents played a key role in promoting its circulation. Ryerson and Hodgins hoped to place a copy in the hands of every teacher in every school section in the province, but this was not immediately possible. By 1850, the Bathurst, Johnstown, Midland, and Prince Edward district councils had ordered copies for every school section, and, in the Niagara District, Dexter D'Everardo had ordered a similar number of copies himself. Several of the other superintendents purchased multiple copies.[43] The journal provided the central office with an important medium for communicating with officials at various levels of the system and for framing inspectoral activity.

From the first numbers of the journal, Hodgins encouraged an active and energetic inspectoral practice, frequently referring to conditions in New York, England, Germany, Ireland, and Holland. At Ryerson's invitation, Thomas Jaffray Robertson, headmaster of the Normal School and one of the first inspectors for the Irish National Board, produced a seven-page article, 'On the Inspection of Common Schools,' for the journal in 1848. This article provided a clear statement of the kind of activity sought from district superintendents.

'The legitimate end of school inspection,' Robertson began, 'is to obtain the most thorough information possible on all points connected with the school.' Inspectors should pay close attention to the nature and quality of the lessons students received, to school records, to the condition of the house and grounds, and to the moral character of the teacher. It was particularly important to discover 'the mode of control adopted by the Teacher, whether it is merely harshness, with its attendant slavish fear and sullen submission, or good-humored firmness, with its concomitant, willing obedience.' To this end, it would be necessary to observe students closely, and 'at their sports, if possible.'

Inspectors were especially advised to examine the progress of students in their studies and to keep detailed and extensive notes of all they observed. The progress exhibited by the students was to be evaluated in terms of their habits of attendance. Robertson stressed that irregular attendance was itself attributable to 'the apathy of parents, which is such as to render them altogether indifferent to the subject.' Only if the school kept good attendance records would the inspector be able to understand the extent to which instruction was allowing the students to advance.

Inspectors were also to provide advice and counsel to teachers in the acceptable method of instruction, especially to those 'who, from age, insufficient pecuniary resources, or other causes, are unable to attend a Normal School.' They should cause teachers to teach before them, to see the extent to which order, energy, and efficiency ruled in the school. Where correction was to be given to a teacher, inspectors were to be careful to give no intimation to students that such was the case.

All this was to be done with 'good humored kindness, coupled with firmness and tact.' Particular care was to be taken to avoid terrifying either teacher or students. The superintendent should remember that he, like the teacher, was 'an officer appointed by law to administer the system under which they both act, and no difference of official rank should for an instant be admitted as an excuse for a harsh and overbearing exercise of authority.'

The activity of the inspector was to extend beyond the walls of the school. He 'should endeavour to make himself acquainted with the feeling of the neighbourhood on the subject of education, with the view of removing prejudice, supporting the authority of the Teacher where necessary, and obtaining such local information as will enable him to afford valuable advice and suggestions on the occurrence of occasional difficulties.'

Two other matters concerned Robertson: the frequency of inspection and the question of secrecy. Robertson himself had witnessed the Irish attempt to inspect schools once yearly and found it a failure. An annual visit could produce statistical information, but could not ensure adherence to rules: for this at least quarterly visits were required by the inspector. These might be supplemented by 'the visits of individuals or committees in the neighbourhood,' as long as such practices did not 'afford opportunity for undue interference on the part of ignorant or inexperienced persons.' Robertson stressed that school inspection demanded expertise: 'The ability to discuss with advantage, and judge with sagacity, of the efficiency of systems of teaching and the organization of schools, requires considerable experience, and no system, whether applied to education or anything else, can be carried out successfully, when unqualified persons attempt to overrule and control it.'

Finally, Robertson insisted that school inspections must by no means be announced in advance. Prior notice would prevent the inspector's observation of a school in its workaday condition and would injure the teacher as well.

How long was such an inspection to take? With a qualified teacher following an approved system and having fewer than fifty students, at least two and a half hours. With an unqualified teacher, or with more students, it would take longer.[44]

This model of inspectoral practice was completely unattainable in Canada West. If all the common schools in the Home District had contained fewer than fifty students, had been taught by qualified teachers according to an approved system, and had been transported to Hamilton Hunter's office in Toronto, it would have taken him 600 five-hour days to inspect them four times: rather more days than there are in a year. The most energetic superintendents in the smallest districts managed to 'see' most of the common schools twice a year. But the journal was concerned to 'improve' educational practice, not simply to describe what real officials could do.

It is impossible to determine with any precision what effects these initiatives of the Education Office had on the practical activity of inspection. They could not be enforced with any rigidity. The Education Office remained highly dependent upon the commitment, cultural understanding, political interests, and moral character of the superintendents themselves. But one should not assume, for that reason, that propaganda was unimportant. Propaganda at least presented a model of desirable practice and a set of standards to educational administrators. It was important as a claim by the Education Office to a monopoly over the expertise needed to be able to recognize a good school.

Determinations

It is striking how little rationalized was the initial lexicon of educational efficiency. Vague terms of evaluation point to the importance of cultural assumptions in educational administration. In 1845, Charles Eliot classified schools in the Western District as 'good' and 'not good'; Thomas Donnelly described schools as 'middling,' 'very bad,' and 'bad.' Jacob Keefer perceived schools to be 'fair,' 'pretty fair,' 'good,' 'middling,' 'ordinary,' 'not forward,' and 'small and backward.'[45] Even when the Education Office printed report forms that demanded the classification of schools in terms of quality, no criteria for making these determinations were specified. The official report forms for 1848 contained a section entitled 'School Houses and their Appendages' in which superintendents were to record information as to the numbers and kinds of buildings and facilities. They were to register the numbers of schools in 'good,' 'bad,' and 'ordinary repair'; those 'suitably furnished' and 'not so furnished'; those with and without 'proper facilities for ventilation' and 'suitable Playgrounds'; and those with 'simple' or 'double' privies and those 'entirely destitute of Privy.'[46] No definitions were given.

The report forms claimed that teachers could be 'naturally divided into three classes.' However, 'the line of demarcation between these three classes of certificates' was 'left to the judgment of each District Superintendent,' for 'further consultation and preparation' were in order before the 'legal classification of teachers could be made.' Only the minimum standard was specified: 'it is recommended, except under very peculiar circumstances, that no certificate of qualification be given to a person who is not competent to teach English Grammar – including Orthography and Orthoepy, as well as Syntax and Prosody – Writing, Practical Arithmetic, Book-Keeping by Single Entry, and the Elements of Geography.'[47]

Remarkably little elaboration of the criteria used in evaluating schools or in distinguishing categories of teachers took place. The inspectors used taken-for-granted standards of evaluation: standards they and central administrators took for granted.

John Flood was one of the few inspectors to discuss his evaluation of schools. 'I am not aware of any established definitions,' he wrote, 'by which to distinguish first class Schools from others but I have arranged in this column all that I considered the best in the District and which always have English grammar.' A well-ventilated school for Flood had a window on two sides.[48] William Hutton found the number of Irish National school books 'used in a school a great criterion of its grade.'[49] That these evaluations were taken by the Education Office as the basis for its annual reports shows that it spoke the same language as its field officers. At the same time, categorical vagueness allowed central authorities to interpret superintendents' reports.

Official knowledge was made, not just taken, and the report forms in use after 1847 themselves framed educational intelligence in keeping with a particular view of what needed to be done and known. The obviousness of the fact that superintendents tended to report the kinds of information the report forms required them to should not lull us into assuming that this information was in any large sense what was 'really' important to know about the schools. The endless inspectoral reports of small and poorly furnished schoolhouses, of low and irregular attendance, and of underqualified and poorly paid teachers are intelligible only within the terms of an implicit model of desirable educational organization. The invariable optimism of inspectors' reports, their unending chant that 'things were improving,' was a declaration of their support for the educational project.

Report forms sought to provide the central authority with quantitative measures of the advance of the educational project and with suggestions from culturally reputable observers as to what needed to be done to continue that advance. Superintendents tended to respond in kind, and the most thorough inspectoral reports were reproduced by the chief superintendent as calls for reform. Official statistics were a 'political arithmetic,' to use William Petty's term, knowledge useful for political ends.[50]

William Hutton's report for 1849 was one of those reproduced in the annual report of the chief superintendent. Hutton revealed not only that he urged people to read the Irish readers at school, but also that he worked to reform their personal habits. 'We are not I fear improving in the delicacy of *feeling* in our school yards,' wrote Hutton in this report,

Most extraordinary and to me unaccountable negligence exists among the Trustees and the People with regard to providing the outbuilding which should be attached to every school house to afford privacy to the children requiring to go to the yard – Scarcely a privy is there to a School house in our whole County & what is more extraordinary still perhaps & scarcely one to our private houses – our wealthy farmers have them not – I have spoken again and again about the necessity of having them but all in vain – Could not some method be devised to encourage the building of them – they form an important item in school architecture.[51]

Hutton did not justify privies in hygienic terms; he was writing before the acceptance of a germ theory of disease. 'Delicacy of feeling,' a bourgeois cultural attribute, was at issue here. Superintendents were placed to agitate for respectable middle-class habits and beliefs. Inspection went well beyond the simple collection of 'facts'; inspection was an instrument of governance whereby respectable men of property sought the cultural, moral, and political reformation of the population. These people believed that their conceptualization of the world reflected the categories of nature. In this transitional period, the power of members of the rising middle classes to make and enforce educational determinations was not decorated with elaborate scientific justifications.

The Annual Reports

In addition to using significantly vague criteria of evaluation, superintendents transformed select bodies of information about the organization and progress of education by applying their 'best knowlege' or 'local information.' From the outset, local superintendents' reports and those of school trustees were described as imperfect, and this fact was recognized by the Education Office. Inspectors' reports were frequently accompanied by hesitations about and qualifications of the reliability of the information submitted. 'The preceeding Report,' wrote Colin Gregor for 1845, 'has been compiled from materials so crude, undigested, and even contradictory, that were there not an imperative necessity for transmitting it, I would crave some delay ... The Reports of the Supt's of Alfred Cumberland and Russell are to me utterly incomprehensible.' Still, Gregor concluded, the schools were improving on the whole.[52] Charles Eliot warned that, in some cases, the township superintendents' 'statements are not perfectly regular' and confessed that, with respect to the schools in Yarmouth Township, he had 'not seen sufficient of many of the Schools in this Township to give a *deliberate* opinion respecting them.'[53] 'I suppose many of the County Supt's would be like myself in reference to the Reports,' Patrick Thornton reflected, 'scarcely know in some instances what to make of the materials handed in under the form of reports from the Township Sup'ts. – I studied to render mine accurate so far as my materials went.'[54]

Several inspectors pointed to cases where the manner in which the Education Office framed its reports either failed to capture or distorted actual educational practice. The debate between Ryerson and Hendry over whether or not room and board should be calculated as a part of the teachers' salaries is the leading case in point, but there were others. John Strachan did not distinguish the time schools were kept open by qualified teachers, as the report encouraged, because 'one half of the Teachers were not qualified nor could qualified Teachers be obtained.' Dexter D'Everardo commented on his report for 1848,

In the Column headed 'Actual number of qualified Teachers' I have put down the number of different Teachers employed in the Section during the year, From the unfortunate practice which prevails here, as in other Districts of frequently changing Teachers, it may often happen that the same person has been employed in two or more Schools at different periods within the year – hence the presumption is that the total under that Column shews a greater number of Teachers than we have, tho many females are employed in Summer who do not teach in Winter and many males teach in winter who do not teach in Summer.[55]

The quality of information inspectors sent to the Education Office was affected by their personal energy and by the size of their districts. 'The accompanying report,' wrote Hamilton Hunter for 1848, 'I have made out with as much accuracy as the nature of the materials with which I was furnished would permit. There are some of the columns which I found it impossible to fill up from the Circumstance of my not having visited the Schools in all the Townships during the year.'[56]

Still, district superintendents were returned their annual reports for correction and revision when these were incomplete. Elias Burnham of Peterborough had this experience repeatedly. 'I have received none anything like as defective as yours,' Ryerson wrote to him about his report in 1849 and, in 1850, told him, 'in its present state your report was comparatively worthless.' After Burnham confessed that the task of filling out the report (there were five sheets and, when assembled, the form was six feet long and three feet wide) so daunted him that he had hired the clerk of the peace to complete it, Ryerson instructed him in detail as to its assembly.[57]

'Knowing how necessary it is in all statistical reports that every column should be attended to,' W.H. Landon remarked in 1849, 'I have supplied these according to the best of my judgement ... in many of the particulars the truth is only approximated.'[58] When James Padfield left some columns in his report blank, Ryerson wrote to him: 'As yours is the only Report deficient in these Items it will be necessary for me with your assistance to approximate as nearly as possible to the truth, so that the grand totals for the Province under the head of "moneys" will exhibit the aggregate of the several totals of the Districts without exception.' Padfield complied and commented, 'I have approximated as near as I could to what I suppose will be the actual results.'[59] 'I have been under the necessity to guess a great deal in trivial matters,' William Fraser remarked, and John Flood echoed, 'I have been obliged to fill up this report in many places from my own knowledge of the schools.'[60] 'The Trustees have left a great deal to be *imagined* by me,' commented Benjamin Hayter wryly.[61] And while John Strachan kept a 'memorandum book' while inspecting schools, which allowed him to supplement the information reported to him by trustees, there is little evidence superintendents acted other than from memory, at times aided by cursory diary entries.[62]

Ryerson and Hodgins themselves worked to order and interpret the information they received from inspectors. When the absconding of William Millar in 1849 led to imperfect reporting for the Eastern District, Ryerson was 'anxious to make the apportionment' of government money to the district 'as near that of last year as possible.' To that end he 'made a liberal allowance for the defectiveness of the School returns.'[63] Hodgins scribbled with exasperation across the top of George Duck's report for 1849, 'Not a particle of this Report added up. The same was the case last year too.' The labour of arranging and interpreting superintendents' reports undoubtedly contributed to the deterioration of Hodgins's health.[64]

My point is not that these reports were inadequate or suspect because they guessed at a set of natural facts that better procedures would have revealed more completely. 'The truth' does not wait patiently upon the design of devices and procedures adequate to its discovery. 'The truth' of the social state is a social, and hence a moral, political, and ideological construct. These reports *were* the truth. Educational facts were the opinions, guesses, judgments, and evaluations of a group of respectable men, interpreted again in the interests of educational improvement by the central authority. Ryerson delivered them to the legislature as the official view of educational organization in Canada West. He used them to defend centralized educational administration against the attacks of the left of the Reform party in 1849. They formed the basis of demands for reform. When the Reform ministry split over the direction of reform in 1849, district superintendents were invited to collect and transmit the views of the most 'intelligent' trustees and teachers in their jurisdictions on alterations to the school acts. In short, the estimates, guesses, and perceptions of inspectors formed a corpus of hegemonic knowledge. The reports themselves were 'read' in ways that educational administrators deemed appropriate or useful in given circumstances. Oppositional voices did not make it into the official record.

The cultural understandings of respectable men formed the central resources in the politics of educational knowledge in Canada West in the 1840s. It was out of the practical experience of their activity that administrative procedures were elaborated. The growing state system tended to organize and connect the activities of these respectable men and once the organization and connection of their activities were formalized and standardized, once their judgments were normalized under the rubric of educational 'efficiency,' these men themselves became replaceable. At the basis of bureaucratic procedure in educational administration lay the class-specific cultural perceptions of respectable, largely Anglo-Saxon men of property. The interests of education were a rendering of their interests, and the practice of inspection created a set of possibilities for the administration of these interests into dominance.

Bureaucratic organization was not simply a neutral and technical response to increases in the scale of educational relations. It was partly the result of efforts by a central authority, operating in a particular context of class and party politics, to coordinate, systematize, and, at times, reform the activities of respectable men of property and education. It involved a double shift of power in educational matters, away from individual members of local élites or 'compacts' and, at once, away from the 'common people,' teachers, students, and ratepayers.

The formation of bureaucratic administration thus involved a double dynamic. An educational authority was created in a particular political economic context, one that was especially a matter of class and party politics. Through the financial and ideological instruments at its disposal, this central authority set in motion an administrative dynamic in which knowledge/power relations figured centrally. The practical experience of administration led to central initiatives that stabilized and formalized administrative practices and procedures. The interests of education became 'public' interests, interests not to be monopolized by individuals, but, at the same time, interests about which most people were held to be unable to judge.

The freeing of the 'interests of education' from popular and élite control was an element in state formation – both as the creation of a new sphere of administrative activity and as the elaboration of an ideology of governance apparently above particular social interests. Yet, as I have repeatedly argued, this educational 'efficiency' was based upon a class culture. It succeeded as the 'way forward' for schooling in Canada West; its success should not lead one to conclude that it was *the only* possible way forward.

Conclusion

The reorganization of state administration in mid-nineteenth-century Canada West was dependent upon a politics of knowledge/power and upon the practice of inspection. By 1850, the right of official inspection as a condition of state finance was firmly established in the domain of public education, and soon followed in other domains. The systematization of central financial power through the Audit Act of 1855 focused the gaze of state servants on the execution of policies at the local level, as it reinforced the importance of inspection. Central authorities were increasingly able to monitor the local fate of their policies, to identify conflicts, to capture and disseminate innovation, to translate legal principles into administrative practices. Inspection was a key resource in the forging of the regime of political representation.

In the case of education in Canada West, the school inspectorate grew enormously under the School Act of 1850. From 20 district superintendents in 1849–50, the Education Office supervised the activities of almost 280 township superintendents in 1852–3, and more than 320 in 1861–2. Forty per cent of these men, for there were no female inspectors, although more than half of elementary school teachers by 1865 were women, were clergymen, and most of the rest were professionals and farmers. But while the act of 1850 increased the numbers of local inspectors, it also increased the authority and capacities of the central Education Office.

The decentralizaton of inspectoral circuits, from two counties in most cases to one township, redistributed powers exercised by a few regionally important men to a corps of lesser officials. The displacement of earlier inspectoral powers over teacher certification and finance to county boards of public instruction and county treasurers, in addition to such things as the introduction of regular audits, allowed the central authority to shape and monitor local practice more completely. The Education Office began to specify standards for teacher certification, and later to produce teacher examinations. The increase in the numbers of inspectors, with statutory requirements for regular inspections and the delivery of public lectures, augmented the sources of information, regulation, and propaganda upon which the central authority could draw. That is not to argue that local educational autonomy was completely abolished; local officials continued to exert a limited discretion in internal school matters, and local conflict over educational practices was intense. But the effect upon general policy that any one inspector's discretion could have was localized and reduced. While township superintendents of common schools were not 'professional' inspectors, in the decades after 1850 the central authority was increasingly able to frame and detail their activity. The resources of the central authority in the administration of the education of the public were markedly increased under the School Act of 1850.

The practice of inspection was applied to grammar schools, by amendments to the Grammar School Act in 1855, which created two inspectors. One of these was T.J. Robertson, headmaster of the Normal School and one of the first Irish National Board inspectors. The School Act of 1871 abolished township elementary school superintendents and replaced them with county inspectors, whose minimum qualifications were defined by the central authority. In 1874, school inspectors were explicitly forbidden to hold any other occupation, and from the 1920s were trained and certified by the central authority. The relative autonomy of the interests of education was solidified, as training and certification criteria for those administering them derived from these very same interests.

The instrument of inspection was at once wielded and shaped by respectable men who were drawn from or spoken for by the rising middle class. Motivated frequently by a sense of public mission, by a desire to encourage a process of social, moral, political, and economic improvement, these men undertook diverse and broad-ranging initiatives in a widely defined educational domain. While many of these men believed themselves to be operating in the interest of the public good, that interest they defined themselves. It was bounded in their minds by political considerations: 'choice men without early educational prejudices' were those fitted by nature and circumstance to make determinations in the interests of education. And while these people could tell at a glance good educational practice from bad, most people could not be trusted to do so.

There were variations on this theme among the men studied here: from Newton Bosworth's and Patrick Thornton's encouragement of self-improvement by organized male teachers and their implicit belief in men's (not women's) capacities to better themselves; to William Hutton's fear that a decade of public instruction was necessary to fit male landholders for self-government; to, at the other extreme, Hamnett Pinhey's deep-seated and paternalistic opposition to electoral representation and property taxation. There were also important individual differences among inspectors in their commitment to and enthusiasm for inspectoral practice.

Still, I argue, these men actively shaped inspectoral practice and, through the routinization of their undertakings, the views of one social class, one gender, and one race were administered into dominance in the educational domain. Class culture lay at the basis of bureaucratic administration.

Inspection was educational for inspectors themselves: as in the political theory of liberalism, participation in local government was practical training. These men learned lessons about record-keeping, account-keeping, and report-making, as well as about interpersonal authority. Increasingly insistent demands from the central authority for complete, consistent, and analytic educational reports constrained the investigative activities of inspectors. William Hutton graduated from this school to become secretary to the Bureau of Agriculture, Registration and Statistics, an important deputy-ministerial post in the Canadian state before Confederation. Hutton's department undertook a very wide range of knowledge-gathering and -diffusing activities, from the oversight of mechanics' institutes, official exhibitions, and agricultural societies, to the design of the census of 1861. And Hutton himself could draw upon a network of relations pioneered in educational administration in his ongoing pursuit of social improvement.

The Generalization of Inspection

While the educational inspectorate in Canada West was the largest in the Canadas of the 1840s, inspection as a political instrument and practice became a constitutive element of the state system in the domains of social policy, public health, and safety. Inspectoral activity generated knowledge, through which interests of state were articulated.

In Canada East, the School Act of 1851 instituted an inspectoral system involving the central appointment of county inspectors. The Public Health Act of 1849 allowed for the central appointment of a five-member provincial board of health upon proclamation of the existence of an epidemic or contagious disease. Local authorities in any place named in such a proclamation could, or, upon the petition of local householders, were required to, appoint a local board of health that was to execute regulations issued by the provincial board. Any two members of a local board were empowered to enter any place in which they believed a person had died from epidemic or contagious disease or which they believed to be in a 'filthy or degraded condition.' These local health inspectors could issue orders with respect to such places, could call on local constables to enforce them, and could cause those refusing to obey to be fined or imprisoned. The capacity of the central authority developed to the point where, during the smallpox epidemic of 1885, two-thirds of the population of Ontario was placed under a condition of sanitary surveillance within a twenty-four-hour period.[1]

The powers of the inspectors of the provincial penitentiary were reorganized by statute in 1851 and extended to cover all prisons and jails in the province. Andrew Dickson, former sheriff of the Bathurst District, was named inspector for Canada West, and Dr Wolfred Nelson, the 1830s reformer, for Canada East. Unlike Dickson's laconic effort, Nelson produced a remarkable report in 1852, which ran to 100 printed pages and which catalogued prison and jail conditions throughout Canada East. Nelson reproduced the circulars he sent to jail managers and their replies, submitted detailed plans and drawings of each provincial prison and jail, and documented prison conditions. He analysed the state of these institutions, suggested plans for improvement, and appended a large number of relevant papers. Inspectoral activity provided the central authority for the first time with a systematic and general knowledge of penal conditions in at least half of the colony.

Legislation in 1857 allowed the executive to appoint five inspectors to investigate all prisons, jails, hospitals, and asylums. The central authority was henceforth able to specify and approve plans for the construction of all new jails and, under the energetic direction of Dr Joseph-Charles Taché, did in fact do so.[2]

After a number of vicious railway accidents caused by scamping contractors, Parliament created a railway inspectorate with powers to prevent the running of trains. Samuel Keefer, younger brother to the first Niagara District school inspector, was one of the first railway inspectors. An earlier act allowed the executive to appoint inspectors of steam vessels who were to conduct yearly hull and machinery investigations and to investigate the condition of firehoses, life boats, lights, safety valves, etc., and who were to issue certificates. Inspectors oversaw colonization road construction and reported on the state of agricultural development, investigated the accounts of agricultural societies, and visited other public institutions. They provided quarterly reports to central authorities about wages, prices, the demand for labour, and the progress of immigration policy.[3]

Educational inspection in Canada West was part of a far larger process of state formation. The instrument and practice of inspection played a major role in the formation of a centralized state system in the Canadas under the Union of 1840.

'Changes in central/local relations,' writes Hennock in a review of the development of English local government, 'were in the first instance due to a feature of the mid-nineteenth century that I have called the centralization of knowledge ... From the 1830s onward inspectors, travelling the country on behalf of central government departments, were able to assemble standardized information about different localities.'[4] These practices were generalized to the

Canadas in the decade of the 1840s, after the reform of local government made possible the execution of systematic social policy.

Panoptic modes of regulation were the necessary complement of the reconstruction of colonial governance under way in this decade. This reconstruction involved a certain democratization of rule by redistributing and extending the governmental powers exercised by adult male proprietors through institutions and practices of representation. These first steps in the creation of the local state were closely monitored by inspection and shaped further by directly educational practices elaborated by the central authority.

Inspectoral practice in education operated initially as a means for the organization and connection of the formerly isolated activities of individual members of the rising middle classes. It remained quite visibly the political practice of members of this class in its formative period, but pressure for effective and efficient intervention, in a context of political conflict that made the presentation of class interest as a general social interest imperative, propelled the standardization of inspectoral practice. Standardization and the neutralization of judgments tended to make implicit, rather than explicit, the class-specific content of educational governance. Once this process of neutralization and standardization was reasonably well advanced, the exercise of the inspective function could be displaced to functionaries drawn from other classes of the population. Anyone, at least in principle, could be trained in the replicable practices, procedures, and valuations established to promote the 'public interest,' an ideological construct that seeks to forge a domain of consensus out of the antagonisms characteristic of capitalist society. Bureaucratic procedure has its roots in the struggle of the rising middle classes for political dominance.

As the technology of rule has become more sophisticated, and as the legitimacy of the right of the centre to know local activity has been solidified, other mechanisms of administration, financial accounting especially, have displaced inspectoral activity. The placing of the Canadian population under a condition of state tutelage has come to be normalized as a natural 'fact of life,' and alternatives to such tutelage survive, if at all, on the margins of popular culture.

But the historical importance of inspection should not be underestimated. Writing in 1851 with only some hyperbole, the Englishman Joseph Fletcher, Her Majesty's Inspector of British and Foreign School Society schools, secretary to commissions on handloom weavers and on the employment of children, and one of two secretaries of the London Statistical Society, observed that 'the instrument of Inspection, while it is one of which the public will never stand in awe, because it is so easy to remove a misbehaving inspector, is of sufficient power to accomplish all that the State can desire.'[5] Charles Leslie Glenn, Jr, director of the Bureau of Educational Equality for the Commonwealth of Massachusetts, writing in 1988, remarks: 'The collection and interpretation of educational statistics, ostensibly a perfectly neutral activity, had and continues to have the power to define perceptions of the salient strengths and weaknesses of schools.' Glenn's observation about Horace Mann of Massachusetts is equally applicable to Egerton Ryerson: his 'requests for information, and the use of the information he received, were in some respects the key elements of his influence over the development of the common school ... he used these reports to show how much needed to be done to improve the schools and, as the years went by, how much he had accomplished.'[6]

A key element of the process of state formation, I have suggested, was the elaboration of relatively autonomous 'interests of education' and the mobilization of expert officials for their administration. These interests were elaborated on the basis of the culture, activity, and authority of select men of property. These interests emerged out of prior relations of power and authority, but they also acquired a momentum of their own; they became responsive, in part, to specifically educational criteria.

In the regime of political representation, official knowledge and knowledge-generating practices have become resources, but they have also become sites of political struggle. They increase the power of central authority to know conditions in localities; they increase the power of local authorities to place their own situations in more general context. They may allow the centre to act against local political reaction; they may allow localities to expose defects, biases, exploitative dimensions of the regime. They juxtapose, and thus may mobilize, central and local interests.

A historical sociology of inspection is not, then, an argument for the abolition of the centralization of knowledge in defence of a (romanticized) vision of local autonomy. Nor is it an argument for the inherent beneficence of the centralization of knowledge. Inspection and the centralization of knowledge *have* become constitutive elements of the regime of representative government. A comprehension of their dynamics is essential for political activity, but they remain *resources* to be judged in terms of the nature of the regime in which they are placed and of the policies in whose pursuit they are enlisted.

Notes

AO   Archives of Ontario
CI   Outgoing General Correspondence
C6C   Incoming General Correspondence
LAC   Legislative Assembly of Canada
LAUC   Legislative Assembly of Upper Canada
MI   Teachers' Superannuation Records
NAC   National Archives of Canada
NLI   National Library of Ireland
NLS   National Library of Scotland
RG2   Record Group 2, Education Department Records
SPEPI   Society for the Promotion of the Education of the Poor in Ireland

Acknowledgments

1 See Robert Lanning, 'Mapping the Moral Self: Biography, Education, and State Formation in Ontario, 1820–1920,' unpublished PHD thesis, Ontario Institute for Studies in Education, 1990.

Introduction

1 Frank Pitkin, 'Dexter D'Everardo,' Welland County Historical Society, *Papers and Records* 3 (1927): 86–103; also, J.H. Love, 'Anti-Americanism, Local Concerns and the Response to Social Issues in Mid-19th Century Upper Canadian School Reform,' unpublished PHD thesis, University of Toronto, 1978
2 Gerald E. Boyce, *Hutton of Hastings: The Life and Letters of William Hutton* (Belleville: Hastings County Council 1972)
3 Rev. S.J. Boddy, *A Brief Memoir of the Rev. Samuel B. Ardagh* (Toronto: Rowsell and Hutchison 1874); A.F. Hunter, *A History of Simcoe County* (Barrie: J.H. Beers 1907)

4 Philip Corrigan and Derek Sayer, *The Great Arch: English State Formation as Cultural Revolution* (Oxford: Basil Blackwell 1985); see also Mao Tse Tung, *Four Essays on Philosophy* (Peking: Foreign Languages Press 1973); Emile Durkheim, *Professional Ethics and Civic Morals* (Glencoe: Free Press 1958); for a recent application of this approach to Canadian material, see Philip McCann, 'Culture, State Formation and the Invention of Tradition: Newfoundland, 1832–1855,' *Journal of Canadian Studies* 23/1&2 (1988): 86–103.

5 See Alison Prentice, 'The Public Instructor: Ryerson and the Role of Public School Administrator,' in Neil McDonald and Alf Chaiton, eds., *Egerton Ryerson and His Times* (Toronto: Macmillan 1978), 129–59; also, S. Houston and A. Prentice, *Schooling and Scholars in Nineteenth-Century Ontario* (Toronto: University of Toronto Press 1989). Compare Janet Ajzenstat, *The Political Thought of Lord Durham* (Montreal and Kingston: McGill-Queen's University Press 1988), 84; earlier, Fred Landon, 'The Evolution of Local Government in Ontario,' *Ontario History* 42 (1950): 5: 'Robert Baldwin thought that the township and county councils would provide a schooling for men who would later aspire to higher honours, and this has been the case.' A key dimension of bureaucratic development is a tendency towards standardization of categories of administration. William Westfall's recent study, *Two Worlds: The Protestant Culture of Nineteenth Century Ontario* (Montreal and Kingston: McGill-Queen's University Press 1989), argues that a parallel process was taking place in the religious domain, especially with the increasing formalization of what he calls the 'religion of enthusiasm.'

6 Ryerson was assistant superintendent from 1844 until the end of 1846, when, largely at his urging, the office of superintendent of education for both parts of the colony was abandoned. One of the earliest revisions of the Ryerson-worship is Robert Gidney, 'The Rev. Robert Murray: Ontario's First Superintendent of Schools,' *Ontario History* 63/4 (1971): 191–204. We still hear loud echoes of earlier tendencies, e.g., Graham Parker, *The Beginnings of the Book Trade in Canada* (Toronto: University of Toronto Press 1985), 124: 'Such, then, were the ways in which Ryerson built up the splendid school system in Ontario, got cheap textbooks into the hands of thousands of school children, and helped develop the public library system.'

7 Philip Abrams, *Historical Sociology* (London: Open Books 1982)

8 I take my distance from social-control approaches in 'Preconditions of the Canadian State: Educational Reform and the Construction of a Public in Upper Canada, 1837–1846,' *Studies in Political Economy* 10 (1983): 99–121; I explore opposition to the public educational project in *Building the Educational State: Canada West, 1836–1871* (Sussex and London: Falmer Press and Althouse Press 1988) and 'Patterns of Resistance to Public Education: England, Ireland and Canada West, 1830–1890,' *Comparative Education Review*, 13/3 (1988): 318–33.

9 Philip Abrams, 'Notes on the Difficulty of Studying the State,' *Journal of Historical Sociology* 1/1 (1988): 58–89 and, more generally, *Historical Sociology* (London: Open Books 1982)

10 Max Weber, 'Politics as a Vocation,' in *Essays in Sociology*, ed. H.H. Gerth and C.W. Mills, 78 (New York: Oxford University Press 1958)

11 Antonio Gramsci, *Selections from the Prison Notebooks* (New York: International Publishers 1971), 12

12 Michel Foucault, *Discipline and Punish: The Birth of the Prison* (New York: Pantheon 1979)

Chapter 1

1 Phillip Buckner notes 'The struggle against aristocratic privilege in Britain was easily translated by reformers into a struggle against a privileged official class in Upper Canada,' *The Transition to Responsible Government: British Policy in British North America, 1815–1850* (Westport, CT: Greenwood Press 1985), 106.

2 See John Garner, *The Franchise and Politics in British North America, 1755–1867* (Toronto: University of Toronto Press 1969)

3 Max Weber, 'Bureaucracy,' in H.H. Gerth and C.W. Mills, ed. *Essays in Sociology* (London: Oxford University Press 1958), 196–244; M.J. Cullen, *The Statistical Movement in Early Victorian Britain* (New York: Harvester 1975); Richard Johnson, 'Educating the Educators: "Experts" and the State, 1833–9,' in A.P. Donajgrodski, ed., *Social Control in Nineteenth Century Britain* (London: Croom Helm 1977), 76–107; R. MacLeod, ed., *Government and Expertise: Specialists, Administrators and Professionals, 1860–1919* (Cambridge: Cambridge University Press 1986); R.J. Montgomery, *Examinations: An Account of Their Evolution as Administrative Devices in England* (Pittsburgh: University of Pittsburgh Press 1967)

4 I have not attempted to unravel the theoretical knot tied by the rise of ultramontanism in Canada East; for the rest, see E.A. Norman, *The Conscience of the State in North America* (Cambridge: Cambridge University Press 1968); Charles Leslie Glenn, Jr, *The Myth of the Common School* (Amherst: Massachusetts University Press 1988); B. Curtis, 'Preconditions of the Canadian State: Educational Reform and the Construction of a Public in Upper Canada, 1837–1846,' *Studies in Political Economy* 10 (1983): 99–121; William Westfall, *Two Worlds: The Protestant Culture of Nineteenth Century Ontario* (Montreal and Kingston: McGill-Queen's University Press 1989).

5 Karl Mannheim, 'The Democratization of Culture,' in *Essays on Sociology* (New York: Oxford University Press 1972); see also Westfall's discussion of attempts by evangelical clergymen to prevent popular usurpation of priestly functions in *Two Worlds*.

6 See Bruce Curtis, *Building the Educational State: Canada West, 1836–1871* (Sussex: Falmer Press; London, ON: Althouse Press 1988)

7 E.P. Thompson, *The Making of the English Working Class* (Harmondsworth: Penguin 1965); 'The Peculiarities of the English,' in *The Poverty of Theory*

(London: Merlin 1978), 92–192; also, Craig Calhoun, *The Question of Class Struggle* (Chicago: University of Chicago Press 1982)

8 Ruth Bleasdale, 'Class Conflict on the Canals of Upper Canada in the 1840s,' *Labour/le Travailleur* 1981: 9–40; Michael Cross, 'The Lumber Community of Upper Canada, 1815–1867' in J.M. Bumsted, ed., *Canadian History Before Confederation* (Georgetown: Irwin Dorsey 1972), 226–40; Daniel Drache, 'The Formation and Fragmentation of the Canadian Working Class, 1820–1920,' *Studies in Political Economy* 15 (1984): 43–90; Kenneth Duncan, 'The Irish Famine Migration and the Social Structure of Canada West,' in M. Horn and R. Sabourin, eds., *Studies in Canadian Social History* (Toronto: McClelland and Stewart 1974), 140–63; L.A. Johnson, *History of the County of Ontario* (Whitby: County of Ontario 1973); R.L. Jones, *History of Agriculture in Ontario* (Toronto: University of Toronto Press 1977); P.A. Russell, 'Wage Labour Rates in Upper Canada, 1818–1840,' *Histoire Sociale/Social History* 16 (1983): 61–80; G.A. Teeple, 'Land Labour and Capital in Pre-confederation Canada,' in *Capitalism and the National Question in Canada* (Toronto: University of Toronto Press 1972), 43–66

9 Grenville to Dorchester, 20 October 1789, in A. Shortt and A.G. Doughty, eds., *Documents of the Constitutional History of Canada 1764–1790,* II (Ottawa: Mulvey 1921), 978

10 Dorchester to Sidney, 13 June 1787, in Shortt and Doughty, *Documents* II: 948

11 Ibid.

12 Dorchester to Grenville, 8 February 1790, in Shortt and Doughty, *Documents*, II: 1003; two half-pay officers served as educational inspectors.

13 This body is not actually named in the act, but was based on later directives from the Colonial Office.

14 Collectors, like most public officials, were paid a percentage of the monies passing through their hands. See also W.S. Herrington, 'The Evolution of Municipal Government in Upper Canada,' Royal Society *Transactions*, 3rd Ser. XXV, sec. II (1927): 1–9. Herrington shows local justices disregarding instructions from the central authority.

15 See Buckner, *Responsible Government*, 60, who writes of the governor: 'Without an obedient corps of lesser officials, his knowledge of conditions throughout the colony and his ability to affect those conditions were extremely limited.'

16 For instance, Colin Read, 'The London District Oligarchy in the Rebellion Era,' *Ontario History* 62 (1980): 195–209; E.M. Richards, 'The Joneses of Brockville and the Family Compact,' *Ontario History* 60 (1968): 195–209. The institution of elective local government after 1840 did not so much unseat local oligarchies as modify the conditions under which they could rule.

17 Bernier and Salée's claim, in 'Social Relations and Exercise of State Power in Lower Canada (1790–1840),' *Studies in Political Economy* 22 (Spring 1987): 101–43, that the 'St. Lawrence valley was home to an aristocracy' must be read in this light. What is at issue here is not land ownership as such, but rather *activity*.

18 I discuss this in more detail in *Building the Educational State*, ch. 1, and in

'Schoolbooks and the Myth of Curricular Republicanism: The State and the Curriculum in Canada West, 1820–1850,' *Histoire sociale/Social History* 16/32 (1983): 305–29.

19 Olga Bernice Bishop, *Publications of the Province of Upper Canada and of Great Britain Relating to Upper Canada, 1790–1840* (Toronto: Ministry of Citizenship and Culture for Ontario 1984), 157–8; Rainer Baehre, 'Origins of the Penitentiary System in Upper Canada,' *Ontario History* 69/3 (1976): 185–207; for the investigation of the penitentiary in 1849, see J.M.S. Careless, *Brown of the Globe* (Toronto: Macmillan 1956). Notice that Brown is sent to tour the American penitentiaries.

20 Bishop, *Publications*, 102. LAUC, *Sessional Papers*, 1839–40, Report on Government Departments, Vol. I, Inspector General's Office. Benjamin Hayter, superintendent of schools in the Newcastle District, worked as a district licence inspector. He was paid half the fine assessed against unlicensed sellers of alcohol.

21 Bishop, *Publications*, 160

22 'The executive authority had no truly efficient local representative. The justices of the peace, traditionally charged with this function, were scattered over an immense territory, and were without effective means to ensure local regulation or respect for order.' Jean-Marie Fecteau, *Un nouvel ordre des choses: La pauvreté, le crime, l'État au Québec, de la fin du XVIIIe siècle à 1840* (Montreal: vlb éditeur 1989), 212

23 This is one of the vital areas of 'police' identified by Adam Smith in *The Wealth of Nations*, Vol. II (London: Methuen 1930). See also, M.S. Cross, 'The Stormy History of the York Roads, 1833–1865,' *Ontario History* 54 (1962): 1–24.

24 Bishop, *Publications*, 169–243

25 The key exception is the Duncombe Commission of 1835–6, appointed by the Assembly to tour the United States to investigate prisons, asylums, institutions for the deaf and dumb, and common schools. For Duncombe's report on common schools, see *Building the Educational State*, ch. 2.

26 See W.D. Rubenstein, 'The End of "Old Corruption" in Britain,' *Past and Present* 101 (1983): 55–86. Philip Corrigan and Derek Sayer, *The Great Arch: English State Formation as Cultural Revolution* (Oxford: Blackwell 1985).

27 J.G. Hodgins, ed., *The Documentary History of Education in Upper Canada* (Toronto: L.K. Cameron 1894–1910), III: 128–9

28 Glenelg to Gosford, 17 July 1835, in W.P.M. Kennedy, ed., *Documents of the Canadian Constitution* (Toronto: Oxford University Press 1915), 410

29 In educational matters in Canada West, as I document in *Building the Educational State*, ch. 4, the communal school meeting was attacked. In the Baptist sect, matters of controversy were settled by a vote of (male?) church-goers. See Stuart Ivison and Fred Rosser, *The Baptists in Upper and Lower Canada before 1820* (Toronto: University of Toronto Press, 1963). A crucial question is the extent to which representation limited the power and influence women may have enjoyed under communal forms of government.

30 'Report of the Committee of the Legislative Council of Upper Canada on Lord Durham's Report, 11 May 1839,' in Kennedy, *Documents*, 478

31 Janet Ajzenstat, *The Political Thought of Lord Durham* (Montreal and Kingston: McGill-Queen's University Press 1988); Ged Martin, *The Durham Report and British Policy: A Critical Essay* (Cambridge: Cambridge University Press 1972); John Manning Ward, *Colonial Self-Government: The British Experience, 1759–1856* (Toronto: University of Toronto Press 1976)

32 Lucas, *Lord Durham*, III: 280–7.

33 Charles Buller, *Responsible Government for Colonies* (London: Ridgway 1840), 34–40

34 Martin, *Durham Report*, 44–7, stresses the importance of Ellice, who, it must be remembered, had substantial Canadian land holdings; also, D.E.T. Long, 'The Elusive Mr. Ellice,' *Canadian Historical Review* 23 (1942): 42–57.

35 John Stuart Mill, 'Lord Durham's Return,' in *Collected Works* Vol. VI (Toronto: University of Toronto Press 1982), 457; my emphasis. Normal schools habituated people to certain norms of behaviour.

36 Russell to Poulett Thomson, 7 September 1839, in Kennedy, *Documents*, 519; my emphasis

37 Russell to Poulett Thomson, 14 October 1839, in Kennedy, *Documents*, 523

38 Ball, *Her Majesty's Inspectorate*. The significance of this will become clearer in what follows.

39 Poulett Thomson to a friend, 20 November and 8 December 1839, in Kennedy, *Documents*, 529

40 Russell to Sydenham, 25 October 1840; Sydenham to a friend, n.d. 1840, in Kennedy, *Documents*, 554–5

41 Sydenham to a friend, n.d. 1840, in Kennedy, *Documents*, 555

42 Poulett Thomson to Russell, 16 September 1840, in Kennedy, *Documents*, 552

43 The importance of the Political Economy Club for the permeation of the state system with Benthamite figures, and the importance of Thomson in this regard is detailed in S.E. Finer's remarkable essay 'The Transmission of Benthamite Ideas, 1820–50' in Gillian Sutherland, ed., *Studies in the Growth of Nineteenth-Century Government* (London: Routledge Kegan Paul 1972), 11–32; see also A. Tyrrell, 'Political Economy, Whiggism and the Education of Working Class Adults in Scotland, 1817–1840,' *Scottish Historical Review* 48 (1969): 151–65.

44 Poulett Scrope, *passim*, *Dictionary of National Biography*, 'Thomson, Charles Edward Poulett.' The School of Art and Design was intended to improve the public taste through the design of public buildings. Notice that Egerton Ryerson's 1850 School Act contained a provision for the establishment of a similar institution.

45 Poulett Scrope, *Memoir of the Life of Lord Sydenham* (London: n.p. 1843), 46, 100. I think Ged Martin, *The Durham Report and British Policy* (Cambridge: Cambridge University Press 1972), leads us astray in his attempts to discount the influence of Durham's report on colonial policy. On education, local government,

land tenure, public works, and other measures, he had the entire support of a broad cross-section of the English ruling class. The question is surely less one of whether these were *Durham's* personal ideas, than one of their currency.

46 In this regard, see the excellent work by Wendie Nelson, 'The "Guerre des Éteignoirs"': School Reform and Popular Resistance in Lower Canada, 1841–50,' unpublished MA thesis, Simon Fraser University 1989.

47 Sydenham to Scrope, 28 August 1841, in Kennedy, *Documents*, 563. Sydenham fell from his horse the day the act was proclaimed, injuring his leg. He was dead in two weeks.

48 LAC, *Sessional Papers*, Appendix Z, 1847

Chapter 2

1 Anon, *A Statement of the Experience of Scotland with Regard to the Education of the People* (Dumfries: A. Constable 1825), 20

2 Nancy Ball, *Her Majesty's Inspectorate, 1839–1849* (Edinburgh: Oliver and Boyd 1971), 1. Kay-Shuttleworth's argument makes the German revolutions difficult to explain.

3 Cesare Beccaria, *An Essay on Crimes and Punishments* (Edinburgh: Bell and Murray 1778); Adam Smith, *The Wealth of Nations* (London: Methuen 1930); Patrick Colqhoun, *A Treatise on the Police of the Metropolis ...* (London: A. Fry 1796); *A Treatise on the Functions and Duties of a Constable ...* (London: Mowman and Hatcher 1803); *A New and Appropriate System of Education for the Labouring People ...* (London: J. Hatchard 1806). I accept the point made by Charles Leslie Glenn, Jr, *The Myth of the Common School* (Amherst: University of Massachusetts Press 1988), that the revolutionary ideas of France were centrally important in this domain, and I deal with some eighteenth-century English work below.

4 A strong case for Irish influence on schooling in Ontario is made by D.H. Akenson, *Being Had: Historians, Evidence and the Irish in North America* (Port Credit: P.D. Meany Publishers 1985). While the case is closely argued, Akenson glosses over key differences between the two systems, especially concerning the position of trustees, the nature of finance, and the nature of opposition. He assumes a perfect identity between school trustees and 'the people,' an assumption manifestly false in many cases. His demographic argument, moreover, is simply ridiculous.

5 I follow O. MacDonagh, *The Inspector General: Sir Jeremiah Fitzpatrick and Social Reform, 1783–1801* (London: Croom Helm 1981), 310–27.

6 For Petty, see M.J. Cullen, *The Statistical Movement in Early Victorian Britain* (New York: Harvester 1975); for Peel, see Galen Broeker, *Rural Disorder and Police Reform in Ireland, 1812–36* (Toronto: University of Toronto Press 1970).

7 By John Howard, for instance, in his widely read *Prisons and Lazerettos*, Vol. 1 (Montclair, NJ: Patterson Smith; reprint of 1792).

8 National Library of Ireland [NLI], Bolton Family MSS, Notebook of Thomas Orde, IQ 1785, 'Miscellaneous Projects.' Orde used the concept 'police' in its common eighteenth-century meaning of things contributing to public order. Roads and bridges were 'forces of police' in this sense, as were ideological institutions. Egerton Ryerson in Canada West occasionally referred to schools as 'police forces,' although this sense of the term was already in decline.

9 NLI, Bolton MSS 15928; 'Thoughts on the Present State of the Police of Ireland'

10 NLI, Bolton MSS 15929; 'F. Trench to Thomas Orde'; 'The Heads of a Plan of Police ...'; 'Extract from a Treatise on the Police of France'; see also 15931, 'A Bill for the better Execution of the Law within the City of Dublin ...'; 'Hints for the Police Bill'; 15934, 'Hints for an Act for the better extension of the Law.' The last document is largely a restatement of Beccaria.

11 John Gifford, *Mr. Orde's Plan of an Improved System of Education in Ireland; Submitted to the House of Commons, April, 12, 1787 ...* (Dublin: W. Porter 1787), 13–4, 26

12 NLI, Bolton MSS, 16372:10, notebook plan of 'System of Education College of Visitors & Inspectors'; Gifford, *Orde's Plan*, 41

13 Gifford, *Orde's Plan*, 112

14 Ibid., 115

15 Key works in this literature included: Robert Stearne Tighe, *A letter addressed to Mr. Orde, Upon the Education of the People* (Dublin: P. Byrne 1787); Anthony King, *Thoughts on the Expediency of Adopting a System of National Education ...* (Dublin: Bowham 1793); T. Blaquiere, *General Observations on the State of Affairs in Ireland* (Dublin: G. Johnson 1797); John Donovan, *Thoughts on the Necessity and Means of Educating the Poor of Ireland, and Attaching Them To Their Country* (Dublin: Mercier 1795).

16 R.E. Burton, 'Richard Lovell Edgeworth's Education Bill of 1799: A Missing Chapter in the History of Irish Education,' *Irish Journal of Education* 13/1 (1979): 24–33, 26

17 Rev. J. Dunn, *Essay on the Present State of Manners and Education Among the Lower Class of the People of Ireland, and the Means of Improving Them* (Dublin: Watson 1799); Anon., *Observations on the Present State of the Charter Schools of Ireland; and the Means of Improving Them* (Dublin: Porter 1806), 28–9; some of this material is discussed in D.H. Akenson, *The Irish Education Experiment* (Toronto: University of Toronto Press 1971).

18 H.J.M. Mason, *Address to the Nobility and Gentry Upon the Necessity of Using Every Exertion at the Present, to Promote the Education of the Poor of Ireland* (Dublin: William Folds 1815), 40

19 NLI, *First Report of the Society for Promoting the Education of the Poor of Ireland (SPEPI)*, Dublin, 1813, Appendix III, 'Extract of a letter from the Superintendent of the Belfast Lancasterian School, 26 December 1813'

20 NLI, SPEPI, *Sixth Report*, 18–19

21 O'Heideain, *National School Inspection*, 13

22 NLI, SPEPI, *Eleventh Report*, 20

23 NLI, *First Report of the Commissioners on Education in Ireland*, 30 May 1825, 99

24 Ibid., 422–4

25 Ibid., 470–519; also O'Heideain, *National School Inspection*, 16–18

26 NLI, SPEPI, *Fourteenth Report*, 20–63

27 NLI, SPEPI, *Twentieth to Twenty-Ninth Reports*; Akenson, *Irish Educational Experiment*, provides the standard account of these events.

28 O'Heideian, *National School Inspection*, 20–31

29 NLI, MS 5529, Minutes of the Commissioners of National Education for Ireland, Volume A, 1831–7, 3 and 21 May, 14 June 1832; 2 September 1833. For Sullivan's education, see O'Heideian, *National School Inspection*, 46. Sullivan was educated at the Belfast Academical Institution, the master of which was the father of Francis Hincks, author of the Canada West School Act of 1843. Sullivan was one of the teachers of John George Hodgins, deputy superintendent of education in Canada West from 1846. T.J. Robertson was appointed headmaster of the Toronto Normal School in 1847 and held that position until his death in 1866. He framed the instructions offered to Canadian school inspectors.

30 *Report of the Select Committee of the House of Lords on the New Plan of Education in Ireland*, 1837, 718, 1411.

31 NLI, *Minutes*, 18 October 1832; 17 October 1833; 8 and 13 February, 6 March, 3 April 1834. These injunctions were not entirely effective. The inspector John Foster Murray, who later led an active campaign against the board, was found to have written 'a political Pamphlet' entitled 'Repeal no Remedy' and was discharged; the board refused his pleas for reinstatement.

32 NLI, *Minutes*, 15 January 1835; 12 and 26 May, 25 August 1836

33 NLI, *Minutes*, 8 December 1836; 16 February 1837; Akenson, *Being Had*, suggests that the model schools were not actually organized until 1843.

34 J.C. Colqhuon, *The System of National Education in Ireland: Its Principle and Practice* (Cheltenham: William Wright 1838), 32, 37–43; also Akenson, *Irish Education Experiment*, 157–228

35 John Coolahan, 'The Daring First Decade of the Board of National Education, 1831–1841,' *Irish Journal of Education* 17 (1983): 35–54, 49. Poulett Thomson – later Lord Sydenham – was Scrope's brother.

36 *Fourth Report of the Commissioners of National Education in Ireland*, 1837, 4; *Fifth Report ...* 1838, 7

37 *Ninth Report of the Commissioners of National Education in Ireland*, 1842, 20–1; Appendix III, 24–6; chapter 8, below

38 *Fifth Report of the Commissioners of National Education in Ireland*, 1838, 6–7

39 Thomas Chalmers, *The Christian and Civic Economy of Large Towns* Vol. I (Glasgow: Chalmers and Collins 1821), 223

40 Ibid., 329–30

41 This is detailed in J.F. McCaffrey, 'Thomas Chalmers and Social Change,' *Scottish Historical Review* 60 (1981): 32–60.

42 Chalmers, *Civic Economy*, II: 39–40, 101. Without the ecclesiastic gloss, this is the substance of the English Radical and Whig argument about the political usefulness of organs of representative local government.

43 For some of the relevant literature, see Ball, *Her Majesty's Inspectorate*, 47, 59–60; Marjorie Cruickshank, 'David Stow, Scottish Pioneer of Teacher Training in Britain,' *British Journal of Educational Studies* 14 (1966): 205–15; David Stow, *The Training System*, 6th ed. (Glasgow: Blackie, 1845) James Pillans, *Principles of Elementary Teaching* (Edinburgh: Adam Black 1828), 94–7; National Library of Scotland [NLS], Pamphlet Collection, 'The Substance of a Speech on the Subject of Irish Education' (1832); 'Three Lectures on the Proper Objects and Methods of Education, in reference to the Different Orders of Society' (1836); *Educational Papers* (Edinburgh: James Gordon 1862); John Wood, *Account of the Edinburgh Sessional School* (Edinburgh: Wardlaw 1829), 38; James Simpson, *Necessity of Popular Education as a National Object; with hints on the treatment of criminals, and observations on homicidal insanity* (Edinburgh: Adam Black 1834), 216–28; George Lewis, *Scotland: A Half-educated Nation* (Glasgow: Collins 1834), 5, 22–9. More generally, see J.V. Smith, 'Manners, Morals and Mentalities: Reflections on the Popular Enlightenment of Early Nineteenth Century Scotland,' in W.M. Humes and H.M. Patterson, eds., *Scottish Culture and Scottish Education, 1880–1980* (Edinburgh: John Donald 1983), 25–54.

44 Well before his educational inquiries, Victor Cousin (1792–1867) was influential for his introduction of Enlightenment and German philosophy to the French universities. From 1814, as *maître de conférences en philosophie*, Cousin exposed his colleagues to the work of Reid, Kant, and later Hegel. His own lively interest in things German was strengthened by visits to that country in 1817 and again in 1818, where he met and studied with Hegel. When the reaction of 1821 cost Cousin his course in philosophy at the Sorbonne and his chair at l'École normale, he returned to study in Germany, but was arrested at the insistence of the French authorities as a liberal agitator. He was restored to his chair in the Faculté des lettres in 1827, and from that period became especially active politically. He was one of the first members of l'Académie des sciences morales et politiques (1832) and took his educational missions to Prussia in 1831, and to Holland in 1836. Cousin served as the French minister of public instruction from 1840: *Grand Dictionnaire Universel du XIXe Siècle* (Paris: Larousse 1869).

I do not deny Glenn's contention, in *Myth of the Common School*, that Cousin took Prussian educational *plans* to be Prussian *practice*. But this was not a criticism levelled at him by his contemporaries; they took the reports as models of what might be done.

45 Victor Cousin, 'Report on the State of Public Instruction in Prussia,' reprinted in E.W. Knight, ed., *Reports on European Education by John Griscom, Victor Cousin, Calvin E. Stowe* (New York: McGraw-Hill 1930), 124–9

46 Ibid., 200

47 Ibid., 226

48 Both Cuvier and Noël were active in French diplomacy, and their own inspection of educational organization in the Hanseatic cities and the Batavian republic was conducted in the context of a more general survey of educational organization in the newly formed French departments. Cuvier, for instance, in addition to studying Dutch educational organization, investigated public instruction in northern Italy and southern Germany, and organized a system of public instruction in Rome in 1813. The organization of cantonal committees for public instruction in France in 1816 is attributed to Cuvier's influence and to his experience in Holland. For his part, Noël had already a lengthy diplomatic and administrative experience before his contribution to the report on schools in the Batavian republic. He had been the plenipotentiary to that republic in 1795–7, and his influence was said to have provoked the transformation from a federative to a unitary Batavian state. Noël was a divisional head at the French ministry of the interior in 1798; the *commissaire général de police* in Lyons in 1800; prefect of the Upper Rhineland, 1800–2; and, finally, from 1802 until his death many years later, an inspector general of public instruction. See the entries in the *Grand Dictionnaire du XIXe Siècle*; *Dictionarie de Biographie Française* (Paris: Letouzey 1961); and *Nouvelle Biographie Générale* (Copenhagen: Rosenhilde et Bagger 1965).

49 Cousin, *Education in Holland*, 127–31. 'We' obviously means men of Cousin's class.

50 As we shall see below, in Canada West the organization of public education was a matter of parliamentary conflict in the 1840s. I have also argued, in *Building the Educational State*, that judicial interference was important in shaping educational administration.

51 Cousin, *Education in Holland*, 135–40; my emphasis

52 Ibid., 142–3

53 Ibid., 147–8

54 J.S. Mill played in Bentham's garden, which was itself laid out in the form of a panopticon. For the Austins and Horner, see the *Dictionary of National Biography*; also Sarah Austin's preface to John Austin, *The Province of Jurisprudence Determined*, 2nd ed. [1861] (New York: Franklin 1970); John Austin performed the theoretical contortions for a theory of bourgeois legal sovereignty. More generally, see W.H.G. Armytage, *The German Influence on English Education* (London: Routledge and Kegan Paul 1969).

55 Cousin, *Education in Holland*, xxxi–lxxii

56 Ball, *Her Majesty's Inspectorate*, 6–8; also Francis Duke, 'The Poor Law Commissioners and Education,' *Journal of Educational Administration and History* 3/1: 7–23. Notice that Sir Francis Bond Head had also been an assistant poor-law commissioner. Dr Kay's first major work was dedicated to Thomas Chalmers. For useful background, see F. Mort, *Dangerous Sexualities; Medico-moral Politics in England since 1830* (London: Routledge and Kegan Paul 1987).

57 Ball, *Her Majesty's Inspectors*, 25

58 Ibid., 64–8

59 Ibid., 76–83, 101–2; also, Fiona Paterson, *Out of Place: Public Policy and the Emergence of Truancy* (Lewes, Sussex: Falmer Press 1989)

60 Griscom (1774–1852) was born of Quaker parents near Salem, New Jersey, and educated at the Friends' Academy. He taught school in Burlington and in New York until 1818, when he visited England, France, Switzerland, Italy, Belgium, Holland, Scotland, and Ireland. His two-volume report on his travels was a popular success and earned him enough to defray all the costs of his trip. Griscom was active in the New York Society for the Prevention of Pauperism, and in support for the establishment of a monitorial high school. In the 1830s and later, he was in close personal contact with leading American educational reformers, including Horace Mann. For Griscom's biography, see Knight, *Reports on European Education.*

61 John Griscom, *A Year in Europe ... in 1818 and 1819*, Vol. II (New York: Collins & Co 1823), 161, 395–9, 472–3, 465–6n. See also, James G. Carter, *Essays upon Popular Education* (New York: Arno Press and the New York Times 1969), 44, 55.

62 J.A. Walz, *German Influence in American Education and Culture* (Freeport, NY: Books for Libraries Press 1935), 9, 15–45; Alexander Bache, *Report on Education in Europe* (Philadelphia: Lydia R. Bailey 1839), 6, 171–2; Horace Mann, *Report of an Educational Tour* (London: Simpkin, Marshall & Co. 1846)

63 Glenn, *Myth of the Common School*, 103. Glenn's study deserves a careful attention for his insights into the international origins of the common school, and for his analysis of the attempts by liberal reformers to create a civic morality out of Christianity. But he reads educational reform only as religious and not as class or gender conflict, an important flaw in an otherwise illuminating study.

64 AO RG2 CIC, 'Circular to District Superintendents of Common Schools,' 15 December 1846; MU1375, Hodgins Papers, Ryerson to Draper, 30 March 1846; LAC *Debates*, 3 June 1850

Chapter 3

1 Anna Brownell Jameson, *Winter Studies and Summer Rambles in Canada* (Toronto: McClelland and Stewart 1965), 31–2. (My thanks to Alison Prentice for this reference.) Jameson's reference is to B.F. Duppa, *The Causes and the Present Condition of the Labouring Classes in the South of England* (London 1831).

2 J.G. Hodgins, ed., *The Documentary History of Education in Upper Canada*, Vol. II (Toronto: L.K. Cameron 1894–1910), 198–9

3 Ibid., 179

4 Mary Jane Duncan, 'American Influences on Ontario's School Legislation, 1836–1850,' MA thesis, University of Rochester 1964, 11; *Doctor Charles Duncombe's Report upon the subject of Education, made to the Parliament of Upper Canada, 25th February 1836* (N.p.: Johnson Reprint Corporation 1966;

Toronto: M. Reynolds, 1836), 38; see also Sir C.P. Lewis, ed., *Lord Durham's Report on the Affairs of British North America*, Vol. II (Oxford: Clarendon Press 1912), 280–8; Bruce Curtis, *Building the Educational State: Canada West 1836–1871* (Essex and London, ON: Falmer Press and Althouse Press 1988), 36–8.

5 For discussion of the act's failure, see R.D. Gidney and D.A. Lawr, 'The Development of an Administrative System for the Public Schools: The First Stage, 1841–1850,' in N. McDonald and A. Chaiton, eds., *Egerton Ryerson and His Times* (Toronto: Macmillan 1978), 160–84; for the overlap in personnel, see below, chapter 5; for contemporary criticism of the township commissions, see *Building the Educational State*, ch. 2.

6 Charles Dent, *The Last Forty Years: Canada Since the Union of 1841*, Vol. I (Toronto: George Virtue 1881), 218–9n. Alexander McNab, in a defence of the education department against Hincks's charges of mismanagement in 1845, described the latter as 'a latitudinarian in religion and a revolutionist in politics': Cobourg *Star*, 8 October 1845.

7 R.S. Longley, *Sir Francis Hincks: A Study of Canadian Politics, Railways, and Finance in the Nineteenth Century* (New York: Arno Press 1981), 6. For Hunter, see AO RG2 MI, 'Teachers' Superannuation Records'; for Hutton, see G.E. Boyce, *Hutton of Hastings* (Belleville: Hastings County Council 1972); for foreign references, see LAC *Debates*, 1843, 933–5.

8 Despite the fact that a great number of superintendents presented cursory, or no, reports and accounts, there is no evidence of this clause having been enforced.

9 In practice, educational organization in Canada West was under the direction of the assistant superintendent, and the chief superintendent was largely a figurehead. See Gidney and Lawr, 'The Development of an Administrative System.' There is no record of any superintendent ever having been fined.

10 An interpretation clause, a product of debates about the eligibility of women teachers for public money under the act of 1841, specified 'teacher' to include both males and females 'except when applied to the Teacher of a Normal School, or of a Model School, in which case it shall apply to a Male Teacher only': 7 Vic., c.XXIX, sec. LXIX.

11 It is not clear what township and county clerks actually did. My impression is that superintendents did most of the work, but see also the later chapter, 'From Class Culture to Bureaucratic Procedure,' n. 20. No history of county clerks exists.

12 AO, MUI375, Hodgins Papers, Ryerson to Draper, 30 March 1846: 'it has been mentioned to me ... as to whether the term *Inspector* instead of *Superintendent* would not be the better designation of District Overseer of schools.' Ryerson did not think the terminological question particularly important. 'Superintendent' was the popular term in the business world for general manager, and perhaps connoted a more general supervision of matters than did 'inspector.' See also Newton Bosworth's mention of his powers as a 'mere inspector' in chapter 7, below.

13 AO RG2: see, for example, C6C, J. Fourré, Sheffield, 26 February 1844; CIB, Murray to Fourré, 18 March 1844; C6C, Daniel McLeod, Nelson, 27 February 1844; CIB, Murray to McLeod, 18 March 1844; C6C, Daly to Murray, 25 March 1844 (with Draper to Daly, 8 March 1844 enclosed).

14 AO RG2 CIB, for example, Murray to Keefer, 14 August 1844

15 See, for example, the case of John Strachan versus Dr MacLean in the Midland District, reported in Kingston *Chronicle and Gazette*, 24 and 28 February, 6 March 1844.

16 AO RG2 C6C, Alex McLean, Treasurer, Eastern District, 26 March 1844; CIB, Murray to McLean, 26 March 1844. Could the same person be a town superintendent and clerk? CIB, Murray to District Clerk, Sandwich: 'the School act did not contemplate such a union, although it is not directly prohibited ... It might be well as far as practicable to avoid the union.' C6C, Don. M'Donald, District Clerk, L'Orignal, 27 March 1844: 'Can a member of the Municipal Council legally or properly undertake the Office of a Superintendent, seeing that his Bond is given to that Body?'

17 For biographical information on Eliot, see Upper Canada Legislative Assembly, *Sessional Papers*, School Report no. 45, 1835; Provincial Revenue and Expenditure, 1836; Gaol Reports, 1836; Appendix to the Report on Banking, 1837; Report of the Common Schools, Western District, 1839; LAC, *Sessional Papers*, Appendix V, 1843; Appendix 3, 1861; Canada *Gazette*, 22 February 1845; R.A. Douglas, ed., *John Prince, 1796–1870* (Toronto: University of Toronto Press 1980), 28ff. Complaints about Eliot's appointments of clerks and bailiffs reached the Executive Council. See NAC RG1 E1, Executive Council Minutes, Canada State Book C, 345, 1 April 1844.

18 AO RG2 C6C, Jacob Keefer, Thorold, 6 March 1844, suggests using American forms; CIB, Murray to Keefer, 12 March 1844, says no forms ready; at least Hutton, Steele, and Bosworth delayed inspecting while waiting for forms.

19 AO RG2 C6C, William Hutton, Belleville, 6 and 30 July 1844; CIB, Murray to Hutton, 1 August 1844; C6C, John Bignall, Goderich, 16 March 1844; CIB, Murray to Bignall, 27 March 1844; McNab to George Benjamin, Belleville, 11 November 1844. In a later chapter, I show that the school monies in Dalhousie were paid until 1848 without the assessment of a tax.

20 For example, AO RG2 CIB, McNab to Daly, 16 and 23 May 1845; C6C, Samuel Hartt, Cornwall, 4 March 1844, and Hamilton Hunter, Toronto, 24 April 1844, both correct Murray's population figures.

21 AO RG2 C6C, Robert Boyd, Prescott, 18 April, 23 November 1844; CIB, Murray to Boyd, 19 April 1844; McNab to Boyd, 4 December 1844. Murray told Boyd in detail how to divide the town, but McNab rebuked him for not having done so and refused to pay the school monies until he did.

22 AO RG2 C6C, Daly to Murray, 17 April 1844

23 For example, AO RG2 CIB, Murray to Rev. Samuel Armour, Cavan, 23 April 1844; C6C, Armour to Murray, 27 April 1844; C6C, Hamilton Hunter, Toronto, 24 April

1844; CIB, Murray to Hunter, 26 April 1844; C6C, *re* John Hopkins, Kingston, 27 April 1844; Samuel Hartt, Cornwall, 19 May 1845

24 AO RG2 CIB, Murray to John Blacksbury, Township Superintendent, Bastard, 25 March 1844; Murray to Neil Eastman, Superintendent, Township of Cornwall, 6 May 1844

25 That is, if we accept Weber's model of bureaucratic positions as salaried. AO RG2 CIB, 'Circular to District Superintendents,' 25 July 1845: 'Be kind enough also to inform me out of what moneys the County and township Superintendents have received their salaries for the past year.' The circular was provoked by McNab's discovery that, in the London District, Council paid the superintendent out of the grant: McNab to William Elliot, London, 10 July 1845. The responses were revealing: e.g., C6C, Samuel Hartt, Cornwall, 28 July 1845: 'the County Superintendents salary (totally inadequate as it is) was fixed by the Distr. Council at a percentage of 4 per cent to be deducted from the Government monies passing thro his hands and that the Salaries of the Township Supts. were to be taken from the school assessments of each Township which were for that purpose levied to a greater amount than that of the government grant.' Some superintendents were paid out of general district revenues, as the act intended. William Hutton, it was claimed, continued to deduct his salary from the school grant throughout the period of the superintendency. See Boyce, *Hutton of Hastings*, 173.

26 I discuss the two cases of absconding later. Henry Clifford's wife was made uneasy by Clifford leaving large amounts of school money in their house when he went off inspecting schools; cf. A.F. Hunter, *A History of Simcoe County* (Barrie: Simcoe County Historical Society n.d.), part 2: 149–51.

27 AO RG2 C6C, Hopkirk to McNab, 25 August 1845, includes McNab to Hopkirk with Draper's opinion on the outside; CIB, McNab to Burnham, 30 August 1845

28 Cobourg *Star*, 19 February, 19 March 1845. One correspondent claimed the meeting in question was rigged. The surplus school monies were a source of contention in this district in 1849. See also AO RG2 C6C, Jacob Keefer, Niagara, 19 November 1844, who wrote that the School Act was confusing and the Education Office should make allowances for defective reports. Still, there was 'a good feeling prevailing towards the School Act.'

29 AO RG2 F3A, Western District Report, 1845; Duck had undertaken himself to circularize trustees, reminding them to send in their reports. He also stressed the need for separate schools for blacks. C6C, John Strachan, Ernestown, 17 March 1846. Paying separate schools in towns according to population might have reduced the funds available to them.

30 AO RG2 C6C, Hamilton Hunter, Toronto, 1 January 1845

31 See *Building the Educational State*, 112.

32 Egerton Ryerson, *Report on a System of Public Elementary Instruction for Upper Canada* (Montreal: Lovell and Gibson 1847), 171–7; also, AO RG2 CIC, Ryerson to Daly, 27 March 1846. In CIC, Ryerson to Thornton, 15 July 1846, Thornton was described explicitly as 'a public guardian of the youth of the country.'

33 Riddell, the Tory member for Oxford, opposed allowing district councils to appoint superintendents, but both J.S. Macdonald and Robert Baldwin argued strongly in favour of this clause: LAC, *Debates*, 14 April 1846

34 9 Vic. c.XX, sec.XII, para. 10

35 For the first quotation, AO MU1375, Hodgins Papers, Ryerson to Draper, 30 March 1846; for the second, RG2 C1D, 'Special Measures,' etc., 22 June 1847. Ryerson pointed to the key distinction between Irish and Canadian schools: the former were under the control of individual patrons; the latter, of elected trustees regulated by the Education Office.

36 AO RG2 F3A, Gore District Report, 1845

37 Elliott's support for the bill was announced in AO MU1375 Hodgins Papers, Ryerson to Draper, 30 March 1846; Hunter's in Ryerson to Draper, 14 May 1846. The latter communication is also interesting for its discussion of ways of including Baldwin and J.H. Price ('my personal enemy') on the general board to break Reform opposition. Ryerson also lamented the paucity of acceptable candidates among dissenters, most of whom were 'not above traders.' In C6C, Hamilton Hunter, Toronto, 13 May 1846, Hunter criticized the amount of work imposed by the bill on district superintendents and argued that there should be a penalty for trustees who made false returns.

38 AO RG2 C1D, 'Circular on the School Act of 1847,' 15 January 1848; also earlier, C1C, Ryerson to Superintendent of Schools, State of New York, Albany, 23 December 1846, refers to his 'school system, from which we have borrowed so largely, especially in your cities and incorporated towns'; for struggles over municipal taxation, see Peter Ross, 'The Free School Controversy in Toronto, 1848–1852,' in M.B. Katz and P.H. Mattingly, eds., *Education and Social Change* (New York: New York University Press 1975), 57–80. Ryerson's initial draft of the 1847 bill also allowed the governor-in-council to remove any district superintendent 'in case of any violation or neglect of duty' and to appoint another until the next meeting of the district council; cf. AO RG2 C1C, Ryerson to Daly, 27 March 1847.

39 AO RG2 C1C, Ryerson to George Vardon, Superintendent General, Indian Affairs, Montreal, 26 May 1847. De Fellenberg's rural industrial school at Hofwyl was Ryerson's model of a good Indian school. Two other things are notable in this remarkable letter. First, Ryerson argued that Indians, like workers, could be civilized only by religion, because they were governed by their emotions. 'Even in ordinary civilized life the mass of the labouring classes are controlled by their *feelings* – as almost the only rule of action – in proportion to the absence or partial character of their intellectual development.' Notice the parallels between the colonized native population and the internal colony – civil society. Again, Ryerson's model of educational adminstration is Dutch.

40 AO RG2 C1C, Ryerson to D. D'Everardo, 30 January 1847

41 AO RG2 C1C, Ryerson to Millar, 18 March 1847

42 'Leonidas' was the pen name Ryerson adopted in his defence of Governor Metcalfe in 1844. Toronto *Examiner* 29 April, 18 November, 9 December 1846;

the *Mirror*, 12 May 1848, quoted in P.N. Ross, 'The Free School Controversy in Toronto, 1848–1852,' in M.B. Katz and P.H. Mattingly, eds., *Education and Social Change* (New York: New York University Press 1975), 57–80, n.42; Huron *Signal*, 12 May, 27 October 1848; the Bignall case is documented below.

43 For example, the *Mirror*, 21 April 1848; the *Examiner*, 12 May 1848; Hodgins, *Documentary History*, VII: 198

44 AO RG2 CIC, Ryerson to Daly, Montreal, 27 March 1847. Ryerson's ability to occupy the 'democratic' terrain on this question likely enabled Stanley Ryerson, *Unequal Union* (New York: International Publishers 1968), to present these as reforms unambiguously in the interest of the working class.

45 AO RG2 CID, Ryerson to the *Globe*, 5 May 1848

46 AO RG2 C6C, Robert Burns, 9 January 1847; CIC, Ryerson to Burns, 14 and 20 January 1847

47 Hodgins, *Documentary History*, VII: 120; AO, Eastern District Council Papers, November 1847. For the reactions of the Gore District Teachers' Association, see *Building the Educational State*, 119–20.

48 AO, reported in Johnstown District Council Papers, 29 September 1847. No resolution by Johnstown Council was taken, but, in the February sessions, the latter set steps in motion that led to the strengthening of the hand of the superintendent, Richey Waugh.

49 Hodgins, *Documentary History*, VII: 120. AO, Municipal Records, Section B, Western District Council Papers, 1842–9, 6 October 1847, 7 February 1848. NAC, RG1 EI, Executive Council Minutes, Canada State Book H, 28 February 1848, 295

50 Reported in the Peterborough *Gazette*, 29 February 1848

51 AO RG2 C6C, 'Report of the Standing Commitee on Common Schools of Colborne District Council,' 8 February 1848

52 This is discussed at greater length in chapter 7.

53 See each issue of the *Bathurst Courier* for July 1848; the original of the memorial is in NAC, RG5 CI, Vol. 224, and dated 9 February 1848.

Chapter 4

1 AO RG2 C6C, Ryerson to James Wallace, Whitby, 9 November 1846. The clause was in the draft, 'but Mr. Baldwin and his friends, and some members on the opposite side of the House of Assembly united to oppose this clause of the Bill and it was lost.'

2 The draft bill with Ryerson's extensive remarks is in AO RG2 CID, Ryerson to Leslie, 14 October 1848. Little of Ryerson's correspondence with the three 'experienced Educationists' on the bill has survived, but see, as above, Ryerson to D'Everardo, 16 March 1848, soliciting his remarks on amendments needed to the act of 1846, thanking him for his 'admirable statistical report' for 1847, and promising that he would be 'recommending it as a model for other District Superintendents'; 4 November 1848: 'I omitted the two Sections to which you objected;

but they have been strongly insisted on by persons in this and two or three other Districts.'

3 This last institution was to design the architecture of the public and was to be modelled on that in England.

4 The superintendents in the districts named were William Landon, William Clarke, Sr, and Dexter D'Everardo.

5 AO RG2 C1D, Ryerson to Leslie, 23 February 1849, contains both the draft of the bill and Ryerson's remarks on it.

6 AO MU1375, Hodgins Papers. In Merritt to Ryerson, 1 February 1849, Ryerson was advised to consult Cameron about amendments to his bill. Ryerson consulted J.C. Morrison instead, on 7 February, outlining how the School Bill could be adapted to the Municipal Bill, and pleading for a wide publication of his report of 1848. Morrison informed him on 11 April that he opposed some of the clauses of the draft bill very strongly, and again, on 12 April, that the worst clauses of the draft had been eliminated. See also, Egerton Ryerson, *Story of My Life*, ed. J.G. Hodgins (Toronto: William Briggs 1883).

7 As Ryerson himself complained to Leslie, AO RG2 C1D, 12 May 1849: 'I have been informed upon authority which I cannot doubt, that the Bill has been chiefly drafted by a person who has, for the last three years, been writing in a District Newspaper against the present School Law and against myself.' Who actually wrote the Cameron act is obscure; Cameron claimed to have consulted a large number of people, but McDonnell was at least directly involved and may, in fact, have produced the whole thing.

8 LAC, *Debates*, 13 April 1849

9 I don't wish to argue that Ryerson's *persona* was insignificant in this matter, but, at the same time, it seems to me naïve to accept Ryerson's claims that the bill was *simply* the product of a personal vendetta. Radical reformers loathed Ryerson, but his political position was, indeed, anomalous.

10 J.G. Hodgins, ed., *The Documentary History of Education in Upper Canada*, Vol. VIII (London: L.K. Cameron 1894–1910), 167–85

11 There was considerable public support for many of these clauses. For instance, Barrie *Magnet*, 27 April 1849, supported a board in place of the chief superintendent, 'instead of having in his hand, solely, the enormous power which the bill confers on him'; also, LAC, *Journals*, petition of the Municipal Council of Halton and Wentworth, 21 May 1850; Brantford Township Council, 28 May 1850, both calling for the duties of the chief superintendent to be 'merged in some one of the Departments of Government.'

12 It is not clear from the draft that advance notice of all visits was to be given; cf. AO MU1375, Hodgins Papers, for Hodgins's marginal note on the visitation clause: 'Does this notice refer to *every* visit he may officially make, or merely the yearly examination visit?'

13 All of the above discussion is in AO RG2 C1D, Ryerson to Leslie, 12 May 1849. Ryerson's concluding remark here should be contrasted with his remarks to T.S.

Shenston, 14 February 1848, in which he claimed those districts demanding greater local control over education were the least efficient in their educational affairs. Hodgins was undoubtedly also actively involved. His copy of the bill with marginal comments is in AO MU1375, Hodgins Papers, and he makes many of the points Ryerson elaborated at length.

14 Ryerson to Hodgins, 27 April 1849, in C.B. Sissons, ed. *Egerton Ryerson: His Life and Letters*, Vol. II (Toronto: Clarke Irwin 1955), 179–80

15 AO MU1375, Hodgins Papers, W.H. Merritt to Ryerson, 26 May 1849

16 A modest misstatement: there were actually four – James Baird for Newcastle, Charles Fletcher for Huron, John Flood for Dalhousie, and William Fraser for the Eastern – and the degree of spontaneity involved is rather debatable. Fletcher, for instance, was initially appointed by the governor-in-council after his predecessor absconded, and was confirmed by Huron Council by a narrow margin over serious opposition to a clerical appointment. Fraser's predecessor also absconded. Baird was appointed on very short notice after Newcastle Council removed his predecessor in a dispute over the school monies, and there was considerable opposition to John Flood's appointment in Dalhousie Council. William Landon was appointed for Brock, but in the fall of 1847, not after January 1849. AO RG2 C1D, Ryerson to Baldwin, 9 July 1849

17 AO MU1375, Hodgins Papers, Ryerson to Baldwin, 16 August 1849; Baldwin to Ryerson, 20 September 1849. For reasons that are not clear to me, Sissons read this as coldness and reserve on Baldwin's part; cf. *Egerton Ryerson*, II: 182–3. Of course, one should recall Baldwin's denunciation of Ryerson's initial appointment as a disgusting 'job' and his attempt to refuse payment to any provincial superintendent who was a minister of religion; see LAC, *Debates*, 25 March 1845.

18 R.S. Longley, *Sir Francis Hincks: A Study of Canadian Politics, Railways, and Finance in the Nineteenth Century* (Toronto: University of Toronto Press 1943), 166–74

19 AO RG2 C6C, Benjamin Hayter, Cobourg, 28 February 1849; and the large bundle of 'Documents in the case of Benj. Hayter,' in October 1849; Hayter to Warden, Northumberland and Durham, 20 March 1850; Warden to Hayter, 25 March 1850; also, Cobourg *Star*, 22 March 1848, a letter from 'Adolphus' stating the district superintendent's duties were too extensive to allow active school inspection, and calling for the appointment of subinspectors; 4 July 1849, Hayter's protest against his dismissal and defence of his position; 8 August 1849, reprinting Ryerson to Hayter; D. Calman, 'Postponed Progress: Cobourg Common Schools, 1850–1871,' in J. Petryshyn, ed., *Victorian Cobourg* (Belleville: Mika 1976), 182–99, shows Hayter served as town superintendent in this the last town in the province to move towards free schools; for Hayter's obituary, see Cobourg *Star*, 6 September 1862.

20 AO RG2 C6C, J.W. Gamble, Pine Grove Mills, 21 June 1849

21 AO RG2 C6C, Richard Graham, Fort Erie, 7 August 1849

22 AO RG2 C6C, A.G. Johnson, Deputy SCS, Albany, New York, 22 August 1849

23 AO MU1375, Hodgins Papers, Hincks to Ryerson, 3 December 1849; Leslie to Ryerson, 13 December 1849; RG2 C6C, Leslie to Ryerson, 15 December 1849

24 AO RG2 C6C, Secretary, Board of Trustees, Hamilton, 28 December 1849, refers to the circular; also *Egerton Ryerson*, II: 186. The circular and Ryerson's correspondence with Leslie appeared in the *Globe*, 20 December 1849.

25 AO RG2 C6C, Hutton to Ryerson, 29 December 1849; 'proper materials' referred to the class of men enlisted in educational improvement.

26 *Bathurst Courier*, 4, 11, 18, and 25 January 1850; 1 March–5 April 1850

27 At least it does not appear in the offical correspondence, where Ryerson's letters to the press are usually copied. Ardagh to Ryerson, and Ryerson's reply of 12 and 23 March 1850, reprinted in the Barrie *Magnet*, 11 April 1850; see also earlier, AO RG2 C6C, 29 March 1849, Ardagh's unsuccessful attempt to permit a teacher to teach the catechism over the objections of the trustees

28 AO RG2 C1E, Ryerson to the editor of the Toronto *Examiner*, 31 December 1849, 2 January 1850

29 There is a copy of the circular in AO RG2 C6C, Hayter to Ryerson, 3 February 1850.

30 AO RG2 C6C, William Fraser, Lochiel, 7 February 1850

31 AO RG2 C6C, Hayter to Ryerson, 3 February 1850: 'I have sent you a copy of a Circular – of a non-descript character!! which, if I were near enough, I would cordially help you to laugh at.' This shows quite a remarkable ignorance of Ryerson's relations with the moderate wing of the Reform party.

32 Cf. S. Houston and A. Prentice, *Schooling and Scholars in Nineteenth-Century Ontario* (Toronto: University of Toronto Press 1988), 130; for the parliamentary exchange, see LAC, *Debates*, 31 May 1850; for McDonnell, see AO RG2 C6C, M. McDonnell, Perth, 30 May 1850, to Hincks. Notice also that McDonnell was appointed to the Lanark County Grammar School Board in 1850. Some of the responses to Hincks's circulars appear in C6C and a few in the Hodgins's Papers; selections were printed by Hodgins in the *Documentary History*, but I have been unable to find any trace of most of the originals. The correspondence Cameron managed to have printed in the *Sessional Papers* for 1850 included none of them and served mainly to recapitulate Ryerson's arguments.

33 Hodgins, *Documentary History*, IX: 60–1. We find the same gentleman writing, AO RG2 C6C, to Billa Flint on 21 May 1850: 'Let us have the management of our own local affairs as much as possible,' and criticizing opposition to alien teachers as something 'not consistent with free trade principles & I am sure it does not look like evincing a desire for *general reciprocity*.'

34 AO RG2 C6C, D. D'Everardo to Hincks, 7 March 1850

35 J.G. Hodgins, *Documentary History of Education in Upper Canada*, Vol. IX (Toronto, 1894–1910), 57. Hodgins omitted much of what Fletcher said because 'it deals theoretically, rather than practically, with the powers of School Teachers, and other matters'!!

36 Ibid., 60

37 Ibid., 61–2
38 AO RG2 F3A, Western District Report, 1849; this is not in Hodgins.
39 Hodgins, *Documentary History*, IX: 59–60
40 AO RG2 C6C, Hutton to Ryerson, 3 June 1850
41 AO RG2 F3A, Talbot District Report, 1849. Clarke reported average annual salaries as £36 for women and £45 for men. Also, Hodgins, *Documentary History*, IX: 58–9
42 Hodgins, *Documentary History*, IX: 62
43 Ibid., 59–60
44 Hodgins, *Documentary History*, VIII: 266–8; misdated 13 February 1849
45 In the Johnstown District, for instance; see below, chapter 6.
46 AO RG2 F3A, Simcoe District Report, 1849
47 AO RG2 C6C, Allan to Hincks, 21 January 1850; to Education Office, 20 and 27 February 1850. Hodgins reprinted only a tiny bit of this and did not indicate the change of heart.
48 AO RG2 F3A, Talbot District Report, 1849
49 Hodgins, *Documentary History*, IX: 60–1
50 Ibid., 62
51 AO RG2 C6C, Elliott to Hincks, 29 January 1850; this did not appear in Hodgins.
52 Hodgins, *Documentary History*, IX: 61–2
53 Ibid., 59–60
54 Ibid., 57–8
55 Hodgins, *Documentary History*, VIII: 266–8. This is also the position of the Gore teachers; see Bruce Curtis, *Building the Educational State: Canada West, 1836–1871* (Sussex and London, ON: Falmer Press and Althouse Press 1988), chapter 2.
56 Hodgins, *Documentary History*, IX: 65–6
57 Ibid., 63–5
58 Ibid., 70
59 AO RG2 C6C, Trustees, section 5 Guelph Township, n.d. March 1850; other correspondents include William Beattie, section 7 Yonge, 28 January 1850; Wendlin Schuler to A. Allan, 15 February 1850; Isaac Crane, Windham, 8 March 1850; Trustees and Teachers, Dumfries, 18 March 1850; Trustees, St George, 18 March 1850; E. Bingham, Glanford, 25 March 1850; J. Ranson, Flamborough, 13 April 1850; also, Hodgins, *Documentary History*, IX: 67–70
60 LAC, *Debates*, 2 July 1850; for other parliamentary reaction, especially in favour of local control over school books, see 8 and 9 July 1850.
61 Hodgins, *Documentary History*, IX: 70–1
62 For one such lecture, see AO, Private Manuscript Collection, Ker Family Papers.
63 The text of the School Act of 1850 is to be found in *Annual Report of the Chief Superintendent of Education* for 1850.
64 S. Houston and A. Prentice, *Schooling and Scholars in Nineteenth Century Ontario* (Toronto: University of Toronto Press 1988), 146, show 44 per cent of the local superintendents in 1861 were clergymen.

Chapter 5

1 See Gramsci's analysis in *Selections from the Prison Notebooks* (New York: International Publishers 1973).

2 See my 'The Speller Expelled: Disciplining the Common Reader in Canada West,' *Canadian Review of Sociology and Anthropology* 23/3 (1985): 346–68, for a discussion of 'improvement' and the movement for the 'diffusion of useful knowledge.'

3 Marx himself stressed, in his fragment on social classes in *Capital*, Vol. 3 (New York: International 1974), 885–7, the complexity of class structure, even in the most developed capitalist society, stemming from the existence of transitional strata and the stratification of classes themselves. He also stressed the further possibility of varying subjective understandings of class position in *The Eighteenth Brumaire of Louis Bonaparte* (New York: International 1972), 40–1.

4 In Ryerson to Secretary Higginson, 12 April 1844, Ryerson had declared that his appointment to the assistant superintendency was supported by 'Mr. Keefer of Thorold (who is a magistrate of wealth, leisure and benevolence ...),' in *The Story of My Life* (Toronto: William Briggs 1883), 348. Ryerson did not report, and may not have known, that George Keefer's name appeared on a petition against his appointment dated 29 March/3 April 1844, NAC, RG5 CI, Vol. 126. For Keefer's income from the mills, see LAUC, *Sundries*, Welland Canal Company Reports, 1833–40; LAC, *Sessional Papers*, Appendix O, 1854–5; the post office was a minor one, paying only £12 in 1843: LAC, *Sessional Papers*, Appendix A, 1844–5; William Ormsby, 'Jacob Keefer,' *Dictionary of Canadian Biography*, Vol. X (Toronto: University of Toronto Press 1972). The two other famous Keefer brothers also served as state inspectors – Samuel as the first railway inspector, Thomas as an inspector of timber slides. I deal with Keefer at more length in 'Mapping the Social: Jacob Keefer's Educational Tours, 1845,' *Journal of Canadian Studies* (in press).

5 Waugh's substantial stone store still stands in Oxford Mills, Ontario.

6 The Crown Lands Agency was worth £58 to Hart in 1845, the first year that he held it, and likely more than that later. LAC, *Sessional Papers*, Appendix EE, 1846; Appendix 11, 1857.

7 For Steele's brewing activity, see LAUC, *Sundries*, paper 26, and Gaol reports, 1836; Public Accounts, 1837; Steele, who supported a household containing thirteen people, including a domestic servant, had a half-acre of potatoes beside his house and store in 1848; see the Haldimand Township census.

8 Naomi S. Heydon, *Looking Back ... Pioneers of Bytown and March.* (Ottawa: MOM Printing 1980), 284; R.D. Gidney and W.P.J. Millar, *Inventing Secondary Education* (Montreal and Kingston: McGill-Queen's University Press 1990); LAC, *Sessional Papers*, Appendix 11, 1857

9 See William Elliott's diaries in the Baldwin Room, Metropolitan Toronto Reference Library.

10 One of the things Higginson brought with him when he came to Canada in 1819 was a magnificent case clock with a hand-painted face. Possession of the clock (which remains with one of his descendants, T. Boyd Higginson) places Higginson as a man of some means. The 1861 Prescott agricultural census claimed Higginson held 85 acres valued at $2,000, with livestock worth $347, and an annual product in butter worth $70. For the railway, see Canada *Gazette*, 4 March 1851.

11 As many as four different farms by the time he was superintendent. These were probably rented out.

12 LAC, *Sessional Papers*, Appendix 11, 1857; Province of Canada, *Statutes*, 1857

13 Eliot's last pension payment was for the summer of 1858. A widow named Jane Eliot is listed in the 1861 agricultural census of West Sandwich Township as holding a 200-acre farm valued at $5,000. This was the second-most valuable farm listed.

14 Province of Canada, *Statutes*, 18 Vic. c. CXCIV; see also Canada *Gazette*, 13 January 1844. Elias was probably related to the influential Burnhams in the neighbouring Newcastle District (Asa A., the district councillor, mayor of Cobourg, and leading merchant; Mark of Port Hope, a merchant; and Zaccheus, the patriarch and pioneer, a substantial landowner and merchant). Elias Burnham was described by his contemporaries as a 'man of means.'

15 Allan was a member of the Society of Advocates from 10 July 1810. He took an MA from Mareschal College in 1806, served as joint legal assessor and clerk to the incorporated trades of Aberdeen, and was a prominent Freemason. He was a burgess in 1813 and an honorary burgess from 1823. He married Anne Davidson in 1824, and they had four children. One of these was, or was named for, Absalom Shade, MPP for West Wellington, 1886–94, and sheriff of Wellington County. Alexander Allan arrived in Preston in 1843 and was immediately named town clerk and was, in the next year, appointed district superintendent, suggesting prior connection to the power structures in this district dominated by the Canada Company. See J.A. Henderson, ed., *History of the Society of Advocates in Aberdeen* (Aberdeen: n.p. 1912), 80–1.

16 Harriet Martineau, *How to Observe Morals and Manners* [1838] (New Brunswick, NJ: Transaction 1989), 94, writes: 'Moral excellence has no regard to classes and professions; and religion, being not a pursuit but a temper, cannot, in fact, be professionally cultivated with personal advantage.' It did pay well to be a clergyman supported from the Reserves Fund!

17 LAC, *Sessional Papers*, Appendix IIII, 1849

18 For a general discussion of clerical salaries, see William Westfall, *Two Worlds: The Protestant Culture of Nineteenth Century Ontario* (Montreal and Kingston: McGill-Queen's University Press 1989), 103–12; for Padfield, see LAUC, *Sundries*, Upper Canada College Accounts and Clergy Reserves Reports, 1836; LAC, *Sessional Papers*, Appendix II, 1848; Appendix III, 1849; Appendix HH, 1851; and Appendix I 1860, which shows a commutation payment of $9,111.03; Westfall would suggest Padfield didn't get this last himself.

19 Cf. R.D. Gidney and W. Millar, *Inventing Secondary Education* (Montreal and Kingston: McGill-Queen's University Press 1990), 85

20 Fraser petitioned repeatedly but unsuccessfully in the late 1850s for a subsidy from the Bureau of Agriculture for the book, which eventually appeared as *The Emigrant's Guide, or, Sketches of Canada: with some of the northern and western States of America* (1867). It is quite a chauvinist piece, a common feature of the genre.

21 For subjects taught at the Burlington Academy, see Gidney and Millar, *Inventing Secondary Education*, 15.

22 His house still stands at 55 Chapel Street, Woodstock, Ontario. The durability of these houses points to the substance of their owners. Landon earned about £20 a year as an agent for the scandal-plagued Woodstock and Lake Erie Railway and Harbour Company; see LAC, *Sessional Papers*, Appendix 6, 1857.

23 For more information on Bosworth and Landon, see chapter 7, below.

24 Westfall, *Two Worlds*, 206; in addition to the information cited above, notice that Bosworth was the author of petitions demanding a secular character for King's College and for the appropriation of the Clergy Reserves for educational purposes; LAC, *Journals*, 29 April 1846.

25 More detail on these teachers follows. Robert K. Smart, Keeper of the Muniments at St Andrews University, suggests that Strachan's payment of the lowest university fees indicates an artisanal background. Notice the school fund paid Hynes and Strachan only £9.9.9 in 1835: LAUC, *Sundries*, Johnstown District School Reports, 1836; Donnelly is listed in the Picton census for 1861. The carriages were valued at $270.

26 Hutton tried unsuccessfully to be named master of the proposed Victoria District Grammar School about 1840, and also attempted to supplement the income of his farm by teaching in Belleville. Of course, what Hutton and others denounced as obnoxious itinerance on the part of common-school teachers did not apply to themselves.

27 There is also a Colin 'Grigory' listed as Ottawa district schoolmaster in F.H. Armstrong, *Handbook of Upper Canadian Chronology* (Toronto and London: Dundurn Press 1985). This is almost certainly the same; Gregor's name was often rendered 'Grigor,' although he advertised himself as 'Gregor' in the press.

28 No record of Hayter's employment survives in any of the histories of Victoria College. Given that he entered the navy at age thirteen, it seems unlikely that he was employed as an academic teacher, although he did have good French. See *O'Hearn's Naval Biographical Dictionary* (London: Murray 1862). (My thanks to Barry Gough for this reference.)

29 LAC, *Sessional Papers*, Appendix A, 1844–5; Appendix EE, 1846

30 Hendry's partnership with John Bain was dissolved after the former's death. His widow, Katherine, a native of Scotland and aged forty, was listed in the 1852 census, living in a single-storey frame house that she shared with her four children and another family.

31 For the Reynoldses, see LAUC, *Sundries*, paper 26, and Revenue and Expenditure, 1836; Public Accounts 1837; Canada *Gazette*, 25 November 1845.

32 AO RG2 M2; Hynes's pension application contains lengthy letters from Sherwood and Smart, among others.

33 Strachan was incorrectly listed in LAC, *Sessional Papers*, Appendix 58, Table G, 1859 as 'M.A. St. Andrews.' R.K. Smart, Keeper of the Muniments at St Andrews, points out in a private communication that, while Strachan did attend the Latin and Greek classes in 1821 and 1822, he certainly did not have sufficient attendance for the MA. The above reference is the only place Strachan is represented as 'M.A.,' and it is not a claim that he ever made himself. However, French was not a regular university subject, but rather was taught by private arrangement, and hence Strachan's claims in this regard cannot be verified.

34 *Aberdeen University Studies*, No. 1, 'Roll of Alumni in Arts, 1596–1860'; *A Catalogue of the Graduates in the University of Dublin*. Volume I lists Ardagh as BA 1827; MA 1832; Gregor's advertisement for the Ottawa District Grammar School described him as a graduate of the university course in Glasgow and a person who had studied Elocution under Sheridan Knowles, Bytown *Gazette*, 21 February 1838; T.W., Moody and J.C. Beckett, *Queen's, Belfast, 1845–1949* (London: Faber & Faber 1959). R.G. Cant, *The University of St. Andrew: A Short History* (Edinburgh: Scottish Academic Press 1970); William Trollope, *History of the Royal Foundation of Christ's Hospital* (London: William Pickering 1834); G.E. Boyce, *Hutton of Hastings* (Belleville: Hastings County Council 1972), 2; AO RG2 M2, Hunter, Hamilton. Out of the total 120 inspector-years served (6 years × 20 districts), these highly educated inspectors served 47.

35 Canada *Gazette*, 7 February, 10 June, 5 August 1843; 22 March, 6 December 1845; 5 June 1847; 12 February, 19 August 1848

36 Hutton, Keefer, Pinhey, Steele, and Wilson. Steele was quickly removed both as warden and as superintendent for 'difficulties' with the district funds.

37 Pinhey was elected in the 1830s, but unseated for rigging the vote by giving tickets of location; Wilson sat in the late 1840s; Higginson sat later; Charles Eliot ran unsuccessfully against John Prince in 1836. Wilson did not take up his Legislative Council seat because he preferred the appointment as district judge.

38 This information is taken from diverse secondary and primary sources and the manuscript censuses.

39 A broadside published by a disgruntled arch-Tory teacher spoke of 'The French quaker, the outlaw or Gold Digger, the Stump orator, the Female Kidnapper,' in addition to other abuses. For more detail, see the discussion in my 'Schoolbooks and the Myth of Curricular Republicanism: The State and the Curriculum in Canada West, 1820–1850,' *Histoire sociale/Social History* 16/3 (1983): 305–29. For more on D'Everardo, the revealing article by Frank Pitkin, 'Dexter D'Everardo,' Wellington County Historical Society *Papers and Records*, Vol. 3 (1927): 86–103

40 See NAC, RG24, 133, and the entries in the *Dictionary of Canadian Biography*; but

compare Leonore Davidoff and Catherine Hall, *Family Fortunes: Men and Women of the English Middle Class, 1750–1850* (Chicago: University of Chicago Press 1987), for an exploration of the rich potential of the English sources.

41 Boyce, *Hutton of Hastings*, 74

42 Hutton wrote of the guests invited to celebrate his wedding anniversary in 1845 (Boyce, *Hutton of Hastings*, 141–2): 'They were the cream of the country, being the best educated amongst us – lawyers, doctors, clergymen, their families and a few merchants. The Lords of the soil are unfortunately, too illiterate as yet.' This speaks once again to the class character of the practice of 'improvement': people not sufficiently cultured to invite to one's house could hardly be expected to be sufficiently cultured to understand the requirements of 'good' schools or the characteristics of 'good' teachers. Hutton, as we see below, could tell the latter characteristics at once.

43 ? indicates no information exists; – denotes a year in which the person named did not serve; % refers to a percentage of the school monies; for Gregor this likely meant about £25, for Hart about £50. The year he had £200, D'Everardo also had costs.

44 Quoted in Boyce, *Hutton of Hastings*, 116.

45 Besides being an able cartoonist, Elliot was 'a great student of literature,' quick with a quotation. *Transactions of the London and Middlesex Historical Society*, 1917–18, 26–9.

46 Wm.W. Judd, ed., *Minutes of the London Mechanics' Institute* (London: London Public Library 1976), Occasional Paper no. 23. Wilson was a member from 1841 to 1849 and first vice-president for 1848–9; He lectured 23 February 1844 on electricity, using a portable machine.

47 LAC, *Sessional Papers*, Appendix 34, 1856, for Keefer (1840), Pinhey (1848), and Steele (1853); Eliot (1839) is cited above.

48 William, Jr, and Charles Clarke organized one of the many temperance petitions of the early 1850s: LAC, *Journals*, 27 August 1852.

49 LAC, *Sessional Papers*, Appendix 32, 1857; their names were used as fronts for the acquisition of land by the Crown agent and his relatives. Keefer's title to the property in question is in NAC MG24 I33.

50 AO RG2 C6C, Hunter to McNab, 18 November 1845. Hunter says clearly he has written to Keefer, and seems to suggest he has contacted or will contact the others as well.

51 'A shrewd man is this Ryerson,' wrote William Elliott in his diary after the chief superintendent's visit to London, 'noting well the feelings & prejudices of the men he has had to deal w/.' William Elliott Diary, Baldwin Room, Metropolitan Toronto Reference Library, 15 October 1847

52 This is detailed in *Building the Educational State*, ch. 2.

53 In 1850, those who served included Alexander Allan, James Baird, William Clarke, Dexter D'Everardo, Thomas Donnelly (for Picton), John Flood, William Fraser, Thomas Higginson, Alexander Mann, James Padfield, Patrick Thornton,

and William Landon. In later years, William Fraser, who moved west to Bruce, Benjamin Hayter (Cobourg), Samuel Ardagh, Henry Clifford, Hamilton Hunter (for London), William Hynes (for Prescott), and John Wilson (London) also acted. London was superintended between 1850 and 1870 by William Clarke (Jr?), Hamilton Hunter, and John Wilson. Alexander Mann for Pakenham, and Thomas Higginson for West Hawkesbury served throughout the period. See the announcements of appointments for 1850 in AO RG2 C6C *passim*, and *Annual Reports of the Chief Superintendent of Education*, 1850–71.

54 It is not clear if this is Clarke, Jr, or Clarke, Sr.

Chapter 6

1 Not until late 1846 did the central government move to provide maps to local districts in fulfilment of its own legal obligations: NAC RG1 E1, Executive Council Minutes, Canada State Book E, 9 September 1846, 694. By 1859, the Crown Lands department had produced a map of the province on a scale of 1 inch to 2 miles – it was 65 feet long and 13 feet wide.

2 AO MU4449, Ardagh Family Papers, Diary fragments, 23 February 1844. He added, 'a most responsible office. May God give me grace to discharge the duty w/fidelity.' For Ardagh, see also S.J. Boddy, *A Brief Memoir of the Rev. Samuel B. Ardagh* (Toronto: Roswell and Hutchison 1874).

3 Baldwin Room, Metropolitan Toronto Reference Library, *William Elliott Diaries*, 6 June 1845

4 AO RG2 C6C, Alexander Allan, Preston, 11 August 1849

5 AO RG2 C6C, Benjamin Hayter, Cobourg, 28 February 1849. This occurred in the midst of Hayter's struggle with Council, and his claims that former superintendent and warden John Steele was attempting to replace him. Hayter claimed that one of the vacant schools was Steele's. In the bundle of documents *re* Hayter in October 1849, see a repetition of the above, dated 2 April 1849.

6 Kingston *Herald*, 3 March 1844

7 G.E. Boyce, *Hutton of Hastings* (Belleville: Hastings County Council 1972), 124

8 Baldwin Room, Metropolitan Toronto Reference Library, William Elliott Diaries, 25 November 1845; 12 and 15 September 1848

9 NAC, MG24, I33, #7, Jacob Keefer notes. Keefer returns to touring the following month. In AO RG2 C6C, 9 August 1844, Keefer wrote 'I have spent about 6 weeks in visiting Schools and have about 2 months work to do yet.' Also, AO RG2 F3A, Niagara District Report, 1845

10 Cobourg *Star*, 23 June 1848

11 AO RG2 C6C, Jas. Baird, Port Hope, 8 March 1850

12 AO RG2 C6C, E. Burnham, Peterboro, 12 April 1849; for Padfield, see below.

13 AO RG2 C6C, John Bignall, Goderich, 12 October 1844

14 AO RG2 C6C, Jacob Bock, Wilmot, 30 August 1844: 'with diffidence did I enter upon the duties of that office as I did not Consider myself fully qualified to fill the

Same, Being a German and a farmer and little acquainted with Business Beyond my own Private Domestic affairs.' E. Burnham, Peterboro, 25 October 1844, reports that no one was appointed in Belmont until September, and that person refused to serve in any case.

15 AO RG2 C6C, *inter alia*, notifications of appointments of township superintendents include, for example, Mr Campion, the councillor and justice of the peace for Marmora; Murdoch McDonnell for Drummond; Henry Clifford – Ardagh's successor as district superintendent – for Oro; Judge J.A. Murdoch for Bathurst; Henry Fowlds for Asphodel; and Benjamin Tett for North Crosby – later a substantial lumber baron and MP.

16 AO RG2 C6C, S.B Ardagh, Barrie, 3 July 1844; 21 April 1845; 5 May 1845

17 For example, C6C, John Strachan, Ernest Town, 17 March 1846; and one of Strachan's former employers and a former township superintendent, John McDonald, Gananoque, 27 April 1845

18 AO RG2 C6C, Philemon Pennock, Augusta, 27 January 1846. Pennock says 'Dist Superintendents,' but he clearly means township superintendents.

19 AO RG2 C1B, McNab to Thornton, 21 November 1845: 'In relation to Township Superintendents, I am of the opinion that their services might be dispensed with, not perhaps without some difficulty however. In case they were discarded could County Supts. perform the duties now performed by both Officers? And who would act as local Treasurers? Please give me your opinion.'

20 AO RG2 C6C, Thomas Moyle, Adelaide, 25 February 1845

21 AO RG2 C6C, P. Thornton, Hamilton, 27 February 1844; C1B, Education Office to Thornton, 11 March 1844; someone has marked all Thornton's spelling mistakes in pencil – I suspect Hodgins in the debate over Mrs Merry in 1849.

22 AO RG2, for the quotation, C1B, McNab to Thornton, 9 January 1845; also, C6C, P. Thornton, Hamilton, 19 March, 12 October, 26 November 1844; C1B, Murray to Thornton, 27 March 1844; McNab to Thornton, 23 November, 4 December 1844. See also C6C, Thomas Donnelly, Bloomfield, 3 October 1844; C1B, McNab to Donnelly, 12 November 1844: 'the *Township* Superintendent, as a general thing, should examine the Teachers, at least, in the first instance.'

23 AO RG2 C6C, P. Thornton, Hamilton, 21 August 1844; C1B, Murray to Thornton, 23 August 1844.

24 AO RG2 C6C, W.G. Stewart, Esquissing, 4 October, 19 November 1844; in the latter: 'if all incompetent persons, are driven from the profession of teaching in Canada West, in the course of the current year, the most enthusiastic theorist, must acknowledge that at least a good beginning has been made.' Stewart accepted the project, he just wanted the teachers he had certified and who had taught to be paid. C1B, McNab to Stewart, 12 November 1844.

25 AO RG2 C6C, James Boyd, Hornby, 1 May 1844; C1B, Murray to Boyd, 15 May 1844

26 AO RG2 C6C, John Hopkins, Teacher, Napanee, 27 April 1844; John Strachan, Ernest Town, 14 May 1844

27 AO RG2 C6C, Henry Clifford, Oro, 5 August 1844; John Chanter, Vespra, 3 August 1844; CIB, Murray to Ardagh, 29 August 1844

28 AO RG2 C6C, W. Williams, Teacher, section 1 Marmora Township, 7 October 1844; CIB, McNab to Williams, 30 October 1844

29 AO RG2 C6C, Henry Parsons, Teacher, section 15, Toronto, 19 September 1846; CID, Ryerson to Barber, 21 September 1846

30 AO RG2 C6C, John Wilson, June 1844

31 AO RG2 C6C, Michael Dumphy, Teacher, Puslinch, 30 August 1844; P. Thornton, Hamilton, 10 September 1844; E.F. Heath, Puslinch, 23 September 1844; Patrick Thornton, Hamilton, 30 September 1844; CIB, Murray to Thornton, 7 and 14 September 1844; Murray to Rev. Thomas Gibney, Guelph, 16 September 1844; Murray to Heath, 28 September 1844

32 AO RG2 C6C, Colin Gregor, L'Orignal, 6 September 1844; CIB, Murray to Gregor, 10 September 1844

33 AO RG2 C6C, Duncan Dewar, Vankleek Hill, 16 June 1845; CIB, McNab to Dewar, 9 July 1845

34 For example, Cobourg *Star*, 20 August 1845, reports on this conflict. Barber lasted as Toronto superintendent until 1859. The *Examiner* repeatedly questioned his competence and behaviour in office in 1845, cf. 12 and 19 March, 16 April, 14 May, 4 and 20 August, 3 and 10 September, 1 October, 5 November. (Thanks to Robert Gidney for this reference.) See also, R.B. Howard, *Upper Canada College, 1829–1979: Colborne's Legacy* (Toronto: Macmillan 1979), 10–12, 42–3. *Journal of Education for Upper Canada* 28 (April 1875): 59. For Hutton and Benjamin, see Boyce, *Hutton of Hastings*.

35 AO, MU957–958, Duck Family Papers; Western District Council Papers; Chatham *Gleaner*, 22 February 1848. The salary was reduced to £100 in 1849.

36 AO RG2 C1C, October 1846

37 AO, District Council Papers, Gore District Council, Appendix to the Report of the Superintendent of Common Schools, a lengthy letter from Thornton entitled 'To the Warden & Councillors of the Gore District in Sessions Assembled,' 13 February 1845

38 AO RG2 C6C, Hamilton Hunter, Toronto, 13 May 1846

39 AO, District Council Papers, Home District Council, *By-Laws and Reports*; Toronto *Examiner*, 14 February 1849

40 AO RG2 C1C, Ryerson to Colin Gregor, 5 May 1847; CID, Ryerson to Hayter, 19 July 1847, 13 March 1848

41 See, *inter alia*, AO RG2 CID, Ryerson to Gregor, 30 July 1847; to Strachan, 30 July 1847; to Donnelly, 7 August 1847; to Hunter, 19 August 1847; to Allan, 2 February 1848; to Burnham, 3 January 1849; C6C, P. Thornton, Hamilton, 20 February 1850; Hamilton Hunter, Toronto, 6 March 1850.

42 AO RG2 C1C, Ryerson to Hunter, 28 January 1847; Ryerson to Cameron, 6 February 1847; Ryerson to Hunter, 10 February 1847

43 AO RG2 CID, Ryerson to D'Everardo, 13 August 1847; in C1C, Ryerson to Millar,

18 March 1847, Ryerson expressed his hope that quarterly examinations and the visitors clauses would capture the benefits of the township superintendency.

44 AO RG2 C1C, Ryerson to Gregor, 5 April 1847; also, Education Office, *Forms, Regulations and Instructions for the Better Organization and Government of Common Schools in Upper Canada* (Toronto: J.H. Lawrence 1847)

45 AO RG2 C6C, Trustees, section 9 West Hawkesbury, with a note from Thomas Higginson, 9 December 1847; C1D, Ryerson to Higginson, 20 December 1847

46 AO RG2 C6C, W. Elliott, London, 4 June 1849; C1D, Ryerson to Elliot, 16 June 1849

47 AO, District Council Papers, Johnstown District, Fifth Report of the Ctte. on Education, 5 February 1848; William Jelly, *A Summary of the Proceedings of the Council of the District of Johnstown ... 1842–1942* (n.p.: 1943), February 1848. In AO RG2 C1D, Ryerson to Waugh, 14 February 1848, a discussion of attempts by district councils to decide questions the province of district superintendents

48 Reference to this case is to be found in S. Houston and A. Prentice, *Schooling and Scholars in Nineteenth-Century Ontario* (Toronto: University of Toronto Press 1988), 151–3; the rebuke to Ryerson is AO RG2 C6C, Leslie to Ryerson, 5 July 1849.

49 Prince Edward *Gazette*, 19 and 26 May 1848

50 AO RG2 C6C, Hamnett Pinhey, Horaceville, 20 November 1844; 20 September 1845; D. Daly, Montreal, 3 May 1845; Js. Fitz. Wm Briedon Healy, Bytown, 11 September 1846

51 AO RG2 C1B, McNab to Elliott, 25 June 1845; C6C, Wm. Elliott, London, 22 July 1845; 17 August 1845; 1 November 1845; C1B, McNab to Elliott, 17 November 1845; C6C, Daly to Ryerson, 7 March 1846; Baldwin Room, Metropolitan Toronto Reference Library, Wm Elliott Diaries, 17 June; 8, 12, 28, and 31 August; 18, 19, and 27 September; 29 and 31 October; 12, 13, 17, and 18 November 1845. *Western Globe*, 5 June 1846. In the educational correspondence of the 1850s, a teacher named Duncan Campbell played an important role in forcing the Middlesex County Board of Public Instruction to alter its certification practices.

52 AO RG2 C6C, John Strachan, Ernest Town, 20 February 1846; 11 December 1849; Leslie to Ryerson, 21 January 1850; C1D, Ryerson to Daly, 2 July 1847. I am somewhat suspicious about the Kingston and Camden East schools; these are the only references to them, while the Newburgh Academy is much better known.

53 Kingston *Chronicle and Gazette*, 6 March 1844; 18 January, 14 May, and 6 December 1845; Notice that Strachan quotes from Pestalozzi and John Locke in his discussions of pedagogy. AO MU3277, Pringle Family Papers, Strachan to Pringle, 22 April 1844. These papers also contain a communication from R.H. Thornton to Pringle, which suggests at least an indirect link between Strachan and Patrick Thornton. Also, F. Burrows, 'Early Education' and G.A. Aynesworth, 'Newburgh,' Lennox and Addington Historical Society, *Papers and Records*, II (1910): 13, 26–35. This kind of activity was encouraged by Murray, AO RG2 C6C, Charles Eliot, Sandwich, 28 August 1844; C1B, Murray to Eliot, 9 September 1844. Mur-

ray wrote: 'The only way in which Teachers of Superior qualifications can be encouraged is by District Supts recommending them to the Trustees of the most important School districts, & where they may be of greater service to the public & obtain better Salaries.'

54 AO RG2 C6C, R. Waugh, Merrickville, 4 April 1845; C1B, McNab to Waugh, 8 April 1845

55 Brockville *Recorder*, 5 February 1846; AO RG2 M1; LAC, *Sessional Papers*, 'Annual Reports of the Chief Superintendent of Education for Upper Canada'; Neilson is on the superannuated teachers' list and still alive in the late 1850s.

56 For the by-law, AO, District Council Papers, Johnstown District, Letterbook A, 15 November 1847; also, RG2 C6C, Johnston Neilson, Kitley, 4 March 1846; C1C, Ryerson to Neilson, 17 March 1846

57 Brockville *Recorder*, 9, 16, 23, and 30 July 1846, where we notice Carroll's conclusion that 'Justice' wanted people to patronize 'the Academy of a certain village not one hundred miles from F__v__e as the Model School.' There were regular advertisements for the Ogdensburgh, NY, Academy in the Brockville paper, and the hints about the disloyalty of Waugh's critics, combined with the marriage of Waugh's predecessor, William Hynes, in Ogdensburgh in 1851, could lead to interesting speculations; also, 13 August, 12 November 1846.

58 AO RG2 C1C, Ryerson to Waugh, 19 September 1846. The reference was likely to the London District Model School.

59 AO RG2 F2, two versions, 'Report on the Model School of the Johnstown District for 1846' and ditto, but signed 'Ogle R. Gowan, Brockville, 6th Nov. 1846'

60 AO, District Council Papers, Johnstown District, Annual Report of R. Waugh, 1 February 1847

61 Brockville *Recorder*, 27 May 1847; AO RG2 C1D, Ryerson to Waugh, 17 October 1848; Ryerson to Sullivan, 25 April 1848

62 Legislative Assembly of Canada *Journals*, Third Session, 1843, Appendix Z, 'Annual Report of the District Superintendent of Education ... 14th November 1843'

63 AO RG2 C6C, S.B. Ardagh, Barrie, 5 May 1845; William Hutton, Belleville, 25 December 1845; also 30 March 1846, where Hutton urged greater financial powers for the district superintendent, which would aid in 'introducing a uniformity in the description of school Books used – a most important consideration – as in every school at present the variety is endless & many objectionable.' Notice, also, AO MU972, Robert McKee Moore's Register and Day Book, West Gwillimbury Twp., 21 August 1846: 'Visited and examined in reading writing & spelling. The children in attendance very small. I beg to recommend the books of the Irish National Schools.' S.B. Ardagh, Supt. of Education, Dist of Simcoe.

64 AO RG2 C6C, Newton Bosworth, Woodstock, 8 April 1845

65 AO RG2 C6C, Henry Clifford, Oro, 15 October 1844; Benjamin Hayter, n.d. 1847. Clifford wanted surplus monies to go to the purchase of books and proposed a detailed monitoring plan. Hayter suggested dividing his district into subdistricts with a book depot and subinspector in each.

66 AO RG2 C6C, John Strachan, Ernest Town, 4 December 1849; Strachan recommended the Rev. George D. Greenleaf's book on the history and geography of Canada to Ryerson. Also, F3A, Ottawa District Report 1849, where Higginson provides a lengthy description of the political benefits of a Canadian history and geography: 'such a work would be a secure basis whereon our young people could and would rest their loyalty Patriotism and country-love, such a work would develope events and circumstances around which, the associations of heart and memory might cluster as around a common centre, making us what we should be, what we require to be, and what we have never yet been a united, a prosperous, and a contented People.'

67 AO RG2 F3A, Home District Report, 1845. Only one Thornton reader apparently exists, the fourth, but it went through two editions. NAC's library has a copy of the second edition, Rev. R.H. Thornton, *The Instructive Reader, Consisting of Moral Instruction, Descriptions of Natural Objects, Places, Manners: And Other Instructive and Useful Information for the Young* (Toronto: George Brown 1845). The cover also bears the inscription: 'The 4th in the Progressive Series by P. and R.H. Thornton.' While the work reprints part of the sections of wages and rich and poor from the fourth Irish reader, the book is far less turgid and contains more narrative material than its official competitor. Notice that, in the report referred to above, Hunter urged the general adoption of the Irish readers.

68 AO RG2 C6C, Patrick Thornton, Hamilton, 30 July 1845; Joseph Fenton, Hamilton, 21 September 1846; CIC, Ryerson to Fenton, 28 September 1846. Thornton's 'Progressive Series' was advertised by James Lesslie as late as 1849.

69 AO RG2 C6C, Patrick Thornton, Hamilton, 5 November 1846; CIC, Ryerson to Thornton, 10 November 1846

70 AO RG2 C6C, W. Elliott, London, 18 July 1846; see also my 'Schoolbooks and the Myth of Curricular Republicanism,' *Histoire sociale/Social History* 16/32 (1983): 305–29; and 'The Speller Expelled,' *Canadian Review of Sociology and Anthropology* 22/3 (1985): 346–68.

71 AO RG2 CIC, Ryerson to D'Everardo, 29 September 1846; C6C, Dexter D'Everardo, Fonthill, 9 November 1846

72 AO RG2 CIC, for instance, Ryerson to Hendry, 1 February 1847; also C6C, Thomas Donnelly, Bloomfield, 16 December 1846; and W. Hutton, Belleville, 8 December 1846. Donnelly urged the support of Cobb's popular *Speller*, which Hutton as strongly opposed. Hutton, at the same time, urged the adoption of Morse's *Geography* as the best available – something the Board of Education did.

73 Brockville *Recorder*, 1 July 1847

74 AO RG2 F3A, Huron District Report, 1847; C6C, Charles Fletcher, Goderich, 29 January 1849

75 AO RG2 C6C, Hamilton Hunter, Toronto, 18 November 1845; CIB, McNab to Hunter, 27 November 1845

76 For example, AO RG2 C6C, William Millar, Cornwall, 23 March 1849, 'I[t] is astonishing that so little interest is felt in this District, respecting the Journal of Edu-

cation. I tried all the Councilors and a great many persons from all parts of the District but could not get a single subscriber – Nor did anyone even call to examine the present of Books from Ireland.' Millar was on the verge of absconding and had already resigned, 'finding the salary of £80.0.0 quite inadequate to support my family'; William Hutton, Belleville, 19 February 1850, sent his subscription and promised to get others; W.H. Poole, Consecon, 1 August 1849, claimed that Prince Edward councillors and the district superintendent, Thomas Donnelly, opposed the circulation of the *Journal* – a fictitious account, since Council actually ordered a copy for each school section.

77 AO RG2 C6C, John Strachan, Ernest Town, 21 October 1844; Strachan wrote, *inter alia*: 'I called a meeting of the inhabitants to try if I could prevail with them to unite and both Protestants and Catholics to send to the same school, to which they agree.' *Re* funding, CIC, Ryerson to D'Everardo, 16 January 1846

78 AO RG2 C6C, Jacob Keefer, Thorold, 25 August 1845; Benjamin Hayter, Cobourg, April 1849; Patrick Thornton, Hamilton, 22 June 1849; Wm Fraser, Lochiel, 9 August 1849; CIC, Ryerson to Fletcher, 11 March 1847; CID, Ryerson to Burnham, 25 September 1847

79 AO RG2 C6C, John Flood, Richmond, 15 May 1845, a staunch defence of the claims of women teachers to a share in the school fund; although, while Patrick Thornton was a teacher in Hamilton the male teachers attempted to prevent female teachers from sharing in the school fund; see Clerk, Hamilton, 10 July 1844; John Carrothers, Teacher, 11 July; CIB, Murray to Osborne, 13 July, Murray to Carrothers, 11 July 1844; later, Thornton at best provided lukewarm support, and at worst regarded teaching as men's work. See also, C6C, 25 April 1844, copy of a circular from John Steele to township superintendents instructing them to pay female teachers.

80 NAC MG24 I33, 7, Jacob Keefer tour notes, 17 October 1845

81 See *The Ecclesiastical and Missionary Record*, October 1860; *The Canadian Congregational Yearbook*, 1878, 22–4; AO RG2 C6C, William Clarke, Simcoe, 2 June 1849; CID, Ryerson to Clarke, 16 June 1849

82 For example, AO RG2 CIC, Ryerson to George Vardon, Superintendent General, Indian Affairs, Montreal, 26 May 1847

83 AO RG2 C6C, Patrick Thornton, Hamilton, 12 October 1844; CIB, Murray to Thornton, 23 November 1844 (the Indian students); C6C, Patrick Thornton, Hamilton, 26 November 1844; CIB, McNab to Thornton, 4 December 1844

84 AO RG2 C6C, John Cowan, Sandwich, 15 October 1845; CIB, McNab to Cowan, 5 November 1845

85 AO, District Council Papers, Minutes of the Western District Council, 11 November 1845, 'by their own teachers.' Council addressed the question of race relations repeatedly, petitioning the government in February 1849, for instance, not to allow coloured people to settle in the district because their presence was 'highly deleterious to the morals and social conditions of the present and future inhabitants.'

86 More on these questions is to be found in AO RG2 C6C, Isaac Rice et al., Amherst-

burgh, 23 January 1846; Robert Peden, Amherstburgh, 23 February 1846; CIC, Ryerson to Peden, 9 February 1846; Ryerson to Rice, 5 March 1846; Ryerson to Peden, 5 March 1846; Ryerson to George Duck, 4 January 1847; Ryerson to John Fraser, President, London Branch Bible Society, 13 April 1847; Ryerson to Allan, 29 May 1847; CID, Ryerson to Reynolds, 13 December 1847; and, earlier, C6C, John Carrothers, Teacher, Hamilton, 11 July 1844. This last, in the attempt of Hamilton's male teachers to exclude women from the school fund, included the charge that women teachers refuse to teach 'any coloured children either boys or girls.'

Chapter 7

1 *Bathurst Courier*, 23 January, 27 February 1844, for Allan's obituary; Also, F.H. Armstrong, *Handbook of Upper Canadian Chronology* (Toronto and London: Dundurn Press 1985), 329; Allan was appointed postmaster in 1837. While Francis's widow had left the village by 1852 (if she had not predeceased him), James had two young men who were likely his brothers living with him, his wife, and three young children. The village's local history collection was destroyed by fire in the mid-1980s.

2 AO RG2, C6C, Dawson Kerr, Teacher, Perth, 15 April 1844; CIB, Murray to Kerr, 17 April 1844; for McDonnell on the school laws, NAC RG5 CI, Vol. 142, Murdoch McDo[n]nell, 20 December 1844

3 *Bathurst Courier*, 23 January, 27 February 1844. McDonnell and Malloch were both thirty-eight years old in 1844; for more information, see the census for Perth 1852.

4 'What Think ye of the Candidates?' *Bathurst Courier*, 9 April 1844. Dick was an important Reformer and man of repute.

5 *Bathurst Courier*, 16 April 1844

6 Dickson was the first prison and jail inspector for Canada West from 1851. He was a leading member of the district council and likely was influential in Mann's appointment.

7 The school report for Pakenham in 1842 noted 'the attendants improving but the number of Scholars under the operation of the School Bill evidently decreasing.' AO, RG2, F3A, Bathurst District Report, 1842. The Pakenham census for 1852 lists Mann, his wife, and five children aged eleven to two living in a single-storey stone house. For the Scriptures, see LAC *Journals*, 26 August 1841.

8 *Presbyterian Record* 12/41 (8 October 1884): 679; Andrew Haydon, *Pioneer Sketches in the Bathurst District* Vol. 1 (Toronto: Ryerson Press 1925), 209; V.R. McGiffin, *Pakenham: Ottawa Valley Village, 1823–1860* (Pakenham: Mississippi Publishers 1963), 103–40. Gifts from parishioners included a riding horse, a silk gown, and a pulpit Bible and psalm books. One of the Mann children was born 21 May 1841. This last work (in the Carleton University Library) reports average wages in the district in the 1840s as £24 with and £36 without board for farm servants per annum and £50–75 per annum for skilled workers.

9 AO, RG2, C6C, Mann to Murray, 4 June 1844; C1B, Murray to Mann, 13 June 1844; Murray to District Council Perth, 1 July 1844, C1B. The £50 is confirmed in C6C, Alexander Mann, 9 August 1845, and Mann adds that, in Bathurst, the township superintendents are paid 6 to 10 per cent of the township assessment.

10 AO RG2, C6C, Alexander Mann, Bathurst District, 14 March 1845; C1B, McNab to Mann, 24 April 1845

11 AO RG2, F3A, Bathurst District Report, 1845

12 *Bathurst Courier*, 28 July 1846

13 AO RG2, C6C, Alexander Mann, Pakenham, 15 October 1846, officially asks Ryerson about the legality of paying the school monies on Council's order; C1C, Ryerson to Mann, 22 October 1846 declares it illegal; for the press coverage, see *Bathurst Courier*, 8 and 15 September 1846; 6 October, where Murdoch McDonnell claimed Mann was 'fully aware too (for he has spoken of it to me), that he paid parties in my township, more than they claimed to be entitled to'; 13 October; 10 November, reporting 9 and 10 October; note also here that Council awarded Mann £30 for postage and stationery while he was superintendent. Earlier, J.A. Murdoch had complained to Ryerson of the evils of the rate-bill system, and noted that many teachers had resorted to the old system of 'subscribing for so many scholars and all sharing alike.' Ryerson had responded that this was illegal. AO, RG2, C6C, J.A. Murdoch, 10 January 1846; C1C, Ryerson to Murdoch, 19 January 1846.

14 *Bathurst Courier*, 9 February 1847; LAC, *Journals*, 14 June 1847; Province of Canada, *Statutes*, 9 Vic. c.LXIX; 9 & 10 Vic. c.LVIII.

15 *Bathurst Courier*, 16 February 1847. The payments and the prohibition discussed are both to be found in LAC, *Sessional Papers*, Appendix III, 1849, Expenditure of Clergy Reserves.

16 *Bathurst Courier*, 4 March, reporting 4 February 1847

17 *Bathurst Courier*, 18 February; 16 March; 6, 3, and 27 April; 4 and 18 May 1847. In 1845, Mann had complained to Acting Assistant Superintendent MacNab that Murdoch had not delivered his school report for 1844 on time. This earned Murdoch a terse letter from MacNab, and probably did not increase his affection for Mann; AO RG2, C1B, MacNab to Murdoch, 8 March 1845. *Bathurst Courier*, 18 February 1847

18 *Bathurst Courier*, 31 August 1847. McDonnell suggests a by-law to tax, with Council then remitting it after its collection; 2 and 16 November, reporting October sessions of Council. As in 14 January 1848, Mann complained that Padfield refused to accept some of the monies for 1845, which Mann still held, and that Mann had not yet been paid for the work he did up to April 1847.

19 *Bathurst Courier*, 16 November 1847

20 Armstrong, *Handbook of Upper Canadian Chronology*, 178; also, T.R. Millman, *The Life of the Right Reverend, The Honourable Charles James Stewart* (London: Huron College 1953), 213; Richard B. Howard, *Upper Canada College, 1829–1979: Colborne's Legacy* (Toronto: Macmillan 1979), 27, 352–3; the reports

of Padfield's income in parliamentary reports are higher than those given by Howard and likely included his house rent.

21 W. Perkins Bull, *From Strachan to Owen* (Toronto: McLeod 1937), 140

22 Millman, *Charles Stewart*, 180. Gourlay tells us that 'March and Huntley were associated for legal and ecclesiastical purposes for a long time. Rev. James Padfield, a very excellent man, was Church of England minister at first': J.L. Gourlay, *History of the Ottawa Valley* (privately printed 1896), 29.

23 Millman, *Charles Stewart*, 180

24 See the *Church*, 13 April 1839. Using 2 Tim. I: 13, Padfield proved 'the Scriptural authority for a Liturgy,' elucidating his quotations by testimony received from Calvin and other continental reformers, Robert Hall, Adam Clark, and other English dissenters. (My thanks to Curtis Fahey for this reference.)

25 *Wilson's Marriage Notices of Ontario* (Lambertville, NJ: Huntendon House 1980); Millman, *Charles Stewart*, 213; personal communication from Curtis Fahey. Padfield is also listed in Smith's *Canadian Gazetter* of 1846. Adams was chairman of the grand jury and a man of property reputed to be a close ally of Malcolm Cameron.

26 *Bathurst Courier*, 11, 16, and 23 March 1847. MacMillan was the Warden for Bathurst, 1841–6, and registrar for Lanark in 1846. Harris was the rector of Perth and a close friend. Padfield performed the marriages of Harris's children. Ryerson responded to the official announcement with a backhanded congratulation to Padfield on 'appointment to your present office, especially in a District where so large a proportion of the inhabitants are not members of the Church of England.' In fact, the Church of England was the largest denomination in the district. AO RG2 CID, Ryerson to Padfield, Bathurst, 10 August 1847; Smith's *Canadian Gazeteer*, 1846, gives the denominational membership.

27 *Bathurst Courier*, 3 March 1848

28 See the *Bathurst Courier*, July 1848

29 See AO RG2, CID, Ryerson to Robert Moffat, Bathurst District Clerk, 16 and 21 March 1848; *Bathurst Courier*, 1 and 22 December 1848; 19 January 1849. Notice also that, in 26 January 1849, Johnston Neilson, late master of the Johnstown District Model School, comes to Ryerson's defence.

30 'Second Report of the Superintendent of Common Schools for the Bathurst District,' *Bathurst Courier*, 10 November 1848

31 'Report of the Rev. James Padfield,' *Bathurst Courier*, 16 and 23 November 1849

32 For example, AO RG2 C6C, Johnston Neilson, Carleton Place, 16 February 1850; Robert Duglass, Perth, 4 March 1850

33 Woodstock *Herald*, 6 April, 13 October 1844; January 1845; February, 5 March 1847; Woodstock Public Library, *Minutes and Records of the Woodstock Public Library, 1835–50*. The remarkable network of Reform- and reform-minded intellectuals and artisans also included T.S. Shenston.

34 *The Aspect and Influence of Christianity Upon the Commercial Character: A Discourse Delivered at Montreal, 15 Oct., 1837* (Montreal: Greig 1837), 7

35 Ibid., 8–25

36 *Hochelaga Depicta* ... (Toronto: Coles facsimile edition 1974). Notice that Bosworth is involved here in mapping part of the social domain. This knowledge was both aesthetically pleasing and 'useful.' See E.R. Fitch, ed. *The Baptists of Canada* (Toronto: Standard 1911).

37 Rev. A.J. Barker, 'A Pioneer Baptist Minister of Lower and Upper Canada: The Reverend Newton Bosworth,' *Canadian Baptist Home Missions Digest* 6 (1963–4): 283–93. Barker quotes Bosworth's diary, now in the Baptist Archives at McMaster University, on his decision to leave Woodstock, 15 December 1844: 'I would rather resign my situation as Pastor than cause any contention in the Church; although I could no longer unite in a practice which appears to me so contrary to the word of God.'

38 D.A. Smith, *At The Forks of the Grand: 20 Historical Essays on Paris Ontario* (Paris: Centennial Committee 1967), 141–4. With respect to the latter lecture, the Mechanics' Institute Report for 1846 noted that it 'was thinly attended, although the subject was such as might reasonably be expected to attract the attention of all classes in the community.' The Mechanics' Institute died from lack of interest in 1850.

39 Woodstock *Herald*, 17 February, 16 November 1844.

40 Ibid.; AO RG2 C6C, District Clerk, Woodstock, 20 February 1844; Bosworth to Murray, 4 June 1844; C1B, Murray to Bosworth, 11 June 1844; C6C, Bosworth to Murray, 31 July 1845. In McMaster University Archives, Newton Bosworth Diary, 1843–7, 16 February 1844, Bosworth hoped the council would consider the question of his salary, which, at £35, he considered too small. Bosworth probably made some small amount of money from his writing and from his congregation, although how much is not known. According to his advertisement in the *Herald*, 9 January 1846, he owned a 'small farm ... within a quarter of a mile of the flourishing Town of Woodstock, on the Macadamized road, consisting of nearly forty-seven acres. A comfortable dwelling house and a newly erected stable are on the premises.' T.S. Shenston, one of the trustees with W.H. Landon of school section 2, and, with George Hendry, one of the organizers of the famous Oxford Reform Dinner for Hincks, had agreed to show the farm.

41 AO RG2 F3A, Brock District Report, 1842. There were no returns from North Oxford, West Oxford, Burford, or Blenheim townships.

42 McMaster University, Baptist Archives, Diary of Newton Bosworth, 1843–7; there are general notes about the schools visited in 1844; Woodstock *Herald*, 16 November 1844, account of the Burford Teachers' Association meeting; 24 January 1845, Bosworth 'To the Teachers of Common Schools in the Brock District.' Bosworth and the Teachers' Association both put forward the staples of middle-class educational reform: teaching to understand, gentle pedagogy, the importance of moral regulation. The key distinction to notice is who is to organize this: for Bosworth, largely, it should be teachers themselves.

43 AO RG2 C6C, Newton Bosworth, 5 October 1844; 8 April 1845

44 AO RG2 F3A, Brock District Report 1845. Hendry actually submitted this after Bosworth's resignation.

45 Woodstock *Herald*, 13 February 1846, 'Report of the Superintendent of Education for the District of Brock for the year 1845.' This document also echoed much of what is reproduced below. It is important to notice, however, that Bosworth clearly believed the act of 1843 was serving the interests of the 'friends of improvement.'

46 NAC RG5 CI, v.172, no.12821; Newton Bosworth to D. Daly, 3 February 1846

47 In this regard, see Walter G. Pitman, *The Baptists and Public Affairs in the Province of Canada, 1840–1867* (New York: Arno Press 1980).

48 Bosworth Diary, 22 December 1845. I think Bosworth saw himself administratively as an agent of the council, not of the Education Office.

49 Woodstock *Herald*, 13 February 1846

50 T.S. Shenston, *The Oxford Gazetteer* (Toronto: Chatterton & Helliwell 1852), 120. The schoolhouse has been moved from its original location to the corner of Bay and Peel streets in the town, and is occupied as a doctor's office.

51 Woodstock *Herald*, 22 September 1840; Woodstock Public Library, Bain Brothers file

52 William D. Reid, *Death Notices of Ontario* (Lambertville, NJ: Hunterdon House 1980). The youngest daughter, Isabella Jane, died aged six months twenty-three days in September 1841. At Hendry's death, Bain was appointed guardian of his children's interest: see Woodstock *Herald*, 22 October 1847. The 1852 census listed Katherine Hendry, aged forty, a native of Scotland, member of the Free Church, and a widow, living in a frame house with her four children and one other family. The children, aged fifteen, ten, eight, and six, were born in Canada. Some of the lectures at the Woodstock Mechanics' Institute while Hendry acted as secretary included the founding member Dr Keast's 'The Structure and Functions of Vegetables in Relation to Agriculture'; G. Beard's 'Light'; P.M.O. Bartley's 'The Progress of Science and the Fine Arts among the Ancients'; and the Rev. Mr Mesley's 'Astronomy'; Woodstock *Herald*, 17 February; 13 October 1844; January; 24 February 1845.

53 LAC, *Sessional Papers*, Appendix MM 1854–5. Woodstock *Herald*, 17 February 1844; there was some debate about the appropriateness of Hendry serving as auditor and township superintendent. Auditors were paid £7.10 in 1844: *Herald*, 16 November 1844.

54 Woodstock *Herald*, 20 February 1846; well acquainted, that is, with the Reform-sponsored School Act of 1843. T.C. Barwick, another councillor, was also one of Hendry's friends.

55 LAC, *Debates*, 14 April 1846; Woodstock *Herald*, 23 October 1846, quoting Hendry's remarks at the Oxford Reform Dinner. The word 'Mechanic' was greeted with cries of 'Hear, hear' from those in attendance at the dinner.

56 AO RG2 C6C, George Hendry, Woodstock, 9 March 1846

57 AO RG2 F3A, Brock District Report, 1845. There is an anomaly here; Hendry re-

ports he visited the schools, but most of the remarks here are Bosworth's. Hendry took office in February 1846, and the report was drawn up in late March, so it is possible that the inspection referred to was made between those dates, but then Hendry was including material that should actually have appeared in his own report for 1846. Or was Hendry acting as Bosworth's proxy?

58 Woodstock *Herald*, 23 October 1846

59 AO RG2 C6C, George Hendry, 12 September 1846. The warrants had not been sent, and Hendry wrote 'I am annoyed, every day, about it by teachers and township Superintendents. They threaten to write in the newspapers about it and "show us all up as a set of bungling incapables, unfit for the duties that we have taken upon ourselves to perform" etc.' CIC, Ryerson to Hendry, 14 September 1846, Ryerson claimed there must be an error in Montreal; Woodstock *Herald*, 18 September 1846. Ryerson was charged by 'Culpam Qui Meruit Ferat' of a dereliction of duty. *Herald*, 25 September 1846: Hendry defended him at length. Bosworth's name had inadvertently been given as superintendent, and Ryerson had written to Daly to have the error corrected so Hendry could draw the money. The fault lay not with Ryerson, but with Daly, 'that smooth faced gentleman whose tenure of office is so easy that he has been compared to the flower which, notwithstanding that it is so elegantly arrayed, it toils not neither does it spin.' Unlike many Reformers, it seems, Hendry distinguished Ryerson from the ministry; AO RG2 CIC, Ryerson to Hendry, 11 January 1847.

60 AO RG2 CIC, Ryerson to Hendry, 1 February 1847; also Ryerson to Shenston, 8 February 1847. Shenston, now district clerk, had written to ask how the council should decide whether or not to tax a school section. Ryerson urged the council to follow the advice of trustees, and not to wait for a petition from the residents. Just as the council expressed the will of the district, so did the trustees express the will of the school section. This matter is discussed below in the section on Landon, since Landon and Shenston were both trustees of the school that petitioned Council for a tax.

61 AO RG2 CID, Ryerson to Hendry, 23 August 1847; the proposed meeting in Woodstock was scheduled for the week of Hendry's death.

62 AO RG2 C6C, George Hendry, 28 October 1846

63 AO RG2 CIC, Ryerson to Hendry, 7 November 1846

64 AO RG2 C6C, George Hendry, 11 November 1846

65 Unlike Bosworth, Landon did not oppose the right of women to speak. Fred Landon, *Western Ontario and the American Frontier* (Toronto: McClelland and Stewart 1967), 100; for a discussion of the role of clergy in attempting to regulate popular enthusiasm, see William Westfall, *Two Worlds: The Protestant Culture of Nineteenth-Century Ontario* (Montreal and Kingston: McGill-Queen's University Press 1989), 58–68.

66 Woodstock *Herald*, September 1847, for the advertisement. This was an academy for the daughters of the middle class, but Landon also noted 'as it is almost universally admitted in New York and the other neighbouring States that females are by

far the most valuable teachers for the Common Primary Schools; and as suitable encouragement is now held out to well qualified female teachers by the Common School regulations of Upper Canada, the subscriber will pay particular attention to such young ladies as are desirous of qualifying themselves to fill, with pleasure and advantage, the honorable office of instructors of the young; and will exert himself to furnish them with all the advantages proposed by Normal Schools.' Landon's views on the social position of women were rather more progressive than those of Newton Bosworth – and of Ryerson, who had recently purged women from Victoria College, and who did not admit the worth of women as primary-school teachers until 1865, – but, in education, he supported centralization.

67 Immediately after the Landons, the enumerator – Landon himself – listed the names of thirty-five male students. Landon was probably conducting a boarding school with his wife. An elementary school now stands near the house on Chapel Street, and John Bain also lived on this street.

68 Woodstock *Herald*, 13 March 1847

69 Woodstock *Herald*, 29 October 1847

70 The possible exception is the question of female teachers, although this was never directly discussed. In AO RG2 C1D, 2 November 1847, Ryerson replied to Landon's query about the applicability of the alien-teachers clause to women that it did not apply.

71 AO RG2 C1D, Ryerson to Landon, 13 December 1847: 'To those who are needy and who do what they really can to help themselves; it will afford me pleasure to give every assistance in my power'; the Lord of the Education Office, like the Lord of Hosts, helped those who helped themselves.

72 AO RG2 C1D, Ryerson to Landon, 3 January 1848. Of course, the fact that Ryerson regarded forms of political and administrative regulation as means to the ends of 'improvement' is key to understanding his own political career, and the disgust with which he was viewed by those committed to other political principles.

73 *Oxford Star and Woodstock Advertiser*, 25 February, 8 March 1848

74 AO RG2 C1D, Ryerson to T.S. Shenston, 14 February 1848; an aggressive reply given the recent accession of the Reformers to power

75 AO RG2 C6C, W.H. Landon, Woodstock, n.d. September 1849

76 My thanks to Edwin Bennett of Woodstock for this reference and for a photograph of Landon's substantial brick house, which still stands on Chapel Street in the town.

77 AO, MU1375, Hodgins Papers, W.H. Landon to Hincks, 28 January 1850; Landon also suggested that the power to distrain for school taxes be with the collector, not the trustees, but this was not accepted; in RG2, C6C, Clerk, Oxford County, 14 March 1850, Landon was himself appointed for Blandford.

78 This is from Roger Hall's entry in *Dictionary of Canadian Biography*, Vol. VIII: 706–7.

79 Naomi Slater Heydon, *Looking Back ... Pioneers of Bytown and March* (Ottawa:

Nemo 1980), 280–8. There are two portraits of Pinhey here, one in 1818, one in 1847.

80 M.S. Cross, 'The Age of Gentility: The Formation of an Aristocracy in the Ottawa Valley,' in J.K. Johnson, ed., *Historical Essays on Upper Canada*. (Toronto: McClelland and Stewart 1975), 226–40.

81 Ibid., 231; Hall, *Dictionary of Canadian Biography*; also, *Historical Sketch of the County of Carleton* [1879] (Belleville: Mikla Press 1971)

82 Pinhey's comment is in NAC, MG 24 I 9, v. 11, Hill Collection, n.d.; AO RG2 C6C, Hamnett Pinhey, Horaceville, 31 May 1844; G.P. Barker, District Clerk, Bytown, 10 October 1844. This is the first model school for which support was sought, and McNab received a lesson from a shirty Dominique Daly about procedure: the report was to be submitted before money was sought. See CIB, McNab to Daly, 29 November; C6C Daly to McNab, 19 November; Pinhey to Daly, 20 November 1844. Later, the master of the school, Js. Fitz Wm Bierdon Healy, who was trained in the Kildare Place Model School, complained that Council refused him a decent salary; C6C, Healy, Bytown, 11 September 1846.

83 AO RG2 C6C, Hamnett Pinhey, Horaceville, 20 September 1845; CIB, McNab to Pinhey, 29 September 1845, 'The Act may well be "deemed to be too complex and too prolix," and will in my judgement require important amendments before it will work comfortably.'

84 AO RG2 C6C, Hamnett Pinhey, 27 June 1846

85 AO RG2 F3A, Dalhousie District Report, 1845

86 AO RG2 C6C, G.P. Balken, District Clerk Dalhousie, Ottawa, 8 February 1847, enclosing Pinhey's annual report for 1846

87 AO RG2 C6C, Hamnett Pinhey, Horaceville, 7 February 1847

88 AO RG2 C6C, G.P. Balken, Ottawa, 8 February 1847

89 AO RG2 C1C, Ryerson to Pinhey, 16 February 1847; even if this assessment wasn't actually levied!

90 AO RG2 C1D, Ryerson to Pinhey, 15 February 1848

91 AO RG2 C6C, Hamnett Pinhey, Horaceville, 12 February 1849; C1D, Ryerson to Pinhey, 26 February 1849

92 AO RG2 C6C, Pinhey to Ryerson, 23 June 1849; C1D, Ryerson to Pinhey, 4 July 1849. This was not just to get shut of Pinhey. Scully had applied to the Normal School, but couldn't get in because he had no certificate of moral character from a recognized clergyman. Ryerson told him that Pinhey's certificate of character would be quite sufficient, and Pinhey gave it. See with Pinhey, as above, Scully to Pinhey, 16 June 1849, and Pinhey to Scully, 23 June 1849.

93 More about the school grant follows, but notice that, in addition to the case of M'Gillicuddy discussed above, that of Wm A. Ross, who had been teaching in Torbolton Township in 1843, and who later was master of the Ottawa District Grammar School and a professor at Queen's College. As the only teacher in Torbolton, Ross was entitled to the entire township appropriation for 1843, something over £13. Pinhey, however, arbitrarily decided to pay Ross only about £3

and to give the rest to Captain Grierson, RN (ret.), towards the construction of a schoolhouse. Ross found out only about five years later, but Ryerson refused to support his claims against Pinhey, despite the fact that, from the correspondence, it is clear Pinhey had acted improperly. See NAC RG5 CI Vol. 240, for this material.

94 AO RG2 C6C, John Flood, Richmond, 20 August, 26 October 1849
95 AO RG2 C6C, John Flood, Richmond, 15 May 1843
96 J.L. Gourlay, *History of the Ottawa Valley* (privately printed 1896), 74–5; the other sources echo Gourlay: H. Walker and O. Walker, *Carleton Saga* (Ottawa: Runge Press 1968), 381; also *Historical Sketch of the County of Carleton* (Belleville: Mikla Press 1978), 205, 259.
97 Wilson's *Marriage Notices of Ontario* (Lambertville, NJ: Hunterdon House 1980), to Sarah Emily Read, daughter of Thomas Read of March Township, 4 August 1842; Kingston *Chronicle and Gazette*, 10 December 1845
98 For all of this correspondence, see NAC RG5 CI, vol. 169, no. 12341, where the original application is; vol. 174 and vol. 199.
99 AO RG2 CID, Ryerson to Flood, 5 April, 18 October 1849
100 AO RG2 C6C, Flood to Ryerson, 5 March, 26 October 1849; CID, Ryerson to Flood, 12 March 1849; CIE, Ryerson to Flood, 31 July, 31 October, 3 November 1849
101 AO RG2 C6C, Flood to Ryerson, 24 December 1849; CIE, Ryerson to Flood, 27 December 1849: just the moment Ryerson regained ministerial support
102 AO RG2 CIE, Ryerson to Flood, 7 February 1850
103 AO RG2 C6C, John Flood, Richmond, 29 March 1849
104 AO RG2 C6C, John Flood, Richmond, 20 August, 18 October 1849
105 AO RG2 F3A, Dalhousie District Report, 1849. Flood also apologized for the blots on his report, excusing himself by the fact that he was so ill-paid he could not afford to do two drafts.
106 See his account of the reasons for low rates of school attendance in Bruce Curtis, *Building the Educational State: Canada West, 1836–1871* (Sussex and London, ON: Falmer Press and Althouse Press 1988), ch. 5.

Chapter 8

1 See R.D. Gidney and D.A. Lawr, 'Who Ran the Schools? Local Influence on Education Policy in Nineteenth Century Ontario,' *Ontario History* 72/3: 131–43; Carl Kaestle, *Pillars of the Republic: Common Schools and American Society, 1760–1860* (New York: Hill and Wang 1983); Carl Kaestle and Maris Vinovskis, *Education and Social Change in Nineteenth-Century Massachusetts* (Cambridge: Cambridge University Press 1980); Michael Katz, *Class, Bureaucracy and Schools* (New York: Praeger 1973) and 'Education and Social Development in the Nineteenth Century: New Directions for Enquiry,' in P. Nash, ed., *History and Education: The Educational Uses of the Past*, 83–114 (New York: Random House 1970); P.V. Meyers, 'Professionalization and Societal Change: Rural Teachers in Nineteenth Century France,' *Social History* 6 (1976): 185–207; for additional

references and a comment, see B. Curtis, 'Policing Pedagogical Space: "Voluntary" School Reform and Moral Regulation,' *Canadian Journal of Sociology* 13/3 (1988): 283–304.

2 The literature is vast and, I hope, well-known by now. A representative contribution is Sidney Pollard, 'Factory Discipline in the Industrial Revolution,' *Economic History Review* (Second series) 16 (1963–4): 254–71. Max Weber himself was particularly interested in the formation of a 'bureaucratic character' distinguished by indifference and political indecisiveness. 'Politics as a Vocation,' in *Selections in Translation*, ed. W.G. Runciman (Cambridge: University Press 1978), 215–25.

3 I'm speaking to old theoretical debates in sociology. Compare Weber's account of the rise of bureaucracy in *Essays in Sociology*, with Durkheim's criticism of a social science claiming to speak only to the validity of means in *The Rules of the Sociological Method*, ed. Steven Lukes (Glencoe: Free Press 1982).

4 I don't mean to suggest that bureaucratic rules are purely formal; bureaucratic relations may change power structures, may cut against arbitrary and idiosyncratic rule by entrenched élites. In the case with which I am concerned, such rules and procedures formalize the power of the middle classes.

5 I take this distinction from P. Corrigan and D. Sayer, *The Great Arch: English State Formation as Cultural Revolution* (Oxford: Blackwell 1985), where it is a central insight. See also, P. Corrigan, 'On Moral Regulation: Some Preliminary Remarks,' *Sociological Review*, 29/2 (1981): 313–37. In the same regard, Douglas Hay's emphasis upon the 'theatricality' of the law as a ritual of power is instructive. See D. Hay, 'Property, Authority and the Criminal Law,' in D. Hay et al., eds., *Albion's Fatal Tree: Crime and Society in Eighteenth-Century England* (New York: Pantheon 1975), 17–64; E.J. Hobsbawm and T. Ranger, *The Invention of Tradition* (Cambridge: Cambridge University Press 1983); Benedict Anderson, *Imagined Communities* (London: Verso 1983).

6 Antonio Gramsci, *Selections from the Prison Notebooks* (New York: International Publishers 1971), 12. While I find the distinction between 'state' and 'civil society' problematic, given that many of the categories of private life and experience are themselves largely political in origin, the distinction between legal-coercive and moral-ideological dimensions of rule seems to me to be useful. A critical reading of Durkheim's work on the state and collective representations in this light, particularly *Professional Ethics and Civic Morals* (Glencoe: Free Press 1958), is also instructive.

7 Weber, in his essay 'Bureaucracy,' in *Essays in Sociology*, points out that bureaucratic rationality is continually dependent upon irrational forces; for instance, upon the unwavering and unquestioning loyalty of bureaucratic cadres. This tension between the rational and the irrational is, for him, a motor force of society.

8 Weber, *Essays on Sociology*, 81

9 AO RG2 C6C, Daly to Education Office, 9 September 1845; C1D, Ryerson to Colin Gregor, Guelph, 10 December 1847. An inspector who resigned was taken to task for not passing books and papers to his successor and was informed 'the Council

will be of course justified in holding you responsible for any loss or evils which may be experienced from such a state of things.'

10 AO RG2 C1D, Ryerson to Hamilton Hunter, 19 August 1847; Ryerson complained that many superintendents continued to give certificates and pay teachers in this way. He told Hunter 'not to be too rigorous in enforcing an entire change in this respect' in 1847, but to notice that 'no further indulgence will be extended in this regard.'

11 Very large sums of money, in contemporary terms, were at issue. For instance, William F. Clarke, according to the Talbot District Auditors, AO RG2 C6C, February 1849, held as much as £1486.14.4 during 1849, and had large balances in hand at the end of the year as well – this, in a period where the Congregational churches were paying ministers like Clarke in principle about £75 per annum (although payment was usually late and often in kind); C6C, 28 July 1845, for example, Samuel Hart, Eastern District superintendent, revealed in response to a circular letter from McNab that his salary '(totally inadequate as it is) was fixed by the Distr. Council at a percentage of 4 per cent to be deducted from the Government monies passing thro his hands.'

12 G.E. Boyce, *Hutton of Hastings* (Belleville: Hastings County Council 1972), shows that William Hutton was attacked in Council after 1850 for taking his salary out of the school monies.

13 AO RG2 C6C, a bundle includes McNab to Hopkirk, 25 August 1845; with Draper's opinion on the outside and Hopkirk to McNab; also McNab to Elias Burnham, Peterboro, 30 August 1845; C1C, Ryerson to Dr McLean, 5, 7, and 27 May 1847; C1D, Ryerson to Burham, 15 September 1847; Burnham was asked peremptorily why he had paid only £6 to section 3 of Druro; Ryerson to Ardagh, 14 July 1847, accepts Aradagh's accounts; also, later, Ryerson to Thornton, 27 March 1849, pointing out that Thornton's accounts did not add up correctly, and asking for a detailed explanation

14 Cobourg *Star*, 10 December 1845. F.H. Armstrong, *Handbook of Upper Canadian Chronology* (Toronto: Dundurn Press 1985), a generally useful compilation, gives Steele's tenure of the wardenship as from 13 August to 4 November 1845.

15 AO RG2 C6C, John Bignall, Goderich, 25 May 1844

16 AO RG2 F3A, Huron District Report, 1847

17 Macqueen lectured frequently on phrenology and analysed people's behaviour in phrenological terms. In the following decade, he was implicated in a number of shady land dealings. Huron *Signal*, 'Politics for the People, No.3,' 18 February 1848; Macqueen also opposed the *Journal of Education* as an organ of the 'antiquated educational system of Prussia,' a view he revised after May 1849. These characterizations of Bignall were veiled and mild compared to those that followed his departure: 17 November, 'a useless mass of sottish indolence'; 27 October, 'all we could ever learn of his qualifications was simply that *he was a great big man with a great big appetite!*'; 'He reminded us of Horace's plough boy,' etc.

18 AO RG2 C1D, Ryerson to Trustees, Goderich, 18 April 1848

19 AO RG2 C1D, Ryerson to Bignall, 30 May 1848
20 In November, the following advertisement ran in the Goderich paper:

$400 REWARD

Whereas John Bignall, Superintendent of Common Schools of the Huron District, has absconded with a large sum of Public Money, the above Reward will be paid to any one apprehending the said John Bignall and recovering the amount stolen; or the reward will be paid in proportion to the amount recovered. The money, *Three hundred and forty eight pounds*, was in $10 notes of the Bank of Montreal. The above John Bignall is a remarkably large man, with course features, about six feet three inches in height; very round in his shoulders, haughty in his address, and about 50 years of age, hair straight inclined to grey, whiskers white.

The *Huron Signal* provides a complete account and post mortem. See especially 17 and 31 March, 14 April, 12 May, 27 October, 3 and 17 November, 15 December 1848; 19 January 1849; also, AO RG2 C6C, Charles Fletcher, Goderich, 2 August 1849; C1D, Ryerson to Fletcher, 22 December 1848, 'I deeply regret the calamity which has befallen your School interests in consequence of Mr. Bignall's villany.' NAC RG1 E1, Executive Council Minutes, Canada State Book I, 29 November 1848, 338–40, for discussion of the matter in Council

21 See AO RG2 C1D, Ryerson to Bignall, 11 September 1848; also C6C, George Duck, Chatham, 17 July 1849; C1E, Ryerson to Hincks, 18 July 1849. In this last, Ryerson suggests that at least half the grant be paid in cash.

22 AO RG2 C6C, William Fraser, Lochiel, to Ryerson, 11 July 1849: 'Mr Millar ... is a defaulter in a sum not less than £500 & according to all appearance has left the country.' Also, F3A, Eastern District Report, 1849, William Fraser: 'my predecessor William Millar who absconded & brought with him a little more than £500 of the publick money.' No Cornwall paper that might provide a fuller account survives for the period; C6C, October 1849, a large bundle of documents concerns the Hayter case, which has yet to receive a systematic examination. I think that Hayter, a Tory, was initially appointed by the governor-in-council after the resignation or removal of John Steele; cf. Cobourg *Star*, 19 August 1846, where we hear Hayter was *re*appointed by Council.

23 Circular from the Chief Superintendent to the Wardens of Counties and Unions of Counties ..., in *Journal of Education for Upper Canada* 3/8 (1850): 114.

24 AO RG2 C6C, 3 May 1845: Ardagh had offered to serve as superintendent gratuitously, if the district council would cover his expenses. 'These including Clerk – Office – Stationery – Postage & Travelling' for 1844 'amounted to about £44.' But the district council 'refused to allow more than £25'; McMaster University Archives, Newton Bosworth Diary, 1843–7, 16 February 1844: Bosworth hoped the council would consider the question of his salary, which, at £35, he considered too small; C6C, William Fraser, August 1849.

25 AO RG2 C6C, William Hutton, Belleville, 25 December 1845; to use Weber's dis-

tinction, *Essays in Sociology*, 84: 'Either one lives "for" politics or one lives "off" politics.'

26 This is a point at which law becomes administration.

27 AO RG2 C6C, John Strachan, Ernest Town, 21 October 1844; C1B, Ryerson to Strachan, 26 October 1844

28 AO RG2 C1B, McNab to S.B. Ardagh, 3 March 1845

29 AO RG2 C1D, Ryerson to George Hendry, 23 August 1847; C1E, Ryerson to Charles Fletcher, 6 August 1849

30 AO RG2 C1C, Ryerson to Hendry, 11 January 1847

31 For example, AO RG2 C6C, Elias Burnham, 24 June 1845

32 Participants in the debate have seen the origins and the nature of these public perceptions in ways ranging from the simple reflection of obvious and pressing problems to the construction by bourgeois intellectuals of collective 'misrepresentations.' For a helpful summary comment, see Peter Gowan, 'The Origins of the Administrative Elite,' *New Left Review* 162 (March–April 1987): 4–34.

33 AO RG2 C1D, Ryerson to Governor General, 28 June; Ryerson to Daly, 29 June 1847. Ryerson asked Daly to have the 1845 and 1846 reports laid before the House and complained: 'In the local reports for 1846, the District Superintendents have furnished me with nothing but the imperfect statistics ... they have offered no observations of a general or practical character as many of them did in their reports for the preceeding year.' Notice, none the less, these figures are used by Ryerson in his defence in 1849.

34 AO RG2 C1D, 'Special Measures etc.,' 22 June 1847

35 AO MU1375 Hodgins Papers, Ryerson to J.C. Morrison, 7 February 1849. *Journal of Education* 2/7 (July 1849): 112; none the less, a copy was sent to each district superintendent and, in that way, made accessible to the district councils. Notice that, by this time, William Hutton's son was articling in Morrison's law office.

36 AO RG2 C1D, Ryerson to Leslie, 12 May 1849

37 *Journal of Education* 2/6 (June 1849): 88–9; Hodgins ladles out the agricultural imagery.

38 *Journal of Education* 2/9 (September 1849): 135–6

39 Cf. AO RG2 C1B, McNab to Daly, 16 and 23 May 1845

40 AO RG2 C1B, Murray to Provincial Secretary, 23 August 1844; C6C, D. Daly, Montreal, 29 August 1844; Murray asked for and got permission to have 5,000 report forms produced, but it is not clear that these were actually printed, or if printed, reached superintendents. For 1846, superintendents produced their own forms.

41 For example, AO RG2 C6C, John Steele, 22 February 1844, sought from Murray 'any Regulations and Instructions, that you may deem requisite and necessary'; W. Hutton, Belleville, 25 December 1845: on the eve of his departure on tour sought from Ryerson 'any suggestions which you think will be calculated to advance the good cause'; Elias Burnham, Petition to Sir Charles Metcalfe, 24 June 1845; C1C, McNab to Burnham, 30 July 1845. When Elias Burnham proposed to use the sur-

plus school monies from 1842, together with what 'he could raise ... by private subscription,' to build two schools in Peterborough, McNab urged him to get up a local petition and send it to the Education Office.

42 AO RG2 C1D, Ryerson to Daly, 30 July 1847, outlines the proposed tour and discusses his need for financial aid to undertake it. The tour could be reconstructed in greater detail from newspaper accounts, but, so far, no one has undertaken this task.

43 For example, *Journal of Education* 2/9 (September 1849): 134. Hodgins's own 'Acknowledgements' at the end of each number document the circulation of the periodical to many members of the dominant classes.

44 Thomas Robertson, 'On the Inspection of Common Schools,' *Journal of Education* 1/5 (May 1848): 129–35; more of the same in 'Inspection and Supervision of Schools,' *Journal of Education* 3/2 (1850): 17–18. Also, AO RG2 C6C, Patrick Thornton, Hamilton, 4 March 1850: 'I am much gratified by the perusal of Mr. Robertson's remarks on the Supervision of Schools, which has appeared in the last No. of the Journal of Education.'

45 AO RG2 F3A, Western District Report, Prince Edward District Report, 1845; NAC MG24 I33, Keefer notes. In reading the school reports, however, both Robert Lanning and I were struck by the similarity in their categorization and framing of knowledge. These are also often remarkable physical documents, some of them enormously large and presented on numerous sheets, sewn together, one assumes, by wives and daughters.

46 AO RG2 F3A, 1848. There are no reports in this collection for 1847, and only three for 1848.

47 *Forms, Regulations and Instructions for the Better Organization and Government of Common Schools in Upper Canada* (Toronto: J.H. Lawrence 1847), 7

48 AO RG2 F3A, Dalhousie District Report, 1849

49 AO RG2 F3A, Victoria District Report, 1849

50 See M.V. Cullen, *The Statistical Movement in Early Victorian Britain* (Brighton: Harvester 1975).

51 AO RG2 F3A, Victoria District Report, 1849; can we imagine Hutton travelling the Victoria District, urging people to reorganize their eliminatory functions? Is not this the best evidence of the tutelar character of this educational state in formation?

52 AO RG2 F3A, Ottawa District Report, 1845

53 AO RG2 F3A, London District Report, 1845

54 AO RG2 C6C, P. Thornton, Hamilton, 8 July 1845

55 AO RG2 F3A, Midland District Report, 1845; Niagara District Report, 1848

56 AO RG2 F3A, Home District Report, 1848. In addition to the Niagara and Home District reports, there is one other that survives from 1848 – that of Charles Fletcher in the Huron District. Fletcher remarked that the accuracy of his report was limited by imperfections in that of his predecessor, John Bignall.

57 AO RG2 C1D, Ryerson to Burnham, 5 April 1848; same to same, 4 April 1849; C6C, Burnham to Ryerson, 12 April 1849; C1E, Ryerson to Burnham, 13 March 1850.

Also, CID, Ryerson to Wm Clarke, 26 February 1849, complaining of omissions in Clarke's report and urging him to fill in the blanks from his own knowledge

58 AO RG2 F3A, Brock District Report, 1849

59 AO RG2 CID, Ryerson to Padfield, 26 March 1849; F3A, Bathurst District Report, 1849

60 AO RG2 F3A, Eastern District Report, Dalhousie District Report, 1849.

61 AO RG2 C6C, October 1849, Documents in the case of Benj. Hayter, Hayter to Hodgins, 2 April 1849, remarks on the annual report

62 AO RG2 C6C, John Strachan, Ernest Town, 15 March 1849: 'When visiting, I always take the Number of Children on the roll, the average attendance &c; so that I was able to refer to my Memorandum Book in many instances in which the Trustees neglected to state any more than the number of Children in the School Section.' The Bosworth, Elliot, Ardagh, and Keefer diaries would not have provided sufficient information to correct or supplement trustee or township superintendents' reports.

63 AO RG2 CIE, Ryerson to Fraser, 16 August, 5 September 1849; C6C, William Fraser, Lochiel, 29 August 1849; still Fraser was not to deduct his salary from the school monies.

64 AO RG2 F3A, Western District Report, 1849, pencil superscript; CID, Ryerson to Leslie, 15 December 1848, describes Hodgins's labours at length; for Hodgins's visits to European schools, see CIC, Ryerson to Daly, 3 August 1846.

Conclusion

1 Province of Canada, *Statutes*, 12 Vic. c.VIII, 'An Act to make provision for the preservation of the Public Health in certain emergencies'; R.B. Splane, *Social Welfare in Ontario, 1791–1891* (Toronto: University of Toronto Press 1965)

2 Province of Canada, *Statutes*, 14 & 15 Vic. c.II, 'An Act for the better Management of the Provincial Penetentiary'; 20 Vic. c.XXVIII, The Youthful Offenders Act; LAC, *Sessional Papers*, Appendix HH, 1852–3

3 For railways, see Province of Canada, *Statutes*, 20 Vic. c.XII '... for the better Prevention of Accidents on Railways.' Many members of Parliament were heavily involved in railway speculation. Notice that one of the first railway inspectors was Jacob Keefer's brother. For ships, see 14 & 15 Vic., c.XXXIV, 'An Act to amend an Act compelling vessels to carry night lights.' For agricultural societies, see 20 Vic. c.XXXII; for houses of entertainment, see 13 & 14 Vic. c.LXV; for settlement and colonization, see LAC, *Sessional Papers*, Appendix 38, 1856.

4 E.P. Hennock, 'Central/Local Relations in England: An Outline, 1850–1950,' *Urban History Yearbook*, 1982

5 J. Fletcher, *Education: National, Voluntary and Free* (London: Ridgway 1851), 33. (My thanks to P.C. for the reference.)

6 Charles Leslie Glenn, Jr, *The Myth of the Common School* (Amherst: University of Massachusetts Press 1988), 123, 145

Index

THE STATE AND ECONOMIC LIFE

Editors: **Mel Watkins**, University of Toronto; **Leo Panitch**, York University

This series, begun in 1978, includes original studies in the general area of Canadian political economy and economic history, with particular emphasis on the part played by the government in shaping the economy. Collections of shorter studies, as well as theoretical or internationally comparative works, may also be included.